Sociology
FOR
DUMMIES®

Sociology FOR DUMMIES®

by Jay Gabler, PhD

WILEY

Wiley Publishing, Inc.

Sociology For Dummies®

Published by
Wiley Publishing, Inc.
111 River St.
Hoboken, NJ 07030-5774
www.wiley.com

WILEY

About the Author

Jay Gabler is a writer, editor, and college teacher living in Minneapolis. He holds a bachelor's degree from Boston University and graduate degrees, including a Ph.D. in sociology, from Harvard University. With colleagues, he has published multiple sociological research studies including the book *Reconstructing the University* (with David John Frank, Stanford University Press, 2006). He currently teaches sociology, psychology, and education at Rasmussen College. He is also associate editor of the *Twin Cities Daily Planet,* where he writes regularly on the arts, and author of the most recent edition of the *Insiders' Guide to the Twin Cities* (Globe Pequot Press, 2010).

Dedication

To David John Frank and Jason Kaufman, my mentors in sociology.

Author's Acknowledgments

I owe gratitude to Susan Hobbs and Erin Calligan Mooney, my editors at Wiley, for everything they've done to make this book a reality. Jennifer Connolly also contributed significantly to the first chapters of this book, with helpful editing and suggestions.

My professional training in sociology took place over the course of a decade at Harvard University; every page in this book benefits indirectly from the insights and expertise of my then-colleagues in the Department of Sociology. My Harvard classmate Felix Elwert was instrumental in suggesting that I write this book and connecting me with the publisher. My current colleagues at Rasmussen College have also been supportive, as have my coworkers at the *Twin Cities Daily Planet.* Much of this book was written at the Macalester College library, and I am grateful to that institution for sharing its resources.

This book is informed by a range of sources, three of which were particularly useful. Randall Collins's *Sociological Insight,* as I mention frequently in the text of this book, was my personal introduction to sociology, and it continues to underlie my perspective on the discipline. I recommend that book in Chapter 17. A book that I would not recommend to beginners but would strongly recommend to readers interested in really sinking their teeth into sociological theory is Peter Knapp's *One World – Many Worlds: Contemporary Sociological Theory,* which particularly informed Chapter 3 of this book. *Essentials of Sociology,* by David B. Brinkerhoff, Lynn K. White, Suzanne T. Ortega, and Rose Weitz, is the text I teach from at Rasmussen and was also helpful as I wrote this book.

Throughout my life I've enjoyed the enthusiastic support of a loving family, both immediate and extended. In particular, my parents, Jim and Jean Gabler, have in every way supported my academic achievements and adventures. As I wrote this book, many friends — in particular, Anna Meyer — helped sustain me with caring encouragement every day. It meant a lot to me.

Publisher's Acknowledgments

We're proud of this book; please send us your comments at http://dummies.custhelp.com. For other comments, please contact our Customer Care Department within the U.S. at 877-762-2974, outside the U.S. at 317-572-3993, or fax 317-572-4002.

Some of the people who helped bring this book to market include the following:

Acquisitions, Editorial, and Media Development

Project Editor: Susan Hobbs

Acquisitions Editor: Stacy Kennedy

Copy Editor: Susan Hobbs

Assistant Editor: Erin Calligan Mooney

Editorial Program Coordinator: Joe Niesen

Technical Editor: Richard Jenks

Editorial Manager: Jennifer Ehrlich

Editorial Supervisor and Reprint Editor: Carmen Krikorian

Editorial Assistants: David Lutton, Jennette ElNaggar

Art Coordinator: Alicia B. South

Cartoons: Rich Tennant (www.the5thwave.com)

Composition Services

Project Coordinator: Sheree Montgomery

Layout and Graphics: Ashley Chamberlain, Samantha K. Cherolis, Nikki Gately, Christine Williams

Proofreader: Evelyn C. Gibson

Indexer: Potomac Indexing, LLC

Publishing and Editorial for Consumer Dummies

Diane Graves Steele, Vice President and Publisher, Consumer Dummies

Kristin Ferguson-Wagstaffe, Product Development Director, Consumer Dummies

Ensley Eikenburg, Associate Publisher, Travel

Kelly Regan, Editorial Director, Travel

Publishing for Technology Dummies

Andy Cummings, Vice President and Publisher, Dummies Technology/General User

Composition Services

Debbie Stailey, Director of Composition Services

Contents at a Glance

Table of Contents

Introduction

. . . .

*W*elcome to sociology! I've written this book to introduce you to one of the biggest and most fascinating disciplines in all of science. Yes, you read that right: Sociology is a science. Sociologists don't use beakers and test tubes, but like natural scientists, they do seek to learn about the world by creating theories and testing them with systematic observations.

What makes sociology both so interesting and so challenging is its subject: the social world. Society is huge, and hugely complex: there are answers to sociological questions, but there usually aren't any *easy* answers. In addition to the challenge of answering sociological questions, there's the challenge of *asking* them — that is, of thinking about society as a subject of objective, scientific study. Your grandpa and your minister and the guy who works at your local coffee shop probably don't have any opinions about how atoms should and shouldn't bond with one another, but they certainly all have opinions about how society should be organized. Studying society scientifically means setting aside — temporarily — your thoughts about how society *should* work.

After you do that, though, you can learn some amazing things about the world. The achievements of sociologists are among the great achievements of the human race because in sociology, people from all different walks of life come together to understand society objectively — so that, in the long run, it can perhaps be made to work better for everyone. However you've come to sociology, I hope this book leaves you with a greater respect not just for sociologists wearing lab coats (yes, some of them actually do) but for your entire species, the first species on Earth capable of conscious self-analysis. What sociologists see when they look at society isn't always pretty, but that fact makes sociology all the more important: Just like you need to know how a car works before you can fix it, you need to understand how society works before you can change it.

About This Book

I've written this book to introduce you to sociology as a body of knowledge about society, but much more importantly to introduce you to sociology as a *way of thinking about the world*.

With a subject as vast and as frequently-changing as human society, it would be foolish to try to write a "user's manual" — it would be outdated before the ink was dry. If this book makes you curious about a specific aspect of society — say, the job market in the United States or the changing class system — that's great. Your local library and the Internet are full of specific studies on these subjects, written by sociologists and other scholars, and I hope this book makes that information more accessible to you.

What I aim to do in this book is to introduce you to sociology as a discipline so you have the tools and understanding you need to succeed in a sociology class or to apply sociological concepts in your professional or personal life. The book is organized to take you from general questions (what is sociology? where did it come from? who does it, and how?) to more specific topics (how do sociologists study culture and socialization? how do sociologists define "class" and "race"?) to applications of those ideas (how can you use sociology in your everyday life?).

Sociologists study a lot of things — in fact, they study just about everything that has anything to do with people interacting — which means that most things studied by sociologists are also studied by people who don't consider themselves sociologists. What is special about sociology is precisely the fact that it involves the study of *all* those things together, not just some of them in isolation. The fact that sociologists consider all aspects of the social world together means that they are able to see connections that people who study only part of the social world cannot. Throughout this book, I emphasize what is unique about the sociological view of the world.

Conventions Used in This Book

Obviously, I can't possibly know each and every person who reads this book, but I can reasonably guess that you're living in the early 21st century, that you have some reason for being curious about sociology, and that you're likely — but not necessarily — living in an English-speaking country. I have not written this book under any further assumptions about who you might be or why you might be reading it.

I've drawn examples and illustrations from a wide array of social situations, but you may notice that there are especially frequent examples from the contemporary United States. In part that's because it's where I live, so that's what I know best. I've written the book in the first person, and often refer to my own life and personal history. Sociology is an objective science, but any given sociologist is a particular person with a unique set of interests and experiences; I hope that as you read this book and see how sociological concepts relate to my life, you'll think about how they relate to your life, too.

I explain terms as I go, so I let you plunge right in without taking too much space going into specifics here in the introduction, but there are a couple of distinctions it may be helpful to mention right here at the outset.

For one, there's the distinction between *society* and *sociology*. They're not the same thing. *Society is what sociologists study*; sociology is the study of society. The term "social" refers to society, people interacting in groups; the term "sociological" refers to sociology, the *study* of people interacting in groups. If this seems confusing to you, you're not alone: Right on up to the *New York Times*, writers often make the mistake of using the term "sociological" when they ought to use the term "social." If there is increasing crime in your community, that is a *social* problem, not a "sociological" problem. If you're trying to study that crime rises but are having a problem with missing data, *then* you have a genuinely sociological problem.

Also — to get a little ahead of myself and preview something I explain more in Chapter 2 — you should know that sociology is not just something that happens in colleges and universities. Sociology is a way of looking at the social world and a tool to use in understanding society; but it's also an academic discipline, and most people who actually call themselves "sociologists" work at colleges, universities, and research institutes. Chances are good that you're reading this book because you're taking — or are thinking about taking — a sociology class in high school or college; but if you're not, don't stop reading! This book is for you, too. You'll find all kinds of information that may help you understand your place of business, your neighborhood, your city, and even some of your family members!

Sociology is Controversial: Brace Yourself!

As I mention earlier, sociology is the study of the entire social world. That means that among the subjects studied by sociologists are some very controversial subjects. If sociologists avoided controversial subjects, that would defeat the whole point of the discipline; and the same goes for this book.

It's part of a sociologist's job to deal with hot topics, and some sociologists have made highly controversial arguments. In delving into sociology, you need to be prepared to encounter some ideas that you may disagree — may *very strongly* disagree — with. Among the ideas you'll encounter in this book:

- ✔ Religion is a way of getting people to give you money, and serves no other constructive purpose.
- ✔ The most effective kind of government is a dictatorship where the smartest person rules.
- ✔ Society works best when women stay home to cook and clean while men go out and earn money.

You don't need to agree with all of those arguments — *I* certainly don't — to study sociology, but you *do* need to be willing to *consider* arguments that you don't agree with. If you don't agree with one or more of those statements, why don't you? Each of the statements above makes an *empirical* argument. That means that those statements can be tested with objective facts. How could you test them? What data would you gather? How would you analyze those data? If you think the truth is not reflected in those statements, how can you prove it? That willingness to think about the social world as a scientist — that is, objectively — is the very foundation of sociology.

I am 100 percent certain that in this book, you will encounter ideas and arguments you don't agree with. When you come across something you don't agree with, think about *why* you don't agree with it and what you would say in a debate with the people who advanced that idea. That's how to think like a sociologist.

How This Book Is Organized

This book is divided into six parts. In this section, I explain what content you'll find in each part.

Part 1: The Basic Basics

This part gives you the what/who/how: what sociology is (the scientific study of society), where it came from (the tumultuous 19th century), who does it (sociologists in academia as well as people outside academia who can benefit from its tools and insights), and how it's done (with a range of complementary methods, none of which are perfect but all of which have value). Reading this part will help you wrap your mind around what this thing called "sociology" really is.

Part II: Seeing Society Like a Sociologist

No matter what aspect of social life you're interested in, there are some key sociological insights that will help you on your way. In this part, I explain how sociologists understand culture (what it is, and what it's not), the micro-macro link (what does "society" have to do with individual people interacting face to face), and the importance of social networks (what's the difference between your "society" and the people you actually know and interact with?). These fundamental insights are of value across all of sociology.

Part III: Divided — er, United — We Stand: Equality and Inequality in Our Diverse World

Just about everyone who studies society is in some way or another concerned about social inequality. Inequality doesn't have to mean stratification — that is, just because two people are different doesn't mean one is in a better or more powerful position than the other — but very often, it does. This part is devoted to that subject in all its various forms. I begin by explaining the general idea of social stratification (who's up, who's down?), then I go into some of the specific lines that divide social groups: race, ethnicity, sex, gender, religion, and the law (in the sense of being on "the wrong side" or "the right side" of the law).

Part IV: All Together Now: The Ins and Outs of Social Organization

People are always interacting, all the time — but as any parent of young children knows, "interacting" is not necessarily the same thing as "being productive." Corporations, nonprofit organizations, governments, social movements, and other social organizations represent people's deliberate attempts to band together to accomplish tasks, and in this part I explain what sociologists know about when those attempts work and when they don't. Cities are a slightly different form of social organization, but people who live together in a city are together in a social organization whether they like it or not; at the conclusion of this part, I look at urban (as well as suburban and exurban) life.

Part V: Sociology and Your Life

Your life is inextricably tied to your society — the life you've lived, the life you're living, and the life you will live. Understanding society can help you understand your own life. In this part, I first explain how sociologists think about individuals' life courses (including childhood, old age, health, and family life) and then look at what sociology can tell us about life in the future.

Part VI: The Part of Tens

This final part contains three chapters that get very specific: What interesting and readable sociology books are out there besides this one? How can you use sociology in your everyday life? The book concludes with the chapter that was my favorite to write: "Ten Myths About Society Busted By Sociology." Flip to that chapter to see how sociological insight will change the way you think about the social world around you.

Icons Used In This Book

As you read, you'll notice a few symbols popping up in the margin. They give you hints about how to understand what you're reading.

This icon highlights information that you should *especially* pay attention to. Make a point of remembering the information in paragraphs highlighted by this icon.

This icon signals that the information near it is of interest to the curious, and delves a little deeper into the specific topic that's being discussed.

When you see this lit fuse, you'll see information about a trap to avoid — a risk of being misled or confused.

When you see this icon, you can be sure that you're getting a significant piece of information that may come in handy in class or in your everyday life.

The Important icon indicates significant information that you shouldn't miss.

Where To Go From Here

Like all *Dummies* books, this book is written to be *modular* — meaning that each part can stand alone. So if you look through the table of contents and see something you're particularly curious about, feel free to head straight to that section. That said, I've organized the book to lead you through sociology from beginning concepts to specific topics, so if you're pretty sure you'll be looking at the whole book, your best bet is to start at the beginning and read your way through.

I'd also recommend flipping through and glancing at some of the text boxes. They provide concrete examples of the material discussed in the main body of the text, so if you feel like things are getting too theoretical or abstract, look to the text boxes for down-to-earth illustrations of what's being discussed. Have fun!

Part I
The Basic Basics

The 5th Wave   By Rich Tennant

"What do you mean I don't fit your desired sample population at this time?"

In this part . . .

*W*hat is *sociology?* It's not a term that usually comes up during dinner-table conversation, and most people have only a vague idea of what it's all about. By the end of this part, you'll know what sociology is, where it comes from, what sociologists do, why they do it, and how they do it.

Chapter 1

Sociology: Getting Your Head Around It

*Y*ou may be holding this book because you're enrolled in a sociology course in college or high school, or are thinking about studying sociology. You may be wondering if sociology can help you in your job; you may just be curious about different ways of looking at society; or you may be wondering about sociology for a different reason. Whatever the reason, you're reading this book because you want to know more about this thing called "sociology."

In this book, I explain the basics of sociology: what it is, how it's done, and what it's good for. Along the way, I do mention a lot of specific findings that sociologists have made, but my main goal is to tell you about *sociology*, not about *society*. After you understand the basics of sociology, you can roll up your sleeves and get online or into the library to see what sociologists have learned about any given place or time.

This chapter provides a road map to the rest of the book. In this chapter, I summarize the book and explain the basic ideas that this book will cover. I've organized the book to proceed from basic concepts to more specific topics, but the chapters are designed to stand alone, so you may not want to start right at the beginning.

Whatever path you take through this book — and through sociology generally — I hope you'll enjoy it and find the topic of sociology as fascinating as I do.

Understanding Sociology

In Part I of *Sociology For Dummies*, I explain the fundamentals of sociology: what it is, how it came to be, and how it's done.

Defining sociology

In a nutshell, sociology is the scientific study of society. Sociologists use the tools and methods of science to understand how and why humans behave the way they do when they interact together in groups. Though social groups — or societies — are made up of individual people, sociology is the study of the *group* rather than of the *individual*. When it comes to understanding how the individual human mind works, sociologists largely leave that up to psychologists.

Most people who call themselves "sociologists" work in universities and colleges, where they teach sociology and conduct sociological research. They ask a variety of questions about society, sometimes wanting answers just for the sake of curiosity; however, many times their findings are used to inform decisions by policymakers, executives, and other individuals. Many people who study sociology go on to conduct sociological research outside of academia, working for government agencies, think tanks, or private corporations. Accurate, systematic study of society is in one way or another useful to just about everyone.

Studying sociology, whether or not you call yourself a "sociologist," means taking a particular view of the world: a view that sociologist C. Wright Mills called "the sociological imagination." You have to be willing to set aside your ideas about how the social world *should* work so that you can see how it *actually* works. That doesn't mean that sociologists don't have personal values and opinions about the social world; they believe that to change the world, you first need to understand it.

The history of sociology

Sociology is considered one of the social sciences — along with economics, psychology, anthropology, geography, and political science (among others). The social sciences were born in the 18th and 19th centuries, as people began applying the scientific method to human life and behavior. The world was changing dramatically and quickly as industrial production replaced agriculture, as democratic republics replaced monarchies, and as city life replaced country life. Realizing how many great insights science had lent regarding the natural world, people decided to try to use the same method to understand the social world.

Among the social sciences, sociology has always been unique in its ambition to understand the *entire* social world — considering all its aspects in combination rather than in isolation. It's a daunting task, and one that sociologists are still struggling with today.

The most important early sociologists had clear ideas about how to study and understand society; these ideas still form the basis for much sociological investigation and discussion today. Karl Marx emphasized the importance of physical resources and the material world; he believed that conflict over resources is at the heart of social life. Emile Durkheim emphasized cooperation rather than conflict: He was interested in the shared norms and values that make cooperative social life possible. Max Weber took ideas from both Marx and Durkheim and argued that both conflict *and* cooperation, both material resources *and* cultural values are essential to social life. (See Chapter 3 for more on Marx, Durkheim, and Weber.)

Over the past century, sociologists have continued to debate the early sociologists' ideas and have applied them to specific societies all over the world. Thanks in large part to the influence of "the Chicago School" of sociologists in the early 20th century (see Chapter 3 for more on them), sociologists today pay close attention to small groups and person-to-person interaction as well as to the grand sweep of social history. Today, sociologists appreciate that the big questions and the little questions regarding society are interlinked, and that you can't understand the macro (the big) without also understanding the micro (the little).

Doing sociology

From a scientific perspective, society is a very difficult subject to study: It's huge, complex, and always changing. A perennial challenge for sociologists is to develop ways to accurately observe society, and to test hypotheses about the way it works.

Fundamentally, sociological research proceeds along the same lines as scientific research in any discipline: You decide what you're interested in, see what other researchers have learned about that subject, ask a specific question, and find data to answer it; then you analyze those data and interpret your results. The next researcher to be curious about the topic takes your results into consideration when they conduct their own study.

Sociologists use both *quantitative* and *qualitative* research methods. (See Chapter 4 for more on these methods.) Quantitative research involves questions that are asked and answered in terms of numbers; qualitative research involves close observation and detailed descriptions, usually written. Quantitative studies usually make use of statistical methods — sometimes very sophisticated statistical methods— for determining whether or not a trend observed in a set of data is likely representative of a general population. In using statistics or any other research tool, sociologists must take great care to avoid any of several potential pitfalls that can lead to inaccurate or misleading interpretations of the data they observe.

Seeing the World as a Sociologist

To help make sense of the very complicated social world, sociologists have developed some useful perspectives — ways of thinking about the social world that both help them to understand that world and to ask interesting questions about it. Unless you understand these perspectives, sociology can be quite confusing. In Part II of this book, I explain a few of the most important sociological perspectives.

Understanding culture

Sociologists differentiate between *culture* (that is, ideas and values) and *structure* (that is, the basic organization of society). Some sociologists tend to focus on culture, whereas others focus on structure; what's safe to say is that both culture and structure can play important roles in shaping the social world. (See Chapter 5 for more on culture and structure.)

Understanding culture means understanding that ideas and values — including those represented in art and in the media — don't always perfectly reflect the way people behave. Sociologists of culture study the production of culture (how culture comes about) and the reception of culture (the effect of culture on people's actions and beliefs) separately. (See Chapter 5 for more.) They also study different types and levels of culture, from mainstream culture (culture that is widely shared) to subcultures (cultures that exist in opposition to mainstream culture) to microcultures (cultures that are self-contained within a broader set of cultures).

Culture can influence how people think about themselves as well as how they think about other people: It can unite as well as divide.

Microsociology

Understanding how society works at the micro level — that is, at the one-on-one, person-to-person level — is especially tricky because it involves understanding how social norms and influences play out in each person's head.

Sociologists, economists, and other social scientists are all tremendously concerned with understanding how people make decisions about their lives. Sometimes those choices make perfect sense (taking a job because you need the money to buy food to live), and sometimes they seem to make no sense at all (betting that money on a casino game you're almost guaranteed to lose, or donating it to someone living on the other side of the world).

A perennial hot topic in microsociology is understanding how and why people make decisions from moment to moment, taking into account both their individual needs and their social circumstances.

Sociologists also study how people use social roles and rules to interact with other people. Sociologist Erving Goffman pointed out that every person is in a way like an actor on a stage: Your social identity is the role you play, and the setting in which you're interacting with others is like the stage you're performing upon. Everyone understands this to some extent, and they sometimes take advantage of the fact to get the things they want in life. (See Chapter 6 for more on microsociology.)

Network sociology

It's not just your career advisor who's talking about the importance of personal networks: In recent decades, sociologists have increasingly come to appreciate the fact that who you know (and how you know them) is of fundamental importance in determining everything from your values to your economic and political power. A society isn't just one big cloud of people who all breathe the same air, it's a highly complex network in which each person is tied to other people by relationships that vary in nature and intensity. (More on network sociology in Chapter 7.)

You're connected — either directly or through friends of friends of friends — to just about everyone in your society, but your ties to some people are much tighter than your ties to others. The people closest to you are sources of great support, but the people to whom you're only distantly connected can be even more valuable when it comes to gaining information that your friends or coworkers can't (or won't) tell you. Your position in the social network determines what options you have when finding a job, making friends, or spreading your influence.

Some sociologists devote themselves specifically to network sociology, but just about every sociologist today uses the insights and methods of network analysis to some extent. In Chapter 7, I mention some of the specific social insights that have come from network analysis.

Understanding Differences Among People and Groups

An issue of paramount importance to sociologists is understanding differences and inequality among different social groups. In Part III of this book, I take a look at some of the principal lines that divide in society: among classes, among races, among religions, and between "deviant" and "non-deviant" people.

Social stratification

The word "stratification" refers to different levels on top of each other, and it can be used for society as well as for rocks. Some people in any given society have more power and freedom than others — sociologists refer to these differences as differences of *social class*. There seems to be class inequality in every society, but it's much greater in some than in others, and sociologists have always debated whether or not significant class inequality is necessary for a society to function. (See Chapter 8 for more on social stratification.)

When you hear that someone is of a "higher class" than someone else, money is probably the first thing you think of, and indeed, money is certainly important. However, sociologists emphasize that there are many different means of social inequality: not just money, but occupation, ability, motivation, social connections, credentials, specialized knowledge, and discrimination by race, sex, caste, or age.

Class systems change over time, and people's positions in those class systems change even more frequently. Social mobility is something sociologists study closely.

Race and sex

Sociologists distinguish between *race* (a label that others assign to you) and *ethnicity* (the cultural group heritage with which you identify). They also distinguish between *sex* (your biological status: male or female) and *gender* (the way you identify your own status). All of these are among the most important distinctions in any society. Race, ethnicity, sex, and gender often serve as justification for discrimination and stereotyping, but they can also serve as common ground for people to bond with one another. (See Chapter 9 for more on race and ethnicity.)

Questions of race and ethnicity are particularly important today, when immigration is common and societies are increasingly diverse; but there are different races and ethnicities in *every* society, so for better and for worse, issues regarding race and ethnicity are timeless.

Institutionalized (that is, official) discrimination against members of particular races or sexes has happily declined sharply in recent decades, but distinctions of race, ethnicity, sex, and gender remain profoundly important in shaping how people see themselves and how they are seen by others.

Religion

Religion may seem like an unusual subject to study scientifically — but sociologists aim to understand the entirety of the social world, and religious beliefs and institutions are at the very center of that world. It is not for sociologists to determine what lies beyond this world, but sociologists can and do observe how religion affects people's lives in the here and now.

Sociologists study both religious values — what people believe about the spiritual world, specifically as it affects their actions in this world — and religious organizations. Like all social organizations, religious organizations have changed over time. What has remained the same is that for many people in all societies, religious groups are among the most important groups in their lives. (More on religion in Chapter 10.)

Crime and deviance

For sociologists, *crime* is one type of activity that falls under the general category of *deviance*. Deviance is defined as any kind of activity that varies from a social group's norms; crime is deviance that is formally punished with sanctions ranging from small fines to death.

Why do people commit crimes? Sociologists have different theories about that, but Durkheim famously observed that some form of crime has been present in every society ever known — in that sense, crime may or may not be good but it does seem to be "normal." What counts as crime in any particular society is a matter of both that society's specific laws and the social interactions surrounding the crime.

Can crime be stopped, or at least limited? Even if there is never a perfectly crime-free society, sociological research provides many clues as to how the worst crimes might be curtailed. In Chapter 11, I provide several examples.

Social Organization

Sociologists are indeed curious about the lines that divide people in society, but they're equally curious about how people manage to work together. In Part IV of this book, I look at three major types of social organization that have been of great concern both to sociologists and to ordinary people who want to work and live together peacefully and productively.

Corporate culture

Whether you're a high school student or a retired worker, you've had plenty of experience (maybe more than you'd like) with what sociologists call *formal organizations*: corporations, nonprofits, and other organizations of people working together to achieve some goal. Well, at least that's what they *say* they're doing.

Sociologist Richard Scott has pointed out that social organizations behave as *rational*, *natural*, and *open* systems. They are *rational* because they do typically work in a machine-like manner to achieve some goal, but they are also *natural* because humans are not machines and they bring their own foibles and idiosyncrasies into the workplace with them. Further, they are *open* insofar as their behavior is influenced by the behavior of other organizations around them. I explain this in more detail in Chapter 12.

Social movements and political sociology

What about organizations founded for a very clear purpose, such as to bring about social change? Do they ever work? Yes, but not always. Many sociologists have studied the circumstances under which social movements are successful: In general, it seems to be a matter of being in the right place, at the right time, with the necessary resources to make your voice heard.

Understanding how and why social movements work (and don't work) is related to the general subject of political sociology: the study of government, or "the state" in sociological parlance. Your government may seem to be big and invulnerable, but in the big picture, governments are quite fragile. (See Chapter 13 for more on the sociology of governments.)

Keeping a functioning government in business is a remarkable act of social cooperation, and when it doesn't work, the resulting revolution can have disastrous consequences for millions.

Urban sociology

Sociology was born in cities; specifically, in the fast-growing cities of the Industrial Revolution. There, people from wildly different backgrounds were encountering one another in what sometimes seemed like a chaotic stew of humanity. There was violence, disease and poverty, and an electrifying mix of languages, values, and ideas.

And 200 years later, the world is more urban than ever. How, and why, do people keep living in cities? Inner-city life is still crowded and excitingly intense, but not all urban life is inner-city life. Over the past several decades, millions and millions of people around the world have moved into suburban communities. As those suburbs have aged, some residents have moved back into the inner cities whereas others have moved even further out, to newly built "exurbs." All along, sociologists have been there to study urban (and suburban, and exurban) change. You can read about it in Chapter 14.

Sociology and Your Life

Getting right to the heart of things, what relevance does sociology have for *your* life? In Part V, I explain how sociology can change the way you understand your past and your future.

The life course

Your life course, of course, is your own: You decide if and when you'll go to school, marry, have children, and retire. Still, at every stage you're affected by social institutions and social norms regarding the life course. What are you "supposed" to do? What happens if you don't? The timing and nature of life-course transitions varies greatly among societies, and sociologists have studied why.

As you live your life, you'll be profoundly influenced by the families you're a part of; sociologists and historians have shattered many myths about the family, and in Chapter 15 I explain how sociology can help you understand your own family. I also address the always-topical subject of health care, which influences not only how long you live but the quality of the life you have.

Social change

The one constant in social life is change: changing norms, changing classes, changing *everything*. Is there any way to make sense of all that change?

Sociologists believe there is, even if they sometimes disagree about exactly how. Marx believed that social change was driven by conflict over material resources. Durkheim thought that change was inevitable, with norms and values changing as societies became larger and more diverse. Weber thought that both material conflicts and changing norms influenced social change.

From the very beginning, sociologists have hoped to predict the future so as to be able to influence it. Sociology is, and will likely remain, a long way from being able to see the future any more clearly than meteorology can — but like weather forecasters, sociologists have a fair idea of when a storm front is brewing. What they may be most curious about is the future of sociology itself. Will sociology survive? What will society look like in the future? See Chapter 16 for my best guesses at the answers.

Sociology for Dummies, for Dummies

Still aren't entirely sure about all this? Try flipping forward to Part VI, "the Part of Tens." In chapters 17 and 18, I mention ten ways to use sociological insight in everyday life; also, I provide a list of ten readable sociology books that you can pick up if this book piques your interest. In Chapter 19, I list ten myths about society busted by sociology — ten things you may have *thought* you knew about the social world around you.

In the end, that's my best argument for why you should read this book: to learn more about the social world around you. Sure, you'll learn something about sociology itself — about Talcott Parsons's public spat with C. Wright Mills, about Arlie Hochschild's conversations with frustrated working mothers, about the sociologists who went to Paducah, Kentucky to talk with families affected by a tragic school shooting. But more importantly, in learning about sociologists' attempts to understand the ever-changing social world, you'll learn about that world itself, the world that gives meaning to your life.

Sociology: What's the point?

I hope you're excited to begin reading this book, but I don't flatter myself that it's the most important thing in your life right now. What *is* the most important thing in your life right now? Are you just starting a romantic relationship — or just ending one? Is something important going on at work? Are you preoccupied with a tough situation involving a loved one, or are you excited about an upcoming vacation or graduation?

All of those things are very personal, but they're also very social. You experience events like that individually, but your experience also involves the people around you — and the people around them, and the people around the people around them. As much as your life is your own, it is fundamentally, profoundly influenced — in

some ways, *defined* — by the society in which you live.

If you've done any traveling, or read books or see movies about other cultures, you realize how much norms, values, and practices vary from one society to the next. The choices you make are your own, but the choices you're given come from the society you're in, as does a lot about the way you regard those choices. If you don't understand how your society works and how it's shaped your life, you're in the dark about important parts of yourself. Only by understanding your society — which sociology can help you to do — can you truly understand yourself.

Chapter 2

What Is Sociology, and Why Should I Care?

*A*lthough you've heard the word *sociology*, you may not really know what it means. Maybe you think sociology is the same thing as social work, or you confuse it with psychology or anthropology. Perhaps you've noticed that sociologists tend to pop up in the news to discuss social problems like racism or violence. You might have an idea that sociologists study social problems, but you don't really know how sociologists actually conduct their studies. Like most people, you probably envision a few guys in tweed jackets sitting in offices and pontificating about why everyone's so screwed up.

In this chapter, I explain in clear terms exactly what sociology is, what a sociological question is, and how, in a general sense, a sociologist would go about finding an answer to it. I list some of the most important settings in which sociology works ⏤ or where sociology is done, even by people who may not consider themselves sociologists. Finally, I explain how sociology affects your life today and how learning more about sociology will help you in the future.

By the end of this chapter, you'll know enough to join the guys in the tweed jackets and do some pontificating of your own. But even if your friends aren't burning up with curiosity about sociology, after you understand a little bit about what it is, you'll be hooked.

Figuring Out What Sociology Is

A student-written university course guide once jokingly defined sociology as the study of "everything in the whole wide world." That definition isn't entirely untrue; sociologists study just about everything people do. And *how* sociologists study just about everything people do defines sociology.

Defining sociology

The definition of sociology, after you've learned it, is easy to remember because the definition is right there in its name: *soci* for "society" and *ology* for "the study of." Sociology is the study of society.

Social sciences take a systematic approach to the analysis of human lives and interactions. And sociology, which is considered a social science, is generally grouped with the following areas of study:

- ✔ Psychology
- ✔ Anthropology
- ✔ Economics
- ✔ Political science
- ✔ Ethnic studies (for example, African-American studies or Latino studies)
- ✔ Area studies (for example, Asian studies or European studies)
- ✔ Gender studies (for example, women's studies)
- ✔ Cultural studies

Sociology shares a general approach with all these fields, and sociologists often read work by or collaborate with experts in these disciplines. But sociologists insist on reserving the right to study *any* of those topics. Politics, economics, culture, race, gender . . . sociologists believe that these all interact with one another, and if you try to study just one of those areas in isolation, you risk missing important information about how a social group or situation works. So, you can study just about anything having to do with humans' social life and call it sociology — but only if you study it in a scientific, systematic way.

Studying society scientifically

If you've ever participated in a science fair, you know how the scientific method works. You:

1. Ask a question.

2. Set up an experiment or a study that can provide an answer to that question.

3. Make very careful observations.

4. Analyze your observations to see what answer they might provide.

Scientists believe the scientific method is the best way to study the natural world, and social scientists believe that's the best way to study the social world, too. However, one of the hardest things to understand about sociology is also one of the most important: Sociologists have asked many important questions about society, but the most important contribution of sociology is *not* the answers to those questions. It's the fact that they were asked at all.

What makes studying society in a scientific manner so difficult, but ultimately so rewarding, is that to do so you have to set aside your own biases and pre-conceptions about how society "should" work. If you're going to study social norms objectively, you're going to have to understand that your own norms and values aren't the only ones that exist, and you're going to have to put aside any question of whether your own norms and values are the "best."

Emile Durkheim, one of the founders of sociology (more about him in Chapter 3) used what has been called an "organic metaphor" for society. Not everyone agrees that his model is the right way to understand how society *works,* but it's a good way to start understanding what society *is.*

Durkheim said society is like a human body — one big thing made up of many smaller parts. Your body is made of many different systems (nervous system, respiratory system, digestive system) that are themselves made up of organs (brain, lungs, stomach), and the organs are made of billions of cells of all different types. In this way, you are your cells because there's nothing in your body that's not made of cells; however, your cells aren't *you.* It's only when your cells all work together that they make you who you are. There's not any one cell that is "you" — you are *all* of your cells, working together in organs and systems to make up the total person who is sitting there, breathing and thinking and holding this book.

Society is like that — but much bigger and even more complicated. A society is made up of many people acting together in groups and systems, all of which act together (even if they don't always cooperate, they at least affect each other). Your country is a society, but no one person — not even the president or the prime minister — *is* the society. The society is all the people in your country interacting together. Just like a body is, in a sense, what happens when a lot of different cells interact together, a society is what happens when a lot of people interact together.

Just as you need to look at an entire body to understand how the body works, sociologists believe that you need to look at an entire society to understand how society works. You can't understand how a liver works unless you understand its place in the body, and sociologists believe that you can't understand how any part of society (a company, an ethnic group, a small town) works unless you understand its place in society.

Asking and answering sociological questions

To study society scientifically means asking scientific questions about society. A scientific, sociological question is a question about how society works — not about how it *should* work, but about how it *does* work. Of course, asking and answering such questions takes some finesse. So the following two sections give you more detailed info on how scientific, sociological questions should be formed as well as answered.

Putting together empirical questions

Sociological questions are in the general category of questions known as *empirical questions.* An empirical question is a question that can be answered by gathering facts. To best understand how to construct an empirical question for sociological study, you may find it helpful to consider the differences among the following types of questions:

- ✔ **Theoretical question:** A question about ideas, which can be answered with other ideas. If I ask, "What is racism?" I'm asking a theoretical question — I'm looking for a general definition of what is called "racism."

- ✔ **Moral question:** A question about how things "should" or "should not" be. If I ask, "Should there be racism?" I'm asking a moral question — I'm asking you to make a value judgment about whether it is right to judge someone by the color of his or her skin.

✔ **Empirical question:** A question that can be answered by gathering facts. If I ask, "Does racism exist in this society?" I'm asking an *empirical* question — I'm looking for information about the world that can be determined by making observations.

In this case, if I want to fight racism, I can do so more effectively if I have accurate information about how, where, and why people act in a racist manner. Sociologists are strong believers in the value of seeing society as it actually is, not as they want it to be.

How I became a sociologist

The story of how I became a sociologist may help you to understand what's unique about the sociological perspective, and to think about how sociology can cause you to think differently about your job and your life.

When I was in high school and looking for a job, I quickly decided that being a babysitter was a lot more fun than being a golf caddy. So I ended up babysitting for many different families. Doing that work, I temporarily took the place of many different parents with many different views on child-rearing: TV, or no TV? Strict bedtime, or whenever the kids get tired? Organized activities, or free play? Needless to say, every set of parents thought theirs was the "right" way to raise children. They might check out a stack of parenting books from the library, but they would usually end up sticking with the one that told them to do whatever it was that they were going to do anyway.

I went on to study education in college, but my favorite course was one on the history of education, where we learned about the many changes in people's views of children and how they learn. Again, I was struck by how in every time and place, people were convinced that they had it all figured out. What made us so sure that we finally had it "right"?

Eventually, I realized that I was interested not in the education of children, but rather in the sociology of childhood — the study of different ideas about what children should do, and what those changing ideas have to do with changes in other areas of society. For my doctoral dissertation in sociology I studied the history of children's books and media: how changes in technology and child-rearing have affected what we value in our children's reading material. I systematically gathered articles about children's books and media and analyzed them to test my hypothesis that, in our concern that kids aren't reading enough, we have become much more open-minded about what we consider "good" reading material for children. I called the dissertation *From Captains Courageous to Captain Underpants.*

Becoming a sociologist allowed me to pursue questions that I felt needed to be answered: How do we decide what's right and wrong whether it comes to kids' books, or anything else? How do our society's norms and values come to be? Why do the people in one neighborhood have completely different ideas about child-rearing than the people in the next neighborhood? Those are fundamentally sociological questions.

Generalizing answers

Sociological questions are questions about society — but of course, you can't just look at "society." You have to look at *a* society, at specific people in a specific place at a specific time. Still, sociologists want to understand how human society works in general — so they try to ask and answer questions in a way that allow them to generalize as much as possible to other places and times. Here are some examples of sociological questions, and studies that might help provide answers.

- ✔ **Does the extent of discrimination vary by the size of the minority group?** A sociologist might look at sexism in companies with different gender ratios — is sexism more or less severe when there are more women in the workforce?

- ✔ **Does the quantity of social ties affect the quality of social ties?** A sociologist might conduct interviews to see whether people with more acquaintances overall have as many — or fewer — close friends compared to people with fewer acquaintances overall.

- ✔ **Is inequality inherited?** A sociologist might conduct a survey to see whether people raised in poverty grow up to have different jobs than people raised in wealth.

These are big, complicated questions, but they're questions that do have answers! The trick is finding out what those answers are when your questions are about something as massive as society. It's not easy, but sociologists are ready for the challenge. (In Chapter 4, I go into more detail about how, specifically, sociological studies are conducted.)

Looking at the previous questions, you probably have guesses as to what the answers are. Your guesses may be right, but remember that they are guesses — these are empirical questions that do have right and wrong answers, and the only way to know for sure is to go out and gather data. Over the course of this book you'll come across many examples of sociological findings that may surprise you, so you need to be careful not to assume that your guesses about how society works are correct.

Discovering Where Sociology Is "Done"

So who studies sociology? Where are all those sociologists hiding? As it happens, they're hiding in plain sight; people in many different settings and organizations use sociology to understand society and help solve social problems. Some of these people call themselves sociologists and some of them don't (depending on their jobs, they might call themselves "researchers" or "program officers" or "reporters"), but they all make use of sociological findings and ideas.

Colleges and universities

The loudest, proudest sociologists are found in institutions of higher learning, where they explicitly teach sociology to (more or less) eager young minds. Many colleges and universities offer undergraduate and graduate degrees in sociology, and coursework in sociology is often a requirement for students majoring in social science (for example economics, psychology, and political science) or in fields where they will be working with people (for example education, social work, and law enforcement). Elective courses in sociology can also be very popular, especially when they deal with interesting subjects like sex and gender, media and culture, or race and immigration.

A lot of sociological research also goes on at colleges and universities, especially at research universities where faculty members are required to have active research agendas. A professor of sociology at a research university might be busy coordinating a team of research assistants working on a major study; training doctoral candidates who will become professors themselves; and teaching undergraduate courses in sociology. Professors with particular specialties may hold joint appointments with other schools (a medical school or law school) or departments (an African-American studies department or an anthropology department) at the same university. Faculty members, graduate students, and even advanced undergraduate students often travel to sociology conferences where they share their completed or ongoing work with colleagues from other institutions.

Sociology is also taught at many high schools, sometimes under the general heading of "social studies." It's relatively unusual for someone to be a full-time sociology teacher at a high school — but there are the lucky few!

Think tanks and research institutes

Research institutes, sometimes called *think tanks*, are organizations that focus on research in a particular area. Often they're more agenda-driven than colleges or universities, and they often receive funding from people who support a certain cause such as:

- A political party
- Children's welfare
- Women's rights
- Access to health care
- A position on abortion
- Free trade

People with an interest in social issues like these have an interest in gathering facts that will help them accomplish their mission most effectively or garner support for their cause. Trained sociologists who are familiar with research findings and skilled in conducting studies often work at these organizations alongside psychologists, political scientists, experienced journalists, and other experts.

These organizations often publish research reports that can affect policy and rally the public around a cause. When you hear a news report about a current study whose results sound provocative — for example, that a large number of young children have TVs in their rooms — it often comes from an organization like one of these.

Nonprofit organizations

Every nonprofit organization, from Greenpeace to the Girl Scouts to the Boston Ballet, has a mission it is seeking to accomplish, and sociologists often work with these organizations to help them do so most effectively and efficiently.

A Big Brothers/Big Sisters organization, for example, may want to know whether it's best to pair kids with big "siblings" who have similar backgrounds, or whether it's more beneficial to introduce kids to mentors from other walks of life who can introduce them to new people and places. A sociologist can help make this decision based on what other sociologists have discovered, or perhaps conduct a study to see what has worked best in other contexts.

The people who do this work may or may not call themselves sociologists, but in systematically gathering and analyzing information about the social world, they are "doing" sociology.

Government

Governments are the biggest non-profits of all, and they face all the same challenges on a much larger scale. At all levels and in all units of government, sociologists can help shape policy and allocate funding so that the many goals of government — from educating children to keeping the peace — are met as successfully as possible.

- ✔ **Legislators** turn to sociologists for advice on which programs and policies might be most effective. What can government do to reduce unemployment, to provide for the elderly, to support single parents? Which foreign policy initiatives are likely to be successful? If a neighboring country becomes unstable and dangerous, what should be done to prevent a catastrophic civil war?

- ✔ **Law enforcement officers** must use their limited resources to prevent crime from happening and, when it occurs, minimize the damage and apprehend the perpetrators. Is there any way to predict how and when crime will occur? Can criminals be rehabilitated, and how can they be supported upon their release from jail so that they don't return to crime?

- ✔ **Social workers** in government agencies help people whose lives are made difficult by troublesome social situations — from poverty to family conflicts to health struggles. What are the best strategies for helping people in these situations? Should government provide financial support, food assistance, skills training, or other resources? How much, for how long, and to whom?

- ✔ **Teachers and educational administrators** find it enough of a challenge to teach reading, writing, and 'rithmatic, but also face a host of other social issues. How can bullying be prevented? Why do students drop out of school, and how can schools get them back? Should schools sponsor extracurricular activities — and if so, which ones?

These are just a few of the difficult and important social questions that governmental agencies face. Sociologists — sometimes working directly for these agencies, sometimes coming in as consultants — can help these agencies make well-informed decisions.

Journalism and reporting

I work as a journalist in addition to teaching sociology, so I've experienced firsthand how a background in sociology can help inform news reporting.

There are important differences between journalism and sociology. Journalists must publish news much more often, and much more quickly than sociologists, so they usually don't have time to conduct the kind of systematic study that sociologists prefer. But journalists share sociologists' interest in understanding what makes society tick, and they're out on the front lines reporting on social change.

When violence flares up in a particular neighborhood, sociologists can lend perspective and later may conduct a detailed study of the conflict, but journalists have to be there immediately. And a journalist who's trained in sociology or who knows what sociologists have discovered about violence and urban life is in a good position to understand what is happening even as it unfolds.

Plus, it's through journalists that the public learns about findings in sociology and other scientific disciplines, so journalists need to be able to think critically about these studies, or they risk misleading readers.

When reading a news story, ask yourself what assumptions the reporter is making. Does the story seem to suggest that things "should" be a certain way? If so, that is an opinion or a value judgment rather than a statement of fact. In the case of a crime report, for example, there may empirically be logical reasons for that crime — whether or not you think it "should" have happened. (See Chapter 11 for more on the sociology of crime.)

Business and consulting

Many sociologists at colleges and universities focus on understanding how businesses and the economy work, but businesspeople aren't about to leave that job entirely to professors! The kind of social analysis that sociologists do is critical to success in business, where the stakes are high and mistakes can be costly. If sociologists are curious about how information flows through different kinds of social networks, you can bet that marketers and retailers are wondering as well. Sociologists need to set aside their personal biases and study a social situation objectively; successful businesspeople understand this as well. Just because you think something is a great idea doesn't mean it's actually going to fly with your customers.

Management consultants are similar to sociologists — in fact, they often *are* sociologists who have earned degrees in the subject. A management consultant's job is not to be an expert in any one industry, but to look at a company and see how problems with its organization may be keeping it from performing as effectively and efficiently as possible. The success of management consultants is proof of the fundamental sociological principle that something you learn from one social situation may be generalizible to another. Whether you're Cap'n Jack's Frozen Fish or Cathy's Computers, you're going to face certain challenges that are universal, such as employee motivation, supply chain management, publicity, and advertising.

Everyday life

Let's face it, it's not easy being you — or being me, or being *anyone* in today's big, complicated, diverse global society. You're presented with a dizzying array of choices every minute of every day of your life, and whether you're choosing a husband or choosing a brand of toothpaste, it can be really tough to know what choices to make. Sometimes you just go with your gut feelings, sometimes you act on your detailed knowledge of a particular situation or person, and sometimes you just choose randomly — but a lot of the time, you're thinking sociologically even if you don't realize it. Consider these situations:

✔ You're going to a job interview or an important party, and you want to know how to dress.

✔ You've started dating a coworker, and you're trying to figure out how to reconcile your professional and personal roles.

✔ You're buying a house, and you want to know what different neighborhoods will be like in ten years' time.

In each of those situations, you're thinking sociologically — you're trying to figure out how society works so you can make it work to your advantage. Sociology affects your life every day. (For specific examples of how you can use sociology in your own life, see Chapter 18.)

Recognizing How Sociology Affects Your Life and Your World

Okay, sociology is everywhere. So what? Why should *you* care? What can learning about sociology do for you besides helping you pass a class or make scintillating cocktail-party conversation?

Sociologist Randall Collins uses the phrase *sociological insight* to describe the way that learning to think sociologically can change your entire perspective on the world. In his book of that title, Collins offers many examples, including the sociological insights that crime is normal (see Chapter 11 of this book) and that being in a relationship is like owning property (see Chapter 6). Understanding these insights doesn't mean you're going to stop prosecuting criminals or start treating your husband like a doormat, but it does put people's behavior in an interesting new light.

Sociological insight may be sociology's greatest contribution to the world, and it can make a difference in your life as well. In this section I mention several ways that thinking sociologically can make a difference in your life.

Thinking about the social world in an objective, value-free way

When I started teaching sociology at a technical college, the dean made clear to me that my number one job was to help my students critically examine their own beliefs about the social world. The students at that college go on to serve as police officers, nurses, teachers, and therapists — all professions where they're certain to encounter people from a wide range of backgrounds. Going into any of those careers with cultural blinders on can lead to unfortunate, perhaps even dangerous, misunderstandings. Consider these hypothetical situations:

- ✔ As a law enforcement officer, you are called to a college campus where neighbors report that a group of boys are skateboarding on a set of concrete benches, making loud noise and damaging the benches. You grew up being told to stay away from "skate punks" who "probably are doing all kinds of drugs" and "have no respect for authority." When you arrive on the scene, you see the boys — laughing, smoking, cheering one another on as they try to perform complicated tricks.

- ✔ As a nurse, you see a female patient who seems to have severe discomfort in her abdomen — but she can't tell you about it directly because she doesn't speak English. Her husband translates for her in his own imperfect English, and they refuse to allow one of your clinic's translators to help. "Only I can speak for my wife," says the husband.

- ✔ As a teacher, you have a student who regularly misses class and is falling behind in her work. When you call her mother in for a conference, the mother explains that she's a single parent of three children, and she's working two jobs to support her family. Sometimes she needs to ask her daughter to skip school to take care of the younger kids. She doesn't see anything wrong with that. "Family comes first," she says.

These are all difficult situations, and it's not obvious what would be the best way to handle any of them. What won't help, though, in any of these cases, is trusting that your cultural values and norms are the "right" ones, and that anyone who disagrees is wrong. Some might say that the skateboarders are deviant, that the husband is abusing his wife, and that the mother is exploiting her daughter. Maybe all those things are true, but it's important to understand that the people you're dealing with in all those situations may have very different definitions of what constitutes deviance, abuse, and exploitation.

To say that sociology can help you to approach these situations in a "value-free" way is not to say that you should check your values at the door, but it is to say that sociology can help you understand the difference between your own values and others' values. No sociologist would say that all criminals are just misunderstood, or that there is no such thing as spousal abuse or child exploitation. Instead a sociologist would emphasize that all those things need to be carefully, objectively defined so that you can deal with people fairly and sympathetically. Applying terms like "deviance" or "exploitation" shouldn't be just a matter of "I know it when I see it." Learning to distance yourself, when necessary, from your own preconceptions is useful in any field of endeavor.

Visualizing connections across times and places

In recent years, sociologists have studied all these topics:

- Neighbors' coordinated efforts to defend Paris when it was under siege in 1871. (Roger V. Gould)

- The organization of the Burning Man festival in Nevada's Black Rock Desert. (Katherine K. Chen)

- Women's mobilization into the Salvadoran Guerrilla Army. (Jocelyn Viterna)

- People's discussions of moral order in Europe during the Reformation and the Enlightenment. (Robert Wuthnow)

- Families going through funhouses at an amusement park. (Jack Katz)

That's just a tiny sampling of the incredibly diverse array of subjects sociologists study. The studies are about wildly different events, places, and times, but they all appeared in mainstream sociological journals or books, meant to be read by all sociologists.

The reason sociologists pay attention to studies about very different subjects is that sociologists believe there are important common elements across all of human experience. Sociologists believe that the organization of the Burning Man Festival may, if carefully studied, have something to teach us about social organization generally; and that women's mobilization into the Salvadoran Guerrilla Army may have something to teach us about women's (and men's) mobilization into political parties or protest movements anywhere in the world. Revealing the connections and similarities uniting very different places, times, and settings is one of the most powerful and important tasks sociology can do.

Uncovering what really matters . . . and what doesn't

The social world is incredibly complicated, and neither sociologists nor anyone else have completely figured out how it works. Sociologists are sometimes criticized for oversimplifying the social world, but believe me, sociologists are painfully aware of just how complicated the social world is! When you spend years of your life trying to design studies that will shed even a little bit of light on a question — such as what causes people to commit crimes — you begin to appreciate how many different factors affect people's lives and how difficult it can be to say anything that's generally true about large numbers of people.

That said, sociologists have developed powerful tools to help understand how society works, and sociology can help to cut through the confusion to focus attention on what really matters. Many sociological studies have shown that what people assumed were very important are, in fact, not such a big deal. For example:

- ✔ Frank Dobbin, Alexandra Kalev, and Erin Kelly studied companies that tried to make their workforces more racially diverse. They found companies that held big, showy diversity training programs became, on average, no more diverse than they'd been before the programs. Companies that actually assigned a person to keep an eye on hiring saw much better results.

- ✔ Jason Kaufman and I studied high school students' exposure to the arts, trying to see what made kids more likely to attend competitive colleges. We found that kids whose parents attended art museums were much more likely to attend elite colleges — and that it made no difference whatsoever whether or not the kids even went along!

- ✔ The "broken windows" theory of policing, famously advocated by New York City mayor Rudy Giuliani in the 1990s, holds that neighborhoods with signs of disorder are more likely sites for crime — that if criminals see a broken window in one building, they figure it's okay to break a window in the next. Sociologists Robert J. Sampson and Stephen Raudenbush, though, found that although it's true that people's perceptions of a neighborhood's "disorder" make a difference in the neighborhood's crime rate, people see evidence of "disorder" not as much in broken windows but in, sad to say, the mere presence of racial minorities like blacks and Latinos.

These studies are examples of how sociologists, rather than oversimplifying the world, have shown exactly how complicated it is. It's more obvious how people should change their actions based on the diversity-training study than what they should do after learning about the college attendance study or the neighborhood disorder study — parents probably aren't going to start visiting art museums to make their kids more likely to go to Yale, and police certainly aren't going to tell African-Americans and Latinos to stay out of sight — but now you know that it's barking up the wrong tree to drag your kids to museums to make them more attractive college candidates or to spend a lot of money fixing broken windows in hopes of keeping crime down. Sociology can help reveal what really matters, and what really doesn't.

It's all in the family . . . or is it?

One of the most controversial sociological arguments about social policy was a report issued in 1965 by Daniel Patrick Moynihan, a social scientist who was then U.S. assistant secretary of labor. The report, a private memorandum to President Lyndon Johnson that was quickly leaked to the press, was called *The Negro Family: The Case for National Action*. The memo, which became known as "the Moynihan Report," was Moynihan's attempt to convince President Johnson to promote marriage and stable family life among African-Americans.

Moynihan saw blacks as still healing from the devastating effects of slavery, which ripped families apart. The high rate of family instability among African-Americans, said Moynihan, caused large numbers of black children to grow up in troubled circumstances, to do poorly in schoolwork and job searches, and to turn to crime and deviance.

Critics of the Moynihan Report said that Moynihan (who was white, and had himself grown up in a poor, single-parent family) was "blaming the victim" and letting whites off the hook for the racism and discrimination that was doing far more than any private family issues to keep blacks from succeeding in the United States. Others — including Martin Luther King, Jr. — said that Moynihan was right on, and that the government should do more to promote family stability.

To this day, sociologists and lawmakers debate the Moynihan Report. Given that government has limited resources and can't do everything, should it focus on ending discrimination or on supporting families? And what does "supporting families" even mean? Is there anything government agencies can do to discourage divorce or out-of-wedlock births? Is that the government's job, or should government stay out of people's personal lives? The answers weren't obvious then and aren't obvious now — but the Moynihan Report has helped inspire decades of sociological research that can help lawmakers make well-informed decisions.

Informing social policy

If you live in a democracy, you're a policymaker — your vote helps to determine which politicians are elected and which laws are passed. Thinking sociologically can help you to choose wisely.

Every social policy is a sociological argument, whether or not the people who created the policy think about it that way. A social policy is a government action designed to change a society in some way. Knowing *which* action to take to achieve a certain goal can be difficult, and as politicians and pundits argue about the merits of various pieces of legislation, they are often having sociological debates about how society works, what (if anything . . . but there's always something) is wrong with it, and how that problem might be fixed.

It's kind of like looking under the hood of a car and trying to figure out what's making that clanking noise, or why one headlight has mysteriously stopped working. If you don't know how a car works, you're going to have a very hard time fixing it — and the same principle applies for society. Without the benefit of sociology and the other social sciences, legislators are just making rough guesses about what policies might work to lower crime or to help small businesses. (In fact, that was one of the reasons sociology was invented — more about that in Chapter 3.)

Keeping a unique perspective for everyday problems

Sociology is about society rather than about the individual, but it would be a mistake to think that sociology has no bearing on your individual life. Sociology can be tremendously liberating when you apply it to the society (or societies) you live and work in every day.

You live in a maze of implicit and explicit rules that tell you how to dress, how to act, who to hang out with, who to hook up with, where to go to school, where to work and how to spend the money you make, what car to drive, where to go on vacation, and even where and when to blow your nose. You don't have to obey those rules, but if you don't, you risk social disapproval or even — if you break a rule that's been written into law — imprisonment. The consequences of wearing an unfashionable outfit to a party are just as real as the consequences of walking into a wall.

But unlike the rules of physics, the rules of society can change. If there's something about society that you don't like, you can work to make society different. Not only can sociology help you to see different possibilities, it can actually teach you effective strategies for bringing change about. The socio-logical perspective is refreshing: it acknowledges that things are the way they are for a reason, that the organization of society is no accident — but that things can change, and if you understand how society works, you're in a much better position to make that change happen.

Chapter 3

Making It Up as They Went Along: The History of Sociology

*Y*es, this is the requisite history chapter — the flashback section, if you will. It's here not just because it "has to be," but because it actually *has to be:* Understanding how sociology was developed will help you understand how sociologists go about doing their thing today.

In this chapter, I start by covering the genesis of sociology; why people needed a new way of looking at the social world. I briefly tell you about the lives of the three most famous and influential sociologists — Karl Marx, Emile Durkheim, and Max Weber — and tell the story of how sociology traveled across the Atlantic, becoming more "down to earth" in the process. Finally, I chronicle the rise and fall of Talcott Parsons (the sociologist who *almost* figured it all out) and bring you up to the present day.

So . . . Who Cares about History?

I can hear you groan. Isn't it enough to understand what sociologists do *today*? Why bother with learning what people *used* to think about society? Well, the following list gives you a few good reasons to learn at least a little bit about the history of sociology:

✔ **Understanding why sociologists think the way they do and ask the questions they do:** Even if sociologists today know a lot more than their predecessors did, they have the same essential concerns about society and social organization. The new approach to looking at the social world — a scientific, systematic approach — developed by the first sociologists continues to provide the foundation of all sociology. The new science of sociology helped thinkers in 1830 cast aside their personal biases and come up with new solutions to social problems; it does the same today.

✔ **Understanding "old" arguments and ideas that are still useful today:** Over the course of sociology's history there have been some pretty smart people who have come up with ideas and arguments that are still very useful today. Even though Karl Marx, for example, died over a hundred years ago, his work still inspires sociologists — and social activists — to be mindful of the conflict and exploitation that can take place in capitalist societies. Emile Durkheim's argument that cultural values change as a society grows and roles differentiate has become all the more important as societies around the world have become bigger and more diverse. Max Weber's discussion of "the iron cage" of modern life can seem eerily appropriate when you're doing your taxes or waiting in line at a government bureau. The concepts developed by Marx, Durkheim, and Weber are a common vocabulary that sociologists use as they discuss society today.

✔ **Understanding which important ideas *didn't* work out so well:** If you have to reinvent the wheel, you might as well reinvent the round one instead of the square one! The name "Parsons" is almost a dirty word among many sociologists today, but Talcott Parsons's work is still widely read. It's a brilliant articulation of an idea about society — that everything is there for a reason, which was a very compelling idea that many of the world's best sociologists were studying for years. It didn't turn out to be the most accurate way to think about society, but learning why can help you avoid Parsons's mistakes.

Thinking about Society before There Was Sociology

Sociology as we know it was developed in the 19th century, but it's not like it took people all those centuries just to notice that there is such a thing as society! For all of human history, people have talked about society and debated its organization. Sociology was invented as a powerful tool for answering the questions that people had been wondering about for ages.

In this section, I explain how people first started thinking about society and describe the seismic social changes that inspired the development of sociology in the 19th century.

People are the same everywhere you go . . . except when they aren't

When I say that people have long been aware of society, I don't just mean that they noticed there were folks hanging around together in large groups — I mean that long ago, people noticed that there seems to be an *organization* to society. Whether you were a tribesman on the African savannah, a citizen of ancient Athens, or a serf in medieval France, you might have looked around and noticed that your group and the next group over and the group beyond that had all managed to get themselves in some sort of order. You might notice certain constants among all groups: the haves and the have-nots, the family, religion and spirituality, and organized production and trade of food and tools.

But just because these constants are always present in society doesn't mean that they're the same everywhere — there's wide variation across social groups. Here's what I mean:

- ✔ There are "haves" and "have-nots" in every society, but in some societies there are vast discrepancies between the fabulously wealthy and the dirt-poor, and in others the differences are not nearly as great.

- ✔ Every society has families of some sort, but in some societies those families are small and in others they are large and multi-generational. Some societies are patriarchal (the male lineage is most important) and some are matriarchal (the female lineage is most important).

- ✔ Every society has some form of religion. In some cases this means strict laws enforced by powerful clerics whereas in other cases it means a free sense of spirituality with religious leaders who serve only as helpful guides.

- ✔ Food and tools are produced and traded in all societies, but think about the difference between traditional Native American cultures (many of which had little concept of "property" in the modern sense of the word) and capitalist society with its elaborate financial system.

Besides this variation in stable societies, there is sometimes outright social breakdown — with leaders toppled and civil wars raging for years or decades. People have always been curious about social organization: Why is society organized the way it is? Is it just random, or is there a method behind the madness? If people could understand how society works, they thought, maybe they could solve social problems like war and poverty.

Pre-sociologists: People with ideas about society

For many centuries, people tended to focus on the similarities rather than the differences in social organization. If societies were different from one another, people thought, it must be because some were "right" and some were "wrong." But who was to decide right from wrong? What follows is a list of people who have tried:

- **Theologians:** They argued that God (or the gods) had a plan for the world, and sacred scriptures might reveal that plan as God (or, again, the gods) intended it to be manifest. Feudal society in Europe and elsewhere was run jointly by church and state leaders who believed they were running things the way God wanted them to be run.

- **Philosophers:** Many philosophers believed that the key to successful social organization lay in an accurate understanding of human nature. If philosophers could figure out, by means of reflection, observation, and discussion, what the essence of human nature was, they could design a perfect society. Plato's *Republic*, one of the greatest works of classical philosophy, lays out Plato's vision of an ideal society.

- **Historians:** Historians looked to the past to understand the present. Many historians were almost sociological in their comparison of past societies with present societies — in fact, the first sociologists were very interested in historical change — whereas others looked to the past for ideals to be emulated in the present. For example, many historians were convinced that when it came to an effective legal system, the ancient Romans had it figured out and that any successful legal system would have to be based on Roman law.

These theological, philosophical, and historical approaches were interesting and, in some cases, quite useful — but by the late 1700s it became clear that a new way of understanding society would be necessary. Society changed more and more quickly, and people became less and less convinced that the answers to society's problems could be found in a 2,000-year-old book of scripture, philosophy, or law.

Political and industrial revolution: Ready or not, here it comes

There's no shortage of tragic conflict, shocking social upheaval, and stunning technological transformation in the 21st century — but even so, it's difficult for people today to understand just how profound and disorienting were the changes that shook Western society in the 18th and 19th centuries. These changes were so shocking that they caused people to question their long-held assumptions about human nature and social organization, and to wonder whether the scientific method — which had been so useful in understanding the natural world — might not also be useful for understanding the scary and exciting new social world they were living in.

This is a topic that's often in the news today: Is it possible to design a political system to be stable, or are some countries or social situations just naturally unstable? Turn to Chapter 13 for more information on government and political revolutions, as well as information about social movements.

Political revolutions

The American Revolution of 1776 was certainly a wake-up call to the entrenched European powers, but it was nothing compared to the French Revolution and its associated conflicts, which tore across Europe from 1789 to 1814. What was especially shocking about the French Revolution was the idea behind it: the idea that society needed to be fundamentally reorganized, with the hereditary monarchy stripped of their powers in favor of a democratically elected government.

And the French and Americans weren't alone. In one country after another, traditional forms of government and social organization were violently challenged. More and more, people believed — and acted on their belief — that things should be *different*, that just because the kings and dukes and bishops had been in charge for centuries didn't mean it had to be that way forever. For leadership to be something you were born into rather than chosen for, the revolutionaries believed, wasn't right and it wasn't fair.

Of course, the tricky thing about overthrowing one system of social organization is that you have to replace it with something — and that is no easy task. Storming the Bastille and stuffing grass in aristocrats' mouths was very liberating, but what, exactly, was the next step? Who should be put in charge, and with what powers, and for how long? It took decades to create the relatively stable democratic institutions we know today, and along the way things got pretty messy. Complicating the whole process was the fact that technology was also changing rapidly.

The Industrial Revolution

From the late 18th century into the 19th century, quickly developing technology revolutionized (hence the name) life in Europe and its colonies. Previously, life for most people had been fairly straightforward: you were born into a particular family in a particular place, and you were more or less destined to do a particular job — probably not a very exciting one, something along the order of planting and harvesting. Maybe, if you were born in a town, you could have a career in the dynamic field of blacksmithing or go to work as a servant for the local royalty, who had themselves been born into their positions. You'd probably do some trading, but you'd likely build your own house and grow much of your own food. You were fundamentally tied to your place, your family, and your job. They defined you.

With the arrival of industrial production, everything sped up and much less could be taken for granted. Farm production became more efficient, so fewer agricultural workers were needed — they flocked to the growing cities, where jobs were increasingly available in settings like factories and slaughterhouses. Workers were paid in cash, which they had to use to buy everything they needed, from housing to food to entertainment. They jostled in among people from other areas, coming into sudden contact with other languages and cultural traditions.

On top of that, developments in transportation and communication technology were making the world a smaller place. People and information were getting around more quickly and more often, so many people whose grandparents would have lived in a very small world found themselves living in a very large, diverse world. Everything was getting bigger, faster, more powerful — and revolution was in the air, with social arrangements that had lasted for centuries being cast to the wind.

Nothing, it seemed, could be taken for granted any more. What was right? What was wrong? Was there any way to make sense out of the chaos? Theologians and philosophers and historians were doing their best to figure things out, but it was clearly time for a new way of understanding the world.

The Development of "Sociology"

The first person to use the word "sociology" was Auguste Comte, a French thinker who coined the word in the early 1800s to refer to the systematic study of society. Still, it took almost a century for sociology to be fully established as a legitimate field of study.

Figuring out life with positivism

Comte was one of a group of philosophers and historians who believed in the idea of *positivism*, the idea that the methods of the natural sciences could be productively used to study the social world. Positivism in the philosophical sense is not the same thing as "positive thinking," but positivism is "positive" in the sense that it represents an optimistic belief in humans' ability to figure things out and improve their circumstances.

In the early 1800s, even natural science was still somewhat revolutionary — it hadn't been that long since natural scientists like Galileo faced death sentences for daring to suggest that telescopes and microscopes could be used to supplement, or even challenge, the Church's teachings about the natural world. If the powers that be didn't care for the suggestion that the earth revolved around the sun, you can imagine how they felt about the idea that social arrangements might also be subject to scientific analysis!

This idea, which the early sociologists shared, continues to inspire sociologists today — and it can still feel revolutionary. In Chapter 2 I warn you to prepare yourself for the surprises that sociology might have in store for you, and those surprises can still hit with some of the shock that the early sociologists' ideas had for their readers. Comte and other early sociologists argued that society might be better organized along principles that were very different from the principles along which it had been organized for centuries, and many people had a hard time accepting that idea. When sociologists today give people information that challenges their long-held beliefs, they meet similar resistance.

Common themes of early sociologists

Comte and the other early sociologists — most of whom would have called themselves philosophers, historians, and/or economists instead of sociologists — had a variety of ideas about the social world, but their arguments shared some common themes. They questioned whether the traditional tools of their trades were really sufficient for the task of understanding the changing society they lived in.

Philosophers began to wonder whether it was time to make systematic observations of the world rather than speculating about human nature based entirely on their own experiences. Historians saw patterns in the progression of social arrangements through time, and wondered whether scientific theories might help explain human history the way, say, geology had helped to explain the history of the earth. Economists saw the power of the scientific method when applied to trade and commerce, and wondered whether it might not be equally fruitful if applied to other areas of human activity — like politics and religion.

Over time, positivist thinkers from all these fields began to share certain ideas about the social world, ideas such as the following that became the underpinning for the new science of sociology.

- ✔ No king, priest, or philosopher could simply declare what social arrangements were best; those should be determined by means of empirical study and systematic analysis.

- ✔ Society was progressing in a manner that wasn't random. Social change, for better and for worse, made some kind of *sense*, and it had some kind of order or meaning to it.

- ✔ Although some amount of inequality might be unavoidable, inequality on the basis of social class, place of birth, or parentage was not only immoral but also inefficient.

Adventures in sociology

The Revolutionary Era was an exciting time to be in Europe, and even though it was a dangerous time to be going around with bold new ideas about society, it was also a time when those ideas carried great weight and had real urgency. Some of the early sociologists lived lives of excitement and adventure such as sociologists today could only dream (or have nightmares) about.

Marie-Jean-Antoine-Nicolas Caridal de Condorcet, one of the founders of sociology (though, preceding Comte, he did not call himself a "sociologist"), lived up to his fancy name by pioneering the idea of the social thinker as an en vogue cultural sophisticate and man-about-town. His wife, it was said, was one of the most beautiful women in France. Condorcet was what today you might call a "limousine liberal": an aristocrat who nonetheless supported the overthrow of the aristocracy. He believed that human history was marked by the destruction of social inequality, and he was personally involved in the French Revolution — in fact, he drew up the declaration justifying the suspension of the king. When things got ugly, he was driven into hiding. He was ultimately discovered along with his heretical manuscript *A Sketch for a Historical Picture of the Human Mind,* and he paid the ultimate price for his daring proto-sociological views: he died in prison, possibly from poisoning.

Claude Henri de Rouvroy, Comte de Saint-Simon (called Saint-Simon, not to be confused with his student Auguste Comte), was another man of action. He was among the troops France sent over to help the Colonial Army during the American Revolution, and was a captain of artillery at Yorktown. He was imprisoned during the French Revolution, which ironically made him a rich man upon his release because, being in prison, he hadn't been able to convert his holdings into the Revolutionary currency that had become severely devalued. What did he do with his wealth? He partied until he was broke, and then he decided he might as well roll up his sleeves and do some writing.

Saint-Simon convincingly argued that only scientists could put Europe back together after the destructive political revolutions it had experienced, and he became a very influential booster of social science. Further, he believed that social scientists should become a sort of secular priesthood, determining the shape of society with the benefit of their extraordinary insight.

After Saint-Simon's death in 1825, his most ardent disciples formed a sort of cult, living together in a commune and advocating progressive social ideas from women's liberation to collective ownership of property to free love. The experiment ended poorly, with the leaders going to jail. Sociologists, it seemed, weren't quite ready to run the world.

Sociology: The most ambitious science

Comte himself believed that the development of sociology was the logical result — in fact, the climax — of the development of science generally.

Comte pointed out that if a village is settled on the bank of a river that sometimes floods, it will be frequently devastated — unless, through scientific observation, the villagers learn to predict the floods. Why, he asked, shouldn't it be the same with wars and other social conflicts? If people can learn to predict these conflicts, they can be avoided — or at least minimized.

The sciences, thought Comte, developed in a hierarchy from those studying the most fundamental subjects (mathematics, physics) to those studying the more complex subjects (chemistry, biology), to those studying the biggest, *most* complex subjects. Nothing is bigger or more complex than society, so sociology (which Comte first called "social physics") sat at the top of the hierarchy as the most ambitious, most important science.

"There can be no scientific study of society," Comte wrote, "either in its conditions or its movements, if it is separated into portions, and its divisions are studied apart." In other words, you can't *just* look at the economy, or *just* look at the government, and expect to really understand how society works. You have to look at the whole enchilada. Comte's argument is still the justification for sociology as its own science — and it's still controversial.

When it came to the social sciences, sociology was not the only game in town even when Comte was writing. Economics had already been established as the scientific study of the economy, and psychology was being developed as the scientific study of the human mind. Comte knew this, and he explicitly made the case for sociology as a separate discipline lending insights that could not be achieved through those other disciplines.

Sociology's Power Trio

From the mid-19th century to the early 20th century, just as sociology was coming to maturity as an academic discipline and a way of seeing the world, three men — working separately, but the later ones being familiar with the earlier ones' work — came up with a series of ideas that deeply influenced sociology. The names Marx, Durkheim, and Weber are still commonly encountered at every level of sociology, from introductory high school classes to seminars on cutting-edge research. One company has even sold a sociology study guide that is a laminated card summarizing what Marx, Durkheim, and Weber might each say about topics from education to crime.

Understanding these men's place in the history of sociology can be a little confusing because "sociology" as a standalone academic discipline took so long to get off the ground. Karl Marx lived after Comte and had some hugely important sociological ideas, but to his dying day he never called himself a sociologist. Emile Durkheim, working around the turn of the 20th century, proudly considered himself a sociologist, but he spent his life trying to convince the rest of the world that sociology was a legitimate discipline. In 1919, three years after Durkheim's death and almost a century after Comte coined the term, the department of sociology founded by Max Weber was still the very first one in Germany. (Meanwhile, way over in America at that time, sociology departments were popping up left and right.) The bottom line is that all three of these thinkers were tremendously important for the development of sociology as we know it today, despite the fact that sociology as we know it hardly existed during their lifetimes.

Take some time to understand the basics of what each of these three men thought. All three have become touchstones of sociological thought and will come up many times throughout this book (for example, their views on culture in Chapter 5, their ideas about religion in Chapter 10, and their theories of social change in Chapter 16), so for now I'll just give you the very basics about who they were and what they thought.

Karl Marx

Karl Marx, born in 1818 in what is now Germany, was the first of these three great thinkers to come along. He never called himself a sociologist — that word was then too new to mean anything to most people — but he was a little bit of just about everything else. He started out studying law, became involved in philosophy and history, and later worked as a journalist and political activist.

Marx's life and work were inspired by his disgust with the capitalist economic system, especially with the way it kept millions of people toiling in dirty factories and parched fields with very little to show for their work at the end of the day. He was convinced there could be a better way, and he worked to support the Communist Party, a group dedicated to creating a society where everyone shared and shared alike. This rabblerousing got Marx kicked out of Germany, France, and Belgium, and he finally landed in England; he died in London in 1883.

Marx, working with his close friend and colleague Frederich Engels, wrote copious amounts. Some of his work, like the fiery *Communist Manifesto*, was widely read in Marx's lifetime, but much of it took decades to be organized, published, and translated. It wasn't until the 1930s that people truly understood everything Marx was trying to say. (A lot of people still don't quite get it.)

Sociologists consider Marx important for two main reasons: his general theory of history and his specific ideas about power and exploitation.

Marx on history

Marx's theory of history is often called *materialism* (or, even more of a mouthful, *dialectical materialism*). You may think of a "materialist" as someone who only cares about money and material things — and though Marx in his personal life was the opposite of a greedy cash hound, he did think that material goods make the world go 'round.

For Marx, the most important forces in history weren't ideas; they were basically economic forces. Every stage in history, according to Marx, was distinguished by its own *mode of production*, a way of organizing the production and distribution of material goods. Each mode of production (ancient slaveholding society, medieval feudalism, and so forth) has its own inherent conflicts among different classes, and those conflicts inevitably lead to the failure of one mode of production and the beginning of another.

This was an important new way of looking at history because earlier thinkers, such as the philosopher Hegel, had often seen historical change as being about ideas and culture. Marx dismissed immaterial ideas as relatively unimportant. Historical change, he said, is about class conflict over concrete things.

Marx on capitalism

Marx was particularly concerned with the mode of production that dominated his time (and, he would be disappointed to learn, still dominates ours): industrial capitalism.

Marx wrote about a number of different class groups that he saw having roles in capitalism, but the two most important were:

- The **bourgeois:** the wealthy, powerful people who own the factories, the farmland, and just about everything else.
- The **proletariat:** the people who don't own much and are forced to work for the bourgeois to feed their families.

Marx thought that capitalism was bad for everyone, but especially for the proletariat.

The proletariat, said Marx, are especially hurt by capitalism because they are viciously exploited by the bourgeois. No matter how much profit a factory owner makes in a day, if his workers don't have anywhere else to work, all the owner needs to do is pay the workers enough to keep them alive — the bourgeois factory owner keeps all the extra profits, earned on the backs of the hardworking proletariat.

In a larger sense, though, Marx argued that *everyone* is hurt by capitalism because it's a system that trades real things (work, food, shelter) for an imaginary thing: money. I might work all day in a factory assembling things that are going to be used by someone else, and I earn money that I use to buy food grown by someone else and to rent a house built by someone else. The value of my labor isn't measured by what good I do for myself or my society; it's measured by how much (or how little) money I make.

Marx thought the capitalist system was fundamentally unhealthy, and that it would one day be replaced by a worldwide communist utopia, where everyone would contribute what they're able and take what they need. Maybe someday it will, but you probably shouldn't hold your breath waiting for it.

Emile Durkheim

Halfway through this chapter that's supposedly about the history of sociology, you may be wondering when someone is finally going to bust out and call himself a sociologist. And . . . *voila!* The French scholar Emile Durkheim spent his life not just practicing sociology, but trying — quite successfully — to convince the world of sociology's importance.

Durkheim was born in France in 1858, studied philosophy and social theory, and ultimately founded the first European department of sociology. His life had much less excitement than Marx's, but he was full of new and provocative ideas about society.

Durkheim's view of society

Compared to Marx, Durkheim had a fundamentally different — and much more positive view — of society. Reading Marx, you almost get the impression that he thinks we'd all be better off on our own, living by the work of our own hands. Marx appreciated the fact that working together in organized settings allowed us to produce magnificent things (like, say, indoor plumbing) that we couldn't create as individuals, but in general Marx thought people were apt to stab each other in the back if given the opportunity, so he was generally suspicious of society.

For Durkheim, humans are fundamentally social. In fact, thought Durkheim, our social life — at home, work, play, and worship — is what *defines* us, what gives us meaning and purpose. It's what makes us truly human, and that fact is what makes sociology — the study of society — so important.

In his book *The Rules of Sociological Method*, Durkheim set out his vision of what sociology is and how it should be done. Specifically, he said that the job of the sociologist is to study *social facts*: facts that are true of *groups* of people rather than individuals. Here are a few examples of social facts:

- Australia is a democracy.
- Thirty-four percent of men have beards.
- The average income of a Porsche owner is $104,000.

Those are facts about groups of people, and though they don't tell you anything about any one individual — for example, whether any given man will have a beard, or the income of a particular Porsche owner — they tell you something specific about a group of people, who might then be compared to other groups (for example, Toyota Camry owners). Those are the facts Durkheim thought sociologists should take as their special area of concern.

Durkheim agreed with Marx that society was changing, but rather than a growing chasm between the haves and the have-nots, Durkheim thought that we were becoming more differentiated from one another in all kinds of ways.

Earlier in history, when society was relatively simple, there were just a few different jobs people performed: hunter, gatherer, farmer, priest. Now, there are thousands of different jobs that need doing, and they're very different from one another: software engineer, preschool teacher, forklift operator, screenwriter. This functional differentiation, thought Durkheim, was both necessary and — in broad terms — a good thing. Our shared social values help us work together productively and, for the most part, peacefully.

Sociology to die for

To prove the usefulness of sociology as a discipline, Durkheim chose to study a topic that would seem deeply personal, much more the domain of the psychologist or philosopher than the sociologist: suicide. By demonstrating that sociology could help us understand something so intensely private and individual, Durkheim showed the power of his newly invented sociological method.

In his book *Suicide*, Durkheim pointed out that though any individual person's decision to commit suicide was, of course, personal — a person's reasons for taking his or her life may be completely unknowable — in aggregate, suicides seem to have shared social causes. Durkheim observed that predictably, year in and year out, some countries have higher suicide rates than others. Whatever combination of factors cause people to commit suicide, they seemed to be greater in Sweden than in Spain; further, they were greater among unmarried people than married people, and greater among men than women. Putting aside the question of any one individual's motivation, Durkheim said that a group's suicide rate is a social fact that ought to be explained by other social facts.

In a pioneering use of social statistics, Durkheim gathered lots of numbers summarizing the suicide rates and other characteristics of many groups and lined them up in tables to see which social facts seemed to be related (see Chapter 4 for more on the use of statistics in sociology today). In the end, Durkheim concluded that there were actually different types of suicide that tended to happen for different reasons. For example, *egoistic suicides* were more frequent in groups with weak social ties (for example, countries with religious values emphasizing individualism) and *altruistic suicides* were more frequent in groups with extremely strong social ties (for example, the military).

The specifics of Durkheim's study are less important than the way he went about doing it: defining and explaining social facts about groups. Explaining an individual's behavior, according to Durkheim, is a different thing than explaining a group's behavior. Whether or not Durkheim's conclusions about suicide were correct, he was right to point out that understanding why one Spaniard committed suicide (a matter of psychology) doesn't tell us anything about why Spaniards in general committed suicide at a lower rate than Swedes; and understanding the causes of Spain's suicide rate (a matter of sociology) doesn't tell us anything about why any one Spaniard committed suicide.

Great sociology from a troubled marriage

Max Weber's best-known book is called *The Protestant Ethic and the Spirit of Capitalism*. It contains Weber's argument that the values spread by Protestant theologians like John Calvin were very influential in Europe's transition from traditional society to modern capitalism. Essentially, Calvin and other Protestant theologians argued for the values of hard work, discipline, and savings. The belief that time is money, and money is good (because an abundance of it suggests that God favors you particularly) is foundational to the capitalist economy.

It's a brilliant sociological argument, and its core insight — the connection between a rigorous religious worldview and the capitalist economic system — may have been partially inspired by the troubled marriage of Weber's parents. Weber's mother was devoutly religious, a strong believer in the moral value of self-sacrifice, strict discipline, and hard work. Weber's father, on the other hand, was a worldly, wealthy man who unapologetically enjoyed the luxuries his money could buy.

Weber's work addressed this paradox: that modern life has some of the ascetic self-discipline of the monk — you must be at your desk from 9 a.m. to 5 p.m., fulfilling a precise list of duties — and yet it has afforded us luxuries and freedoms unimaginable to people who lived in the pre-modern era. It may be dehumanizing to work in exchange for money rather than to work growing food for your family, but now you have money that you can spend on whatever you want: maybe food, maybe a vacation, maybe a rubber chicken. Whatever!

In The Protestant Ethic, Weber tells the story of a landowner who hires some farmers to work his land. To motivate the farmers to work harder, the landowner increases the amount he pays per acre mowed; however, the landowner discovers, to his astonished frustration, that the farmers then proceed to work less hard because they only want to make enough to live on and after their "raise," it takes less work to do it. If we all behaved that way, capitalism would never work. We're the "good" farmers who work harder for greater financial reward — but to what end? Even Calvin believed that you can't take it with you.

Max Weber

Marx and Durkheim are easy to compare and contrast because their views about what matters in society were so strikingly different. Marx thought it was all about conflict; Durkheim thought it was all about cooperation. Marx was concerned with the material world; Durkheim was concerned with the world of ideas and values. Max Weber (pronounced *VAY-ber* if you want to say it the way he did) is much harder to pigeonhole because for Weber it was not such an either/or question. If they had to choose which of the three great sociological thinkers was most "right," most sociologists today would say Weber because Weber appreciated that social life is marked by both conflict and cohesion. Sometimes we fight, sometimes we get along; the trick is to understand *why* and *when*.

Max Weber was another German, and unlike Marx he largely stayed there, teaching at Freiburg and Heidelberg; in 1919, he founded the first German department of sociology. Despite some serious mental health issues (he suffered from what were then called "nervous collapses") and a troubled personal life (he married his second cousin, and while that made them kissing cousins, they probably didn't do much more than that), he had an amazing work ethic. By the time of his death in 1920, he'd written many important books and articles that, as with Marx, took decades to be translated and published for the benefit of a global audience.

Both Marx and Durkheim had grand views of history; they both presented the march of history as more or less inevitable. For Marx, class conflicts had inevitably led to capitalism and would inevitably lead, in the end, to communism. For Durkheim, developing technology and growing population had inevitably led to functional differentiation. For Weber, history was more like a game of Clue: We know how society turned out, but it takes some detective work to figure out *who* made it turn out that way, and *when*, and *how*. None of those answers can be taken for granted.

So how *did* society turn out? According to Weber, modern society is marked by *rationalization*: Most things are organized according to standard rules and systems that are meant to apply to everyone, with society meant to run like a well-oiled machine. In your job, for example, you don't have the responsibilities you have and get paid the amount you do just because you're *you* — those things go with the job, and if you quit, the next person to take your job would perform the same tasks and get paid the same amount.

This is exactly the capitalist system that got Marx so riled up, and although Weber didn't quite share Marx's desire to overturn the whole system, it did make Weber a little uneasy. He referred to modern society as an "iron cage," where for better and for worse we're locked into well-defined roles.

And how did we get here? The development of rationalized industrial capitalism wasn't inevitable, said Weber, pointing out that Europe had taken that path whereas other societies that had been around even longer —for example, China — had not. The development of a set of religious values (specifically, Calvinist Protestant values) that promoted hard work and savings had worked, said Weber, like a "switchman on the tracks" to ensure that European society would turn in that direction — and when the train went down that track, there was no going back.

Sociology in the 20th Century

In the first years of the 20th century, Durkheim was still trying to make the case for why a discipline called "sociology" needed to exist; today, sociology is one of the biggest and most frequently-studied subjects at colleges and universities around the world. As I explain in Chapter 2, sociologists do important work in a wide range of jobs.

Sociology was born in Europe, but much of its explosive growth in the 20th century happened in the United States. In this section, I highlight the most important events fueling that growth.

Taking it to the streets: The Chicago School

The first sociology department in the United States was founded at the University of Chicago in 1892. That department became home to several of the most important sociologists of the early 20th century, whose arguments and studies are collectively known today as *the Chicago School* of sociology. ("School" being used in the sense of "a school of thought.")

The concerns of the Chicago School were strongly influenced by the fact that the University of Chicago is an unmistakably urban campus, located near south Chicago neighborhoods that were — and remain today — dense and diverse, with people from all walks of life interacting at close range. It's not the wealthiest section of town, and those neighborhoods also have more than their share of conflict and crime.

If you've found yourself thinking that sociologists like Marx and Weber, with their grand arguments about the sweeping forces of history, were getting a little out of touch with the reality of everyday life, you're not alone! The members of the Chicago School urged their students to close their books, get out of the classroom, and plunge right into the social Petri dish they were sitting right in the middle of. They emphasized the importance of on-the-ground research methods like *ethnography* and *participant observation* (see Chapter 4 for more on these methods). Although Durkheim dismissed individuals as outside sociology's area of concern, sociologists in the Chicago School — and in America generally — preferred to study society from the bottom up, from the perspective of the individual in society.

Chicago, similar to the rest of America, was in the midst of a massive wave of immigration, and the Chicago sociologists saw people from completely different social backgrounds learning to interact together. Besides putting race, ethnicity, and immigration among the top concerns of American sociologists (as you may have noticed, those subjects weren't at the top of most European sociologists' research agendas) the sociologists of the Chicago School popularized the study of *symbolic interactionism* — the study of the way individuals interact through a (more or less) shared understanding of words, gestures, and other symbols. (See Chapter 6 for more on symbolic interactionism.)

Mass society: Are we, or are we not, sheep?

In 1954, for the first time ever (and, so far, the *only* time ever), a sociologist made the cover of *Time* magazine: David Riesman, author of *The Lonely Crowd*. Although Riesman taught at the University of Chicago, he wasn't a member of the Chicago School. His focus was on the big picture.

In *The Lonely Crowd*, Riesman argued that Americans had lost their inner compasses and become "other-directed" — in other words, instead of following their own moral values, they just did whatever everyone else was doing. This is still a concern often voiced about America (and other countries) today, and it particularly resonated in the *Ozzie and Harriet* era, when it seemed like everyone was moving to the newly-built suburbs to buy a house that looked just like every other house on the block and have the same 2.2 children as every other family on the block.

Riesman's compelling book introduced sociology to an unprecedented popular audience — it remains the all-time bestseller in sociology. But among academics, Riesman's influence was not as great as that of a man named Talcott Parsons. Parsons shared Riesman's interest in mass society, but unlike Riesman, Parsons thought that it was by and large a good thing.

Parsons was a great believer in Durkheim's view of society, and espoused a view of society that is known as *functionalism*. In functionalism, social phenomena are explained by reference to the purpose they serve: If a certain phenomenon, such as education or religion, is observed in many different societies, it must be there for a reason. It must *do* something for society, or it wouldn't exist. (If this sounds a lot like biological evolution, that's no coincidence. See Chapter 2 for a description of Durkheim's "organic metaphor.")

Parsons was one of the most ambitious sociologists of all time. He believed that the social sciences should be united instead of separate, and with like-minded colleagues in anthropology and psychology, he co-founded a Department of Social Relations at Harvard to bring the disciplines together. His 1951 book *Toward a General Theory of Action* was his manifesto, a 500-page attempt to Explain It All.

Parsons's theory was outrageously elaborate, and for years many sociologists in America and abroad were occupied trying to explain everything from business to politics to popular entertainment on Parsons's terms. For a while, it almost seemed like Parsons was realizing Comte's dream of creating a kind of owner's manual for society.

The Power Elite: Marx's revenge

If the Chicago School had brought sociology down to earth, Parsons brought it right back up into the theoretical stratosphere, with everything explained from the sociologist's perch on high. In fact, Harvard built Parsons a literal ivory tower — William James Hall, which still stands today — to house his multidisciplinary Department of Social Relations. Parsons's quest for a grand unified theory of society hit the rocks, though, as an increasing number of sociologists criticized his theory.

Though functionalism is still an appealing way to think about society, most sociologists today think Parsons was misled in seeking to explain social features by way of their functions. Although social institutions such as government and education may be necessary because of the tasks they perform, sociologists today recognize that social institutions are created by people, not by functions — and although people may have society's interests in mind, they also have their own personal motivations. Plus, even when people do act "for the good of society," they're often mistaken in the choices they make.

Because of his belief in social evolution — in other words, survival of the fittest societies — Parsons became a defender of the status quo. There was no country more advanced or more powerful than the United States; in fact, Parsons said, the United States was close to the ideal of social organization.

One sociologist, C. Wright Mills, thought this was completely wrong. Reminding his readers and students that the whole reason sociology was founded was to change society, Mills pointed out that society was still rife with social problems such as poverty, crime, racism, and to say these things were "necessary" or even "normal" was absurd. In his book *The Power Elite* (another bestseller of sociology), Mills argued that society was run by a small group of wealthy, powerful individuals who basically arranged things for their own benefit.

Sound familiar? If Parsons was a Durkheimian, Mills was a resolute Marxist. The debate between the two — which unfortunately ended with Mills's untimely death in 1962 — was fiery and fascinating. Both were brilliant thinkers, but they represented completely different approaches to understanding society.

Mills mocked Parsons outright, saying that not only were Parsons's ideas wrong, they were stated in ridiculously convoluted language that was almost incomprehensible to anyone who wasn't intimately familiar with Parsons's complex theory. Parsons fired back that Mills himself was empirically wrong, that there was no such thing as a unified "power elite" that somehow secretly conspired to run the world. *Someone* had to be in charge, said Parsons, and he pointed out that political, economic, and cultural leaders often had different agendas that conflicted with one another.

The Cold War and the "sociology gap"

Few social thinkers have had the real-world impact of Karl Marx. Marx's ideas about the evils of capitalism and the redistribution of wealth have inspired political revolutionaries including Vladimir Lenin, Mao Zedong, and Fidel Castro, thus shaping the lives of billions of people in the communist societies they founded.

From 1922 to 1991, several Asian republics were incorporated as the Soviet Union, a communist nation that became a powerful rival to the United States and its allies. In the decades following World War II, the United States and the Union of Soviet Socialist Republics (U.S.S.R.) waged a "Cold War" in which they battled for economic and military dominance. Stanley Kubrick's classic movie, *Dr. Strangelove*, satirizes the panic that characterized that era, with characters taking the real-world concern over a "missile gap" (one country having significantly more warheads than the other) to absurd levels, worrying about a "mineshaft gap" (a gap in provisions to protect citizens underground) and a "doomsday gap" (one country having a doomsday machine and the other not).

It's not a coincidence that the Cold War era saw a boom in popular interest in sociology.

Though it was known that the Soviet Union was a repressive regime that severely limited certain of its citizens' freedoms, the U.S.S.R. was a huge and powerful country organized along fundamentally different principles than Western democracies. Though most Americans were staunchly opposed to any adoption of socialist policies — in fact, citizens who had even so much as attended meetings of the Communist Party were persecuted as "un-American" — many became uneasy about the American way of life.

Russians were known (accurately or not) for adhering to a rigorous work ethic and putting their country ahead of themselves; had Americans grown lazy and complacent in the prosperous 1950s? Had Americans lost the drive, vigor, and individual initiative that had made their country great? It was these concerns that helped pique average Americans' interest in books like David Riesman's *The Lonely Crowd* and William H. Whyte's *The Organization Man*, both of which argued that American society had become marked by a mindless conformity. Both books — especially Riesman's — are still widely-read today.

Neither Parsons nor Mills "won" the debate — most sociologists today consider themselves neither functionalist nor Marxist — but Mills re-injected sociology with some of the sense of purpose and populism that had marked its founding.

WARNING!

When you read sociological books and articles, look out for sociologists who use convoluted language. C. Wright Mills criticized Talcott Parsons for writing sentences like, "Coordinate with the importance of order as formulated in the hierarchy of control and the place of normative culture in action systems, is the pattern of *temporal* order imposed by the functional exigencies of systems." Just because a concept is challenging doesn't mean it has to be written in a way you can't make any sense of. A textbook, a dictionary or encyclopedia of sociology, or a good teacher can help you decipher challenging passages in sociological books and articles.

Sociology Today

No individual or institution today dominates sociology as completely as the Chicago School did in the early 20th century or as Talcott Parsons did in the mid-20th century. Most sociologists today take inspiration from a range of different thinkers, and most are more concerned with answering specific empirical questions than formulating or testing grand theories about society.

Robert K. Merton was a sociologist who appreciated Parsons's insights — Parsons was one of Merton's advisors in graduate school — but thought that sociologists would do well to focus on smaller, solvable problems rather than trying to explain everything at once. Merton argued that sociologists should focus on "theories of the middle range" — that is, that sociologists should ask questions they can actually answer. So instead of asking "Why does education exist?" a sociologist might ask, "How does education in this particular country serve to make people more equal — or less equal — in wealth?" That's still a huge question, but it's much easier to answer than a grand abstract question about the nature of society. There are still sociologists who pursue grand theories, but that tends to be an exercise for experienced sociologists who've earned tenure and have time to write fat books.

Although Parsons's dream of the unity of the social sciences hasn't been achieved — sociologists still talk mostly to sociologists, psychologists still talk mostly to psychologists, and so on — sociologists in recent decades have increasingly collaborated with scholars from other disciplines to share knowledge and theory. Sociologists work with physicians to study the spread of disease, with businesspeople and economists to study corporate organization, with psychologists to study small-group interaction, and with anthropologists to study cultural change.

Besides enjoying the accumulated wisdom of all the sociologists mentioned here and many, many more, sociologists today also have the benefit of access to data and analytical tools that are light years beyond what was available to sociologists just a few decades ago. Huge sets of survey data are publicly available, and with the right software, any personal computer has the capacity to perform highly sophisticated statistical analyses.

In Chapter 16 I have more to say about the future of sociology. For now, suffice it to say that though answering sociological questions has become a lot easier since the time of Comte, asking the right ones is just as tricky as it has always been.

Chapter 4

Research Methods: Because You Can't Put Society in a Test Tube

. . . .

In This Chapter
▶ Examining the steps of sociological research
▶ Choosing a research method
▶ Using analytical tools
▶ Watching for potential pitfalls

. . . .

So what happens when the rubber meets the road? How do sociologists actually go about devising and conducting research studies? It's important for you to know how sociological knowledge is created even if you never intend to conduct your own research study. The scientific process of conducting, evaluating, and building on empirical research is at the core of sociology. Without empirical research, sociology would just be a lot of theories that may or may not be true.

In some ways, as I mention in Chapter 2, the sociological research process is similar to the research process in any other scientific discipline, including the natural sciences. (When I was a graduate student in sociology, Professor Barbara Reskin used to wear a white lab coat just to make the point that sociologists are "real" scientists, too.) In other ways, though, it's very different. Society is enormously complex and constantly changing, so making generalizable statements about the way society works is a tricky matter that requires precise thinking and careful research methods.

In this chapter, I explain both the basic steps of sociological research and the methodological choices sociologists have to face when figuring out how to answer their sociological questions. I also outline the analytical tools available to sociologists and highlight some of the many things that can go wrong in the complex process of gathering and interpreting sociological data.

The Steps of Sociological Research

In this section, I run through the essentials of conducting sociological research. How do you turn a general question about society into data that may be interesting and useful to others — in sociology and beyond? Although there are a large number of different methods and approaches used in sociological research, the basic process I outline in the following sections is nearly universal.

You can't put society in a test tube — you normally can't conduct experiments in sociology like you can in chemistry, physics, or even psychology. Sociological studies almost always consist of observing people in the "real world" rather than the laboratory.

Ask your question

Sociologists sometimes envy scientists who work in disciplines — like, say, astrophysics — where the phenomena being studied are so far removed from everyday life that laymen have a hard time even understanding what they do. That's not an issue for sociologists who study phenomena that a lot of people give quite a bit of thought to: social inequality, social networks, the organization of social groups such as corporations or clubs. When a sociologist talks about their work, sometimes it seems like *everyone* has an opinion.

Frustrating as that may sometimes be, it's also what makes sociology exciting. Sociological studies begin with a hunch about the social world, a sociologist's idea about how a certain process might work, or a question about why people seem to behave in a certain manner. Here are a few questions that led to actual sociological studies:

- ✔ Why is the sport of cricket, which British colonists taught to natives of the lands they colonized, most popular in places like India and Africa, where the relatively recent colonial era was characterized by violent conflicts? Shouldn't people in those countries have the *least* interest in playing a quintessentially British sport? (Jason Kaufman and Orlando Patterson)

- ✔ Why do companies consistently pay so much money to hire charismatic CEOs who seem to do little or nothing to raise those companies' profits? (Rakesh Khurana)

- ✔ When people stop on the street to talk to each other, why do they stand right in the middle of the sidewalk, where they're in everyone's way? (William H. Whyte)

- ✔ Why are people in wealthy neighborhoods more likely than people in working-class neighborhoods to hang abstract art in their living rooms? And do they care if it matches the couch? (David Halle)

For ordinary people, these are questions that may come up around the water cooler at work or over the backyard fence, conversations that may conclude with a shrug. But for sociologists, these are empirical questions that can actually be answered.

Next time you're curious about something in the social world, think: is there an empirical question here? Am I just trying to decide how I feel about something — or am I actually curious about how something works? Is there any information that could be gathered to answer my question? Sociological questions are questions about how the world works. A sociologist may not agree with the values or decisions of the people they study, but they are curious about those values and why people make the decisions they do.

After you have your question in mind, you likely have a *hypothesis*: a guess about what the answer is. This hypothesis, whether you realize it or not, rests on a *theory* about how the world works. Whether or not your theory is supported depends on whether or not your hypothesis proves to be correct.

Check the literature

When sociologists have an interesting question worth pursuing, they head to the shelves (or, more often, the Internet) to see what has been published in "the literature" that may be relevant to their question. When sociologists and other scientists talk about "the literature," they usually don't mean *Moby Dick* and *The Brothers Karamazov*. They mean the peer-reviewed scientific literature in their discipline.

For a scientific study to be *peer reviewed* means that it's evaluated by other scholars who are experts in the area being studied.

In sociology, peer-reviewed publications include:

- ✔ **General sociology journals:** Journals such as the *American Sociological Review* and the *American Journal of Sociology* contain studies so important that they're worth the attention of all sociologists.

- ✔ **Field-specific journals:** In sociology there are hundreds of journals such as *New Media and Society* or *Sociology of Education* intended primarily for scholars studying those specific subjects.

- ✔ **Books:** Sociologists also sometimes publish books, which are peer-reviewed if they come from an academic press.

Reviewing the literature lets you learn from other sociologists' work and avoid merely repeating what someone else has already done.

But *which* books and journal articles should you read? There are thousands and thousands of books and articles — and sometimes work that is not peer-reviewed or labeled as "sociology" can also be important to your research. Sociologists normally search the literature for all these types of material:

- ✔ Sociological studies specifically on the topic they're interested in researching. (For example, if you're interested in studying political parties in Kenya, look for other sociological studies of political parties in Kenya.)

- ✔ Sociological studies on similar topics. (In this example, look at sociological studies of political parties in other African nations, or even political parties in other countries around the world.)

- ✔ Sociological studies using methods or approaches that may be useful. (For example, if you want to use a specific type of statistical technique or interview strategy, look at other studies using that same method.)

- ✔ Articles or books not in the sociological literature that are nonetheless informative about the topic at hand. (In this example, look at news reports on Kenyan politics, a book on the political history of Kenya, or relevant articles in political science or African studies.)

It's always a possibility that you'll discover someone's "scooped" you — has already conducted the study you were interested in conducting. Much more often, though, you might discover that other scholars have studied your topic but that a lot of questions about the topic still remain unanswered. You then have to decide whether you have the information and/or resources to answer them.

Operationalize your question and find your data

The word "operationalize" sounds like something meaningless that you'd say to try to impress your boss in a meeting — but if your boss is a sociologist you actually *will* impress them because the word describes one of the most difficult and most important aspects of sociological research.

As I explain in Chapter 2, what distinguishes an empirical sociological question from a theoretical question or a moral question is that you can actually find an answer to it — but that doesn't mean finding an answer is easy! To *operationalize* a question means to turn it from a general question (for example, are fans equally supportive, or critical, at men's sports and women's sports?) to a specific question that you can actually find an answer to (for example, how many audible player criticisms per fan are heard at each of 20 men's basketball games, and how many at each of 20 women's basketball games?).

The word *data* refers to pieces of information (one *datum*; multiple *data*). In a perfect world, you'd operationalize your question and then go right out and grab the data you need to answer your question. But we don't live in a perfect world, and what happens more often is that you find the best data available and then operationalize your question as precisely as the data allow.

Here's a real-life example from my own research. A colleague and I were curious about which subjects had become more frequently studied in universities around the world over the past century. But what data were available? We couldn't find much information on universities' budgets, so we didn't know how much was spent on, say, the study of law in any given year. The United Nations had collected some data on student enrollments, but it didn't go back very many years — and anyway, some other researchers were already looking at those data. What we *did* have were lists of faculty members at universities around the world, stretching back to the beginning of the 20th century!

So our general question was

> Which subjects have become more frequently studied in universities around the world since 1900?

Our data were lists of faculty members at universities around the world. We thus were able to operationalize our question as

> Which subjects have seen the most growth in the number of faculty members studying them since 1900?

After we found useful data and operationalized our question, it was easy to find an answer: We just started counting!

Finding data sounds like the most boring part of sociological research, but it can be one of the most creative. There are several big surveys available to the public (the U.S. census, the General Social Survey, the National Education Longitudinal Study); they make for high-quality data, but for exactly that reason they're very often used in sociological studies, and it can be difficult to squeeze new information out of them.

Collecting original data is time-consuming and can be expensive, but it makes your study automatically interesting, even for readers who don't agree with your analysis of your data. Here are just a few sources of original data:

- ✔ **Data gathered for other purposes and not yet used for sociological analysis:** You might use corporate records, public government records, and historical records, for example.

- ✔ **Newspapers and magazines:** You might search for articles documenting some kind of activity or showing people's perspectives on the social world.

✔ **Original surveys:** You might conduct your own survey, trying to capture as many respondents as possible for a few key questions.

✔ **Original interviews and ethnography:** You might gather qualitative data by talking with or observing people.

(Later in this chapter, I provide more information on specific types of data and analysis.) After you have operationalized your question and gathered your data, you're ready to begin your analysis!

As you operationalize your question, you need to be sure you've done so in a *valid* way. In other words, your data need to actually be relevant to the original question you asked. If you're not careful about this, you could end up with a data/theory mismatch. (More on that in the last chapter of this section.)

Analyze your data

Some empirical questions require data to answer, but don't really need much analysis. Imagine you want to know whether you remembered to let the dog in. That's an empirical question: The dog is either in or out. For data, you open the door and look out in the yard. Either you see the dog, or you don't. There's the answer to that particular empirical question.

Sociological questions, though, usually aren't quite so easy to answer — even after you've found data and operationalized your question. What you usually end up with is hundreds of pages of interviews or a massive spreadsheet of survey data. It would be nice if you could just open the spreadsheet, look at its thousands upon thousands of cells worth of numbers, and say, "A-ha! I see that gender discrimination remains severe in higher-paying jobs whereas it has lessened somewhat in lower-paying jobs!" Unfortunately, it doesn't really work that way.

Later sections in this chapter cover specific analytical methods in more detail; for now, I'll just say that in almost all cases, you're going to need to analyze your data to find an answer to your question. If you've found useful data and operationalized your question in a valid way, then the answer is there . . . you just need to get at it. Not only is this an essential step, but it's a step where you need to be especially conscious and responsible because it's going to be much easier for people reading your research report to spot an error in your interpretation than in your analysis.

Interpret your results

Okay, you've found your data, operationalized your question, and conducted your analysis. You have your results: a trend on a graph, or a repeated theme in interviews, or a number resulting from some statistical procedure. But what does it mean? *Interpreting your results* is the last step of sociological research. It means thinking about what you've learned and how it relates to the sociological literature. The trick is being honest with yourself — and your readers, if you're hoping to publish your study — about exactly what your results say (or don't say) about your topic.

You probably began your research process with a *hypothesis*: a guess about what the results of your study are. If your guess turns out to be correct, that supports your theory about why things were going to be that way. Depending on your question and your data, there's probably still some room for doubt, but now at least now you have some important new information on the subject. Before presenting your results to your fellow sociologists, you want to be ready with your argument about what new light your results shed on the topic you're researching.

Say you believe that the wage disparity between U.S. men and women has shrunk since 1950; that is, that men and women in the United States today make salaries that are more similar than the salaries of men and women in 1950. You find data on employee salaries at three big companies in New York City, and your analysis shows that sure enough, in 1950 women made an average of two-thirds as much money as men did whereas today women and men make almost the same amount of money. This result supports your hypothesis and provides sociologists with important new information about men's and women's salaries.

Every study needs some interpretation, but it's particularly important in cases where the results are ambiguous. What if you find that women's salaries crept closer to men's for 40 years, but in the past 20 years the disparity has been growing again? Does this support your hypothesis? Yes and no. If that is your result, you need to modify your theory. What happened to account for that change? You need to suggest a possible explanation.

If you're confident in the validity of your data and analysis, you now know something you did not know before. But wait! How do you know that happened across the United States, not just in New York? You don't know — and further, you have no idea what happened in other countries. To answer those questions, you have to — that's right — gather more data. When you present your research, you need to acknowledge this need for more data — but that doesn't mean you're just going back to square one! You can pat yourself on the back for finding important new information that helps inform sociologists' understanding of gender and wages in the United States.

Nearly every sociological study ends with a call for further research. That's just the way it works: the world is big, and sociologists will never know *everything* there is know about it. To point to the need for further research is appropriately modest — you admit that your study doesn't completely close the book on your topic — but it also highlights your achievement. In the previous example, sociologists needed to know *what* happened (whether or not the wage disparity has decreased) before they can ask *how* it happened.

Choosing a Method

Getting an accurate picture of the social world is tricky business, especially because it's a moving target! Society changes every day — usually not *too* quickly. Depending on the nature of your question and the resources available to you, you'll have to make some fundamental decisions about what methodological strategy to use. In this section, I explain what those choices are.

Quantitative vs. qualitative

The most fundamental decision you have to make is whether your study is going to be a quantitative study or a qualitative study. Those words look similar, but they mean completely different things. A *quantitative* study is a study where data are gathered as, or translated into, numbers. A *qualitative* study is a study where data are gathered as words, narratives, and impressions that would lose their meaning or value if they were somehow turned into numbers.

When are sociological data too old?

When a colleague and I studied college attainment, we were lucky to have a very large set of survey data collected by the U.S. Department of Education from 1988 to 1994. One day in 2007 we received a call from a *New York Times* reporter who was writing an article about college attainment. She was very interested in our study — until she learned that our data concerned students who had started college in 1993. Things had changed too much since then, she thought, for our study to be of any interest to her readers.

And yet our study was published in a good sociology journal. Are sociologists less concerned than journalists are in being accurate and up-to-date? Not at all! There are at least two reasons that sociologists found our 14-year-old data of interest when a journalist didn't.

First, a journalist can write an article based on far less data than you typically need for a sociological study. If I want to publish a newspaper article on college attainment, I can just summarize the results of one or two recent studies, interview a couple of kids who are on their way to college this fall, and I'm done. But if I want to publish a sociological study of college attainment, I'll need to do a lot more research. We couldn't just call up 14,000 kids who were going to college in 2007, such as the government did in the early 1990s. We would certainly have liked to, but a major survey like that can cost tens of thousands — even hundreds of thousands — of dollars.

Also, as I note in Chapter 2, sociologists are interested in the fundamental patterns of social interaction. Even in different social situations, sociologists believe general patterns of human interaction are fairly constant. That's why a historical sociologist can study something that happened in the 1800s, or even in the 1200s, and discover that a large number of their colleagues are interested if the study is done well. Fourteen years? That's nothing.

Quantitative analysis

In a quantitative study, data may be gathered as numbers. Some information about society exists as numbers already. For example:

- ✔ Annual income, in dollars
- ✔ Test scores
- ✔ Unemployment rates

Other information can be fairly easily translated into numbers. For example:

- ✔ Sex (1=female, 0=male . . . or vice-versa)
- ✔ Race or ethnicity (1=Latino, 0=non-Latino)
- ✔ Marital status (1=unmarried, 0=married)

Still other information is trickier to translate into numbers, but it's possible to at least try. For example:

- ✔ Self-esteem (How happy are you with yourself? 2=very happy, 1=fairly happy, 0=unhappy)
- ✔ Cultural tastes (Have you been to a jazz concert in the last year? 1 if yes, 0 if no)
- ✔ Social networks (Here is a list of people in your company; answer 1 for each person you consider a friend, answer 0 for each person you do not)

The benefit of quantitative research is that it allows you to consider many cases (people or countries or whatever you're studying) because you don't need to "get to know" each case — the important facts about each case are right there in the numbers. With statistical analysis, you can easily analyze a huge amount of information. (More on that in the next section.)

Qualitative analysis

In a qualitative study, data are gathered as statements, experiences, or impressions and are usually recorded as words. Examples of qualitative studies include:

- ✔ An interview study, where you conduct hour-long interviews with 50 people and record their comments.
- ✔ An ethnography, where you spend weeks, months, or even years in a particular social setting and write about your experiences.
- ✔ Participant observation, where you join a group of people and make sociological observations even as you walk in your subjects' shoes.

✔ A historical study, where you read and research extensively about a particular place and time with an eye to particular features of the social environment.

The benefit of qualitative research is that it allows for a much more in-depth understanding of a situation. Because of the intense work involved, you can't study as many cases as you can with a quantitative study — but you're much less likely to miss something important about any given case.

Cross-sectional vs. longitudinal

Most sociological studies involve questions of causality. In other words, a sociologist asks whether or not one thing causes another. But when you aren't taking people into a lab and conducting experiments on them, it can be very difficult to sort out what causes what. Certain research methods can make this easier — but at a price. In this section, I explain the difference between a *cross-sectional* study (where data are gathered at one point in time) and a *longitudinal* study (where data are gathered from multiple points in time). Longitudinal data allow sociologists to make more confident statements about causality, but they can be difficult to gather.

Say you're studying the effect of television on violence. Psychologists have the benefit of using a laboratory setting: If you take two groups of randomly selected people and have one group play violent video games while the other group play peaceful video games, and the first group gets more violent than the second, you have a good idea that the games caused the violence. But when studying people in the real world, sociologists can't just drop video game systems into some houses and not others. If people who are more violent are also more likely to play violent video games, how do we know that the games made them violent — rather than that they chose to play violent games because of the violent nature they were born with? We don't.

A *cross-sectional* study is the most common form of sociological study. In a cross-sectional study, data are gathered across multiple groups at one point in time. For example, you may visit 1,000 families from different socio-economic backgrounds, see what media they have in their homes (video games, TVs, computers, stereos, and so forth), and ask about or observe their children's behavior. From this information, you do your best to infer what the relationship might be between media use and children's behavior. If families with violent games tend to have children who are more violent, regardless of other factors (family wealth, school quality, neighborhood), that looks incriminating for the games.

Even better would be to conduct a *longitudinal* study, where you follow a group of cases over time. For example, if you revisit those 1,000 families five years later, many aspects of their lives will have changed. Some of the families that did not have violent games five years ago will have bought them in the meantime, and you can observe whether that's had an effect on their children's behavior. If it has, that's a much more convincing finding than a finding from cross-sectional data.

So why isn't *every* sociological study a longitudinal study? Largely because of reasons of time, money, and access. It takes a lot of resources to conduct a sociological study, and conducting a longitudinal study takes at least twice as many resources — plus, of course, you have to wait around while people live their lives. (People can disappear in the meantime — see the final section of this chapter for a discussion of missing data.)

Hybrid methods

Increasingly, sociologists appreciate that the ideal is to use both qualitative and quantitative, and both longitudinal and cross-sectional, methods to answer a question. Because no research method is perfect, you can cover your bases by using multiple methods.

For example, I used all these methods in my study of children's media. My study had two main parts:

First, I tracked newspaper and magazine articles about children and media over time, assigning numerical codes to the articles to indicate which themes they addressed. That was a *quantitative*, *longitudinal* study: I retrospectively "followed" a number of publications over time, and translated their content into numbers on a spreadsheet.

Then, I sat down with teachers and parents at two schools — one urban and one suburban — to interview them about their views on children and media. That was a *qualitative*, *cross-sectional* study: I talked with people from two different social groups, and wrote about what they said without turning it into numbers.

That was a useful approach, but in the end I decided that the issues were just too complex to be distilled into numbers, and I presented a qualitative analysis rather than a quantitative analysis of the newspaper and magazine articles.

Conducting a sociological study is kind of like fixing a car: You'd better bring your whole toolbox because you don't know ahead of time what (methodological) tool is going to be the best one for the job.

Analyzing Analytical Tools

Whether your data are quantitative or qualitative, cross-sectional or longitudinal, you're going to have a whopping task in front of you when you sit down to analyze them. Fortunately, social scientists — with help from natural scientists, mathematicians, and computer programmers — have developed some powerful tools. When used correctly, these analytical tools can lead to astonishing insights.

Statistics

You've probably heard the phrase, "I don't want to become just another statistic." It usually means that someone doesn't want to have something bad happen that will add them to a tally of highway casualties, drug addicts, or other people in undesirable circumstances. In quantitative sociology, though, *everyone* is a statistic. Statistics aren't just about tallying disasters; they're about taking account of the full range of observed circumstances and helping to spot trends and patterns.

The statistical techniques most commonly used by sociologists (and other scientists) address a core problem: You want to know whether a given pattern or trend is present in a very large population, but you can't observe every single member of that population. You can observe a lot of members of that population and see whether a pattern or trend is present in that group you observe . . . but how sure can you be that your group is representative, that you aren't just looking at a group that happens to be in some way peculiar? That's always a risk. If you have a bag with an equal number of black and white marbles, you might reach in and grab a handful of marbles that happen to be all white. That's very improbable, but not impossible. Statistics can help to tell you just how improbable it is that the patterns you observe in your sample are representative of patterns in the total population.

A survey of a group you're a member of isn't automatically invalid just because you weren't among those who were given the survey! Surveying just a few thousand members of a population will yield results that are very close to the results for the entire population, just as long as people surveyed are representative of the population — that is, that they're evenly selected from all parts of the population and there isn't any one part that's overrepresented or underrepresented.

Say you're curious to know whether, in your country, boys drop out of high school more frequently than girls. You're asking a question about *every high school student in the country*, but obviously you can't gather data on every high school student in the country. You'll have to make do with a *sample* of high school students.

Maybe you know that there were 15 boys and 15 girls in your freshman home-room, and that by senior year 2 boys and 1 girl had dropped out of school. Should you then conclude that in your country, boys drop out of high school twice as often as girls? Of course not! That sample is way too small. So imagine you find data on your entire school, and learn that of 354 boys and 373 girls who started high school with you, 32 boys and 20 girls dropped out. Now you can be more confident that boys drop out more often than girls . . . but just *how* confident? Maybe you can find data on your whole school district, and learn that of 4,909 boys and 5,012 girls who started freshman year, 489 boys and 318 girls failed to graduate. Now you can be even more confident that if you were to look at all high schoolers in your country, you'd consistently find boys dropping out in greater proportion than girls.

But where do you stop gathering data? When can you be confident *enough*? Here's where statistics come in. A statistical test would tell you that if your district wide sample is representative, we can be 99.99 percent confident that, in fact, in the general population of high school students, boys drop out more often than girls. That's pretty confident.

That's just a very simple statistical test; programs that can be run on an ordinary personal computer are capable of performing much more complex analyses on huge sets of data. The general principle, though, remains: Statistical analyses tell you how confident you can be that a pattern you observe in your sample holds in a general population. You can never be 100 percent confident, but with a few thousand cases you can often be 90 percent, or even 99 percent, confident.

To be valid, statistical tests rely on a number of assumptions — and the more complex the tests get, the more assumptions they rely on. A crucial assumption is that you're testing a representative sample of the population. In the previous example, what if there's something unusual about your school district? What if it's unusually wealthy, or unusually poor? If that's the case (and it probably is), your district is not really representative of your country's high schools. You would need to take a broader sample, from a wide range of different school districts, to get a representative sample. The thing to remember — about this example and about sociological studies generally — is that if you don't have a representative sample, *your statistics program doesn't know that*. It will happily carry on applying tests and reporting results, trusting you to interpret those results appropriately. See the next section for more on this problem and other things that can go wrong with sociological studies.

Bias and the body

Researchers in all fields, the social sciences in particular, need to be aware of the danger that their beliefs and expectations will bias their results. When you *believe* that something is true, you are more likely to pay attention to information that supports your belief than information that contradicts it.

There's no surefire way to avoid biased results, but working in a team can help to ensure that no individual researcher's bias can dramatically affect the results. This was what I advised my student Kim to do when she proposed a study of women's bodies as they appeared in advertisements over several decades. Kim believed that a "fit," muscular ideal for women's bodies had come to replace the Barbie-style hourglass ideal of the 1950s, and she expected that the change would be reflected in women's bodies as seen in magazine ads.

The problem, though, was in deciding just how muscular any given body was. Kim couldn't test the muscle mass of a model in a *Cosmo* ad —

she'd have to eyeball it. Of course Kim would try her best to accurately specify just how muscular (on a 1 to 5 scale) any given model was, but I was concerned that if Kim tried to publish her research, critics would say that she may have conveniently "seen" more muscle on models in later ads so as to support her hypothesis.

What to do? I advised Kim to enlist a classmate to serve as backup: Each ad was evaluated for "muscularity" by two people whose scores were then compared and averaged. Kim gave her classmate sample pictures of body types across the scale, so both Kim and her classmate could see what should count for a "2" in muscularity and what should count for a "5." It turned out that Kim and her classmate were usually in close agreement on just how muscular any given model was, so Kim could present her results with confidence. (You may be wondering whether her hypothesis was supported. The answer is: yes!)

Qualitative data

The upside of qualitative data is that they present a rich picture of the social world. In a quantitative study, you might ask someone a series of ten multiple-choice questions about their life; in a qualitative study, you might sit down with them and ask a few open-ended questions that they take an hour or more to answer. Obviously in the qualitative study you get to know your subjects a lot better — but the downside is that you're left with dozens, hundreds, or even thousands of pages of interview transcripts or field notes that you can't just feed into a stats program for analysis.

There's no real shortcut for analyzing qualitative data: You have to go over your notes carefully, multiple times, and take note of trends and patterns which you then present to readers or listeners, usually with representative quotes from your interviews or notes. Readers or listeners who doubt your analysis can ask to look at your original data and draw their own conclusions. (In fact, they rarely do.)

Some computer programs are now available to help researchers analyze qualitative data. These programs can help tabulate uses of key words or phrases and let researchers highlight and tag themes to make it easier to see where and when they show up in the data. These programs can't conduct your analysis for you, but they can help you work more quickly and efficiently as well as help you to collaborate with colleagues who may be looking at the same data.

Preparing For Potential Pitfalls

It's exciting when you look at your data and see a pattern you hadn't expected, or realize that you have an eye-opening finding to share. But again, you need to be cautious lest you fall into one of these traps.

Data/theory mismatch

As I mentioned earlier in this chapter, in a perfect world you'd go out and gather precisely the data you need to answer your question. But in the imperfect world we actually inhabit, you often need to settle for the best data available. This creates the dangerous possibility of using inappropriate data: data that don't actually answer your question. Your *data* (the information you gather) need to match your *theory* (the question you're asking, and your hypothesis about it).

For example, when my colleague and I studied the effect of kids' high school activities on college attainment, as our outcome we took a measure of whether or not kids *enrolled* in college. What if, instead, we had taken a measure of whether they had *graduated* from college? That would have been a data/theory mismatch because it would have missed all the kids who enrolled in college and then dropped out. Our question was whether or not the students had enrolled in college, and we had to be sure our data actually spoke to that question. What makes students more or less likely to graduate from college after they enroll is an interesting question — but it's a different question from the one we were asking.

Getting overzealous

Statistical analysis can tell you how confident you can be that a pattern observed in your sample is typical of the general population — but that applies only to the general population of people like those you sampled, not necessarily the whole population of everyone in the whole wide world. It can be tempting to suggest that your findings are relevant to a broader range of situations than you've actually observed — and often, in fact, they are! Still, you need to be cautious when it comes to telling the world what you've discovered and what its significance is. You don't want to overgeneralize.

Another danger is oversimplifying: presenting your findings as being simpler than they actually are. Often, the most interesting result of a study will be a kernel of data that jumps out of one of several regression analyses; you have a responsibility to explain to your readers and listeners that the effect you've discovered may vary depending on what analysis you conduct or the presence of a certain situation. If the wording of a survey question may have influenced respondents' answers, you need to explain that. The world is a complicated place, and it's okay to acknowledge that when you present the results of your study.

This is a valuable lesson you can take away from the study of sociology: If you take some time to look closely at sociological research findings, you'll see that the research process that leads to a discovery is long and complex. Although this doesn't make the discovery invalid — indeed, if a researcher is properly attentive to details and analyses, it makes the discovery *especially* valid — it does mean that any quick-and-dirty summary of the findings, such as you might find in the media, is bound to leave out important details.

For example, say you conduct a qualitative study of parents at an elementary school, and several of your respondents mention that they feel intimidated by the school staff and hesitant to call their children's teachers to discuss concerns they have. You notice that the children of these parents, on average, earn unusually low grades given their standardized test scores. You also notice that of the several respondents who mention this, most are nonwhite. In your paper, you write:

> These findings suggest that parents who vocally advocate for their children may reap a reward in terms of higher grades awarded to those children. The findings further suggest that this effect may particularly disadvantage minority children. Further research should focus on the content of parent-teacher conversations and the context in which they occur.

The journal in which you publish this research is excited by your finding, and they send a press release summarizing your work. Your research is then reported in a two-paragraph newspaper blurb with the headline sociologist: minority parents hurt their kids by refusing to grade-grub. That headline is not exactly inaccurate, but it seriously oversimplifies your findings. That kind of thing happens frequently in media coverage of scientific findings, and scientists sometimes play into it by presenting their work in such a way as to make their findings sound especially "sexy" — that is, intriguing and important in a way that even a layman can understand. Responsible sociologists try to avoid this.

Slipping up on shacking up

A data/theory mismatch may sound like an elementary mistake that can be easily avoided, but there have been examples of data/theory mismatches that have gone unnoticed for years, even in major studies that garner lots of attention.

Sociologist Felix Elwert was curious about the effect of cohabitation — living together as romantic partners — on marriage and divorce. He wasn't the first one: Many sociologists had studied the topic, and several studies by different sociologists had found that married couples who lived together before getting married were more likely to divorce than were couples who had not lived together before marrying. The conclusion? Cohabitation makes divorce more likely. Readers interpreted these studies to suggest that if society didn't make it acceptable to "shack up" without marrying, the divorce rate would go down.

But Elwert pointed out that there was a major data/theory mismatch in that conclusion. The studies, he pointed out, considered only couples who actually *got married*. What about all the couples who moved in together and later decided to break up, without ever having been married? If they had not been permitted to live together without marrying, some of them surely would have been married, and probably would have divorced . . . so it might actually be that "allowing" couples to cohabit made the divorce rate lower than it would have been otherwise!

Further, Elwert and others noticed, many of the studies had a mistaken assumption about causality. The data didn't prove that cohabitation *caused* divorce. How did the sociologists who conducted the studies know that there wasn't something else — perhaps a risk-taking disposition — that caused couples to be both more likely to cohabit and more likely to divorce? Without more complete data, they could not know the answer to that question.

The missing links

When you sit down to analyze a large data set, it may seem like you have way more data than you know what to do with. You may have a survey administered to 10,000 respondents, each of whom answered 100 questions — giving you a million little pieces of data to sort and analyze! That's a lot of data. Even so, there's still a lot more you *don't* know than you *do* know. That's fine, but if you're missing particularly relevant information, the conclusions you draw from your analyses may be flawed. The two major categories of missing information are *missing data* and *missing variables*.

Missing data

Statistical analyses depend on your having a truly random, representative sample of the population you're studying; but that's harder to achieve than it may seem. If your data over-represent any particular group, then your data don't really tell you about the whole population.

Traditionally, surveys have been conducted by phone. Sociologists call a bunch of numbers pulled randomly from the phone book and record the responses they receive. This has never been a perfect method because often people aren't home or, if they do answer the phone, they refuse to participate. As long as that happens only randomly, it's fine — but what if it doesn't? What if the people who are not home or refuse to participate tend to be relatively poor? That means that your data overrepresent the wealthier people in a society. Today, this problem is compounded by the problem that more and more people are trading their landlines for cell phones, which don't appear in the phone book — so a sample of people who are home, have a phone, answer the phone, *and* agree to participate in a survey is looking less and less like a sample of the general population.

Then there is the problem of missing data on particular variables. What if someone takes a 100-question survey and refuses or forgets to answer 5 questions that figure in your analysis? Do you throw out that person's response entirely? Do you try to guess what they might have answered, based on what other people like them answered? There's no obvious answer as to the right way to handle that situation, but on many surveys, a huge fraction — even *most* — of the respondents have missing data on some variables, so it's potentially a big problem.

Missing variables

This is even a trickier problem. What if there are important questions that you simply forget to ask people? Usually, you just don't know. That may lead you to believe that something you *do* know is more important than it is in actuality.

For example, say you're called in to consult for a company that wants to improve its employees' reliability. The company gives you a large set of data on its employees: their work responsibilities, their salaries, their ages, their performance ratings . . . and how often each employee misses work. You run a multiple regression analysis on these data and discover that the most significant variable is age: The younger an employee is, the more often he or she misses work. You report this to the company, which assumes its younger employees are simply partying too much and instructs the human resources department to screen more carefully for serious-minded applicants.

But what *don't* you know about those employees? You don't know where they live or how they get to work. What if younger employees are less likely to own cars and more likely to rely on public transportation, which may be unreliable. How do you know *that's* not the problem? You don't, because information on transportation is simply missing from your analysis. Again, there's no obvious way to avoid this problem — you need to be mindful of the possibility that there's important information you don't have, which may cause your analysis to suggest that some variables are more important than they actually are.

Statistical snafus

Fortunately, expert statisticians have developed a range of sophisticated mathematical techniques for addressing these problems and others. Statistical analysis programs come loaded with so many features and tools that it can seem like magic. Missing data? No problem! Just use this exciting new imputation technique. Missing variables? Don't worry! We have a reliability analysis that you can use to assure your readers there's no significant problem.

These techniques are indeed powerful, and in the hands of a knowledgeable statistician, they can help solve some very tricky problems. The risk comes for the many sociologists (and other scientists) who are less than expert in the use of statistics. Each of those techniques depends on certain assumptions being true and yields results that need to be carefully interpreted, and a sociologist with a less than perfect understanding of statistics may misuse or misinterpret them. If you misuse a statistical technique, your conclusions are off-base . . . but you don't even know that they are!

How does this become a problem? Let's say you're an expert in the sociology of education, with working knowledge — but not expert knowledge — of statistics. You have a great data set that you really want to use, but you know private-school students are underrepresented in that data set. You mention this to a colleague, who says, "Oh, have you tried the Blahdeblah technique for solving that problem?" It sounds good to you, so you run your data through the Blahdeblah analysis on your statistics program, and it spits out some results that look intriguing. You write a paper about them and send it to a journal on the sociology of education. The editor sends it to two sociologists who are experts on education but not on statistics; they like your paper and just have to take your word that you've used the Blahdeblah technique correctly. They recommend your paper be published, and there you have it: a paper published in a peer-reviewed journal, based entirely on a technique that no one involved really understands. What if you misused that technique or misinterpreted your results? No one except a statistics expert would know, and they're all busy reading statistics journals — not education journals.

How big a problem is this in sociology? Some statistical experts guess that the majority of all quantitative papers published in sociology journals contain significant errors due to the misuse of statistics. It's a serious problem.

Mistakes . . . just plain oops!

And then there are those mistakes that are just plain bloopers. If they happen "behind the scenes" of an analysis, they may go completely unnoticed unless someone decides to check and run the analysis for themselves.

A notorious example of this concerned the 1994 book *The Bell Curve*, written by Richard J. Herrnstein and Charles Murray. Very controversially, Herrnstein and Murray argued that genetically inherited differences in intelligence significantly disadvantage members of minority racial groups. This conclusion was so outrageously counterintuitive that social scientists looked very carefully at Herrnstein and Murray's analyses. Could that *really* be what their data showed? The *Bell Curve* analyses were subjected to a level of scrutiny that very few studies ever receive.

In the end, many of Herrnstein and Murray's analyses and conclusions were shown to be seriously flawed. Murray himself, re-examining the analyses, discovered that several people whose years of education were unknown (missing data) had accidentally been incorporated into the analyses as each having negative five years of education! (Which is, of course, impossible. You can't actually have fewer than zero years of education . . . but a statistical analysis program wouldn't know that.) Um . . . oops! Needless to say, mistakes like that left Herrnstein and Murray with results that were highly dubious . . . but they might never have been discovered if the book's conclusions hadn't been so implausible.

So mistakes do happen, often. The research process is complicated, and there are a lot of things that can go wrong — but that doesn't mean you ought to go around mistrusting everything a sociologist tells you! It means simply that you need to be aware that just because a conclusion happens to be backed by fancy statistics or comes from a sociologist at a prestigious university, the study is not necessarily flawless or infallible. In sociology as in everything else, there's always room for improvement.

Part II

Seeing Society Like a Sociologist

The 5th Wave   By Rich Tennant

MUSEUM EXIT

NEANDERTHAL MAN

"And believe it or not children, some of your ancestors could be related to this fellow right here."

In this part . . .

One of the great discoveries of sociology is that there are some common processes and similar challenges across a range of social phenomena. No matter what you study in society, you have to know what *culture* is (and what it isn't), how to connect big social structures with everyday person-to-person interaction, and how to make sense of social networks. That's what this part is all about.

Chapter 5

Socialization: What is "Culture," and Where Can I Get Some?

*W*hen I say that people are in a society together, it generally means that they interact in some way, either directly with one another or by interacting with the same social institutions (the government, for example). It also means that they share a common *culture*.

In this chapter, I tell you what culture is and how sociologists study it. I explain how sociologists have developed strategies for studying everything from hip-hop music to fashion to first names to our deepest values and unquestioned assumptions about the world. I also explain how culture is spread, and how a person learns about culture from the first moment he or she opens his or her eyes and ears to the world.

Understanding how this process works means understanding that you're not born into a single culture, but actually into many cultures: the microculture of your family; the intersecting cultures of your neighborhood, church, and school; the broader cultures of your city, region, and country; and even the global culture shared, in some part, by nearly every single person on Earth.

Socialization is the process through which you learn this culture. Some socialization happens through the media and people you encounter at work and school, but the most important way you learn about culture — and your place in culture — is at home. I explain the concept of *primary group* as sociologists use it, and as you can use it to understand your own socialization.

Understanding What Culture Is — and Isn't

Norms are commonly accepted expectations for behavior in a society; *values* are commonly shared ideas about what is important. When you think of the term *culture*, you likely envision shared ideas, norms, and values, all of which sociologists consider to be the broader sense of culture. However, when sociologists study those shared ideas, norms, and values, they often make a distinction between the following two categories:

- ✔ **Culture:** Ideas, norms, and values that may vary widely across a society.

- ✔ **Structure:** The fundamental organization of society into its institutions, groups, statuses, and roles. Members of a society tend to agree on the nature of that society's structure.

Although the idea that the broad sense of "culture" has a subcategory called "culture" can be confusing, different sociologists handle the broad definition of culture in different ways. So breaking culture into two subsets — culture and structure — helps you understand the basic idea of how culture is studied. To help you understand the breakdown further, in the next sections I explain what culture and structure mean as well as how they may even overlap.

 Culture and structure — and the even broader sense of culture — don't have hard-and-fast definitions. Understanding how they correlate to one another and how others might define them is essential to understanding sociological arguments.

Defining "culture"

In contrast to structure (for more on structure, check out the next section, "Breaking down structure"), sociologists define culture as ideas and values that change relatively quickly and that may vary widely within a single society, neighborhood, or even family. People are allowed or even encouraged to hold these ideas and values for themselves, and those same ideas and values may change over their lives.

You can define culture simply as *shared understandings*. Everything in your head that you somehow share with other people — whether you talk about it or not — might be considered culture. For example:

✔ **Tastes in music, movies, books, and art:** Do you prefer classical music or rock music? Who's your favorite actor? Who's your favorite author? (Records, movies, books, and paintings themselves are referred to as "cultural products.")

✔ **Religious views:** Are you Catholic? Protestant? Muslim? Hindu? A Jew? Do you believe there is a holy text that should be read and followed?

✔ **Political views:** Are you a Republican, a Democrat, or neither? Do you think we should raise taxes or cut them?

✔ **Moral values:** Is it right or wrong to eat animals? What are people's moral responsibilities to one another?

Although the average person doesn't normally change political views or musical tastes every day, people can and do change these views without their everyday lives necessarily being affected very much.

Of course, if these elements of culture can change so easily and vary so widely, you may wonder if they even matter. Some sociologists say *yes*, absolutely, they make a huge difference; other sociologists say *no*, not really, they're just window dressing. Even moral values, which are deeply important to each individual, don't directly affect the overall organization of society. What everyone agrees on is the importance of *structure*. For more on the debate, see Chapter 3.

Adding to the potential confusion of understanding culture is the fact that sociologists sometimes draw a distinction between "real culture" and "ideal culture." When those terms are used, *ideal culture* refers to the values that a society professes — for example, that college students shouldn't drink alcohol — and *real culture* refers to the values that a society actually acts on — in this example, that drinking is generally understood to be a normal part of the college experience. Cultural values aren't always consistent, even in the same society.

Breaking down structure

In sociology, the word "structure" (or "social structure") refers to the fundamental organization of society. The overall structure of your society determines what statuses are available and how easy (or difficult) it is to move from one status to another. Your *status* in the social structure determines what rights and responsibilities you have.

"Status" update

Status isn't just something you update on Facebook. Status is a very important concept in sociology. A status is a place in the social structure. Because society today is very complex, each person has many statuses, all of which may have different implications in different situations. Here are just a few of my own statuses:

✔ Male

✔ White

✔ German-American

✔ College teacher

✔ Employee

✔ Son

✔ Brother

✔ Uncle

✔ Boyfriend

✔ Friend (in real life)

✔ "Friend" (on Facebook)

✔ Minnesotan

✔ Licensed driver

✔ 33-year-old

✔ Graduate of St. Agnes High School

✔ Member of the Dairy Queen Blizzard Fan Club

Each of these statuses comes with its own rights and responsibilities, and sometimes it's hard to keep them all straight! In Chapter 6, I explain more about what happens when statuses come into conflict.

As opposed to "culture," things referred to as "structure" are things that people in the same society tend to agree on, things that form the fundamental organization of society. Members of a society share basic understandings about that society's structure, and they can't be easily changed without seriously disrupting the entire society.

The foundations of social structure include:

✔ **Technology:** A technological change — for example, the invention of the automobile — can spur tremendous changes in the way we live and the culture we share. Technological changes may start small, but eventually come to affect everybody. Even if you don't drive a car, cars affect your life every day. They cause problems (pollution, accidents) as well as help us get things done, but whatever happens in the future, they can't be "uninvented."

✔ **The economy:** When the economy is booming, there are many jobs and resources to share; when the economy is hurting, unemployment is high and everyone has to make do with less. You can debate what the best strategy for economic recovery is, but you can't argue about the fact that unemployment is rising. Even the leader of a country can't snap his or her fingers and turn a national economy around — the economy lies deep in our social structure and is difficult to change.

✔ **The government:** Democracies are organized a certain way; communist governments are organized another way; and military dictatorships are organized yet another way. A government's organization affects the lives of all its citizens. The statuses available to people in the Soviet Union were very different than those available to people in Russia today. Compared to when they lived in a communist society, Russians today have more freedom to make significant amounts of money — but they also run a greater risk of being unemployed and impoverished.

✔ **The military:** Those who have access to weapons and command over armies can often force their will on others. A gun may be fired for reasons having to do with culture, but whatever culture you belong to, a bullet is a bullet. A group or an individual with enough military power can overthrow a government and bring about a new way of life (for better or for worse) for millions of people.

In a society we agree on what our structural situation is, and it is not easy for us to change — sometimes it changes in ways we can control, and sometimes it changes in ways beyond our control. Technological revolutions, economic upheavals, and military coups can transform social organization in ways that may or may not be welcome, but are hard to control or predict.

Examining the culture-structure continuum

To say that structure is more stable than culture is not to say that structure never changes, or never varies. It's helpful to make a distinction between culture and structure, but keep in mind that the word "culture" can be used to describe even the kind of basic understandings that change slowly and vary relatively little.

As an example, look at our economic system. The thousand-dollar bills in my wallet are real, but their value is a social construction — they have value only because the people in my society agree that they have value. If I visited England, I would need to trade my dollars for pounds before I could buy anything — and if I visited a completely different society, such as an isolated tribe in the South American rain forest, my dollars would be completely worthless. Our economic system is a basic component of our social structure, but still, in some ways it behaves like the things we call "culture."

Because the line between "culture" and "structure" can be drawn in different places — and is, in fact, drawn in different places by different sociologists (confusing, I know!) — it's helpful to think about the distinction between "culture" and "structure" as a continuum rather than a split between two fixed categories (see Figure 5-1). Some sociologists consider "culture" to be only relatively frivolous things like fashion and style; other sociologists consider "culture" to include *everything that's in your head.* You can define "culture" as broadly as you want, but the more broadly you define it, the bigger the picture you have to look at if you want to see significant change and variation.

Sociologists who study changes in economic values or fundamental ways of life have to look at hundreds of years of history and compare entire nations to one another; sociologists who study changes in clothing styles or musical genres can see much more change over a shorter period of time. You've seen plenty of hairstyle trends come and go in your lifetime, and you may even have converted from one religion to another — but unless you've moved around the world, how many different economic systems or types of government have you lived under? Here's another example: over the past century, America has welcomed millions of immigrants who have brought diverse religious views and lifestyles to our country and significantly changed our culture — but our social structure has remained, fundamentally, that of a capitalist democracy. *Structure* is more resistant to change than is *culture*.

Are language and symbols (like red for "stop") *culture* or *structure*? It's confusing because they're widely shared and resistant to change like structure, but they're also kind of arbitrary — what language you speak doesn't matter, so long as you get your meaning across. Because they're so fundamental to society, and so universal within a society (everyone has to know what a stop sign means), from a sociological perspective they are closer to "structure" than to "culture."

Cultural – most variable, most subject to change and debate

Art (paintings, music, books, movies)

Religion (beliefs about the spiritual world)

Politics (political leadership, policy debates)

Law (system of government, basic legal principles)

Economy (economic organization, currency, trade patterns)

Language (fundamental basis of communication, widely understood symbols)

Figure 5-1:
The structure-culture continuum.

Technology (level of scientific knowledge and development)

Structural – least variable, least subject to change and debate

Culture and the end of slavery

Slavery in the United States officially ended with the Emancipation Proclamation of 1863 — a change in the law of the land. The end of slavery, though, was a sweeping social change associated with changes up and down the structure/culture continuum. All were important in bringing an end to slavery, but notice how change came most quickly (yet least decisively) at the *culture* end of the continuum.

✔ **Art:** Editorial cartoonists and writers like Harriet Beecher Stowe created works of art that criticized slavery and helped convince Americans that change was necessary.

✔ **Religion:** Many spiritual leaders took up emancipation as a religious issue, arguing that holding human beings as property was morally wrong and displeasing to God.

✔ **Politics:** Slavery was a central issue in American politics of the 19th century, hotly debated among candidates for political office. Abraham Lincoln was elected president without the support of a single southern state.

✔ **Law:** Even an executive order from President Lincoln couldn't make slavery unconditionally illegal in the United States; that required the Thirteenth Amendment to the U.S. Constitution, ratified in 1865.

✔ **Economy:** Slavery was fundamental to the economy of the southern states, and it took decades for those states to adjust to emancipation. Economic arrangements like sharecropping, which became widespread after the Civil War, in some ways were not very different than slavery.

✔ **Language:** One significant barrier to former slaves' upward mobility was the fact that many slaves had not been taught to read or write, and had relatively little experience with the vocabulary and speech patterns of people of influence. Debates about race and education are with us to this day, and there is still a distinctive speaking style associated with African-Americans.

✔ **Technology:** By the 1860s, the ongoing development of agricultural technology making unskilled labor less valuable to farmers certainly didn't hurt in convincing northerners and southerners alike to accept the idea of a world without slavery.

Studying Culture: Makin' It and Takin' It

It's slippery enough to figure out what culture *is*, but that doesn't stop sociologists — the whole point of defining culture is to figure out how it works and how (or even whether) it's important.

Cultural sociologists argue that it's crucial to separate the *production of culture* from the *reception of culture*. Knowing how or why a cultural product is produced doesn't necessarily mean knowing what happens when someone sits down and looks at it, reads it, watches it, or plays it.

Both of these approaches have been used to study aspects of culture besides paintings, books, movies, and TV shows — but most studies have focused on cultural products such as those.

Other angles on culture

Sociologists don't have a monopoly on the study of culture, but there are important differences between the sociological study of culture and the way other writers and thinkers approach the subject. It's important to have some idea of these differences because as widely as the word "culture" is used in sociology, it's used even more widely used in other disciplines. Understanding how other disciplines study culture will also help you understand what's distinctive about the sociological approach generally.

Sociologists can be wrong (and how!), but they aim to make their arguments about culture with solid data — the more data, the better — and reasonably precise analyses. Rather than becoming deeply familiar with any one culture to the exclusion of others, sociologists want to see what the commonalities and differences are across a range of cultures. This means that you're much more likely to find numbers and statistics in a sociological study of culture than in an anthropological study, but what defines the sociological approach to culture is an interest in making scientific observations to find patterns that may be common across a wide range of different societies.

Looking at how other academic disciplines in the following list study culture helps in understanding how sociologists study culture:

Anthropology

Anthropology is a discipline that is all about understanding culture. Anthropologists are deeply interested in culture — with an emphasis on *deep*. Anthropologists appreciate that social values and perspectives may vary widely from one society to another, and when they set out to study any society, from a rural Chinese village to a bustling neighborhood in central Berlin, they are careful to question their preconceptions about what is "right" and "wrong."

Anthropologists document not only everyday practices (for example, methods of preparing food) but also the values that underlie those practices. The emphasis of most anthropologists is on precisely observing and really getting to know the groups they are studying. They do compare culture across places and times, but intercultural comparison is less important for anthropologists than it is for sociologists. Sociologists and anthropologists share a desire not to take anything for granted, but most sociologists would rather look for patterns across many cultures — or over a long period of time — rather than focusing so thoroughly on any one particular culture at any one particular time.

Cultural studies

In the field of "cultural studies," scholars are similarly thorough and analytical in examining cultural practices and products. What does the movie *Invasion of the Body Snatchers* say about American society in the 1950s, when it was produced? What does the portrayal of women's bodies in music videos from the 1980s have to do with the way women were viewed at that time? A scholar of cultural studies would likely be interested in those questions. They're similar to the kind of questions that a sociologist might ask, but as with anthropology, the emphasis is more on achieving a deep understanding of a particular place and time than on making comparisons across places and times. Rather than writing an entire article or book about *Invasion of the Body Snatchers*, sociologists would be more likely to try to study a wide range of films produced in the 1950s and compare them with a similarly wide range of movies that came out in other decades.

Liberal arts

Of course, there may be no one more interested in culture than those people producing cultural products like books, movies, and music. Books like F. Scott Fitzgerald's *The Great Gatsby* and songs like Grandmaster Flash's "The Message" have a great deal to say about culture and society — but writers of fictional stories and song lyrics are not scientists, and they don't want to be! An artist's goal is to say something with emotional impact and broad resonance, not to prove a point using systematic observations and analyses. It's hard to *prove* a book or a song wrong, but sociologists support their arguments with hard data, systematically analyzed. As with any scientific study, a sociological study can be supported or challenged when new evidence comes to light.

The production of culture

Sociologists studying the production of culture concentrate on how and why cultural products are made. Sociologists working in this field have shown that *structural* changes behind the scenes can have a huge impact on the *culture* that we see. In the modern world, this means looking at the people, organizations, and technology important in the production of , for example:

- ✔ Movies
- ✔ Music
- ✔ Books
- ✔ Art

One classic study of the production of culture was conducted by the husband-and-wife team of Harrison and Cynthia White, who studied the rise of Impressionism in French painting. There's no doubt that Claude Monet and Vincent van Gogh were artistic geniuses, but the Whites' historical study showed that the sweeping transformation of art from precisely painted historical scenes to beautifully fuzzy water lilies could only have happened after changes in organizations (the French art market spread beyond a single, central market to a system of independent dealers), the economy (rising affluence meant that more people were able to buy art), and technology (paint became cheaper and easier to use). If Monet had come along 100 years earlier, he would have been out of luck.

This study is an example of how *culture* (art and music) is affected by *structure* (organizations, the economy, technology). As communications technology has developed, allowing culture created by a small group of people to quickly reach a very large group of people, understanding the production of culture has become increasingly important. Still, sociologists have shown that the same cultural product (say, a TV show) may have very different effects on different groups of people.

The reception of culture

Studying the reception of culture means looking at how people use and interpret culture — especially cultural products like books and TV shows. Sociologists working in this area have proven that people bring their own views and values to the culture they encounter; books, TV shows, movies, and music may affect everyone, but they affect different people in different ways. People seek them out for different reasons and make their own interpretations of what they see, hear, and read.

In a fascinating study, Neil Vidmar and Milton Rokeach showed episodes of the sitcom *All in the Family* to viewers with a range of different views on race. The show centers on a character named Archie Bunker, an intolerant bigot who often gets into fights with his more progressive family members. Vidmar and Rokeach found that viewers who didn't share Archie Bunker's views thought the show was very funny in the way it made fun of Archie's absurd racism — in fact, this was the producers' intention. On the other hand, though, viewers who were themselves bigots thought Archie Bunker was the hero of the show and that the producers meant to make fun of his foolish family!

This demonstrates why it's a mistake to assume that a certain cultural product will have the same effect on everyone. This doesn't mean that cultural products have *no* effect — other studies have shown, for example, that TV shows depicting the dangers of drunk driving can actually make people less likely to drink and drive — but it does mean that the interaction between culture and people's actions is a little more complicated than it might seem.

Paddling the "Mainstream"

There are different ways of studying culture, different ways of producing culture, and different ways of interpreting culture — isn't there *anything* we can all agree on?

In a word, no. But there are some things that come close! There are some very widely shared cultural norms and some very popular cultural products: things that just about everyone likes — or, at least, knows about. These things can be called *mainstream culture*. In this section, I explain how mainstream culture can be a common point of reference, even for people who disagree with it and are trying to tear it apart. I'll also bring up the argument that mainstream culture is disappearing, as everyone runs off to join tiny cultural groups and ignoring other groups.

Even if people in a given society have different interpretations of, say, a popular book or television show, certain cultural products, ideas, and values are so widespread across society that they form *mainstream culture:* culture that has relatively wide agreement and awareness across a society. Parts of mainstream culture include:

✔ **Mainstream products:**

- Blockbuster movies and popular songs

- Flags and other popular symbols

- Sacred texts

✔ **Mainstream ideas and values:**

- Widespread religious beliefs

- Ideas about what type of people are most important (men or women? white or black?)

- Ideas about what type of government is best (democracy? communism?)

✔ **Mainstream practices:**

- National holidays

- Rituals such as saying a prayer or a national pledge, watching a popular sport, or voting

- Dating and marriage practices

You're not going to surprise or offend many people by setting off fireworks on the Fourth of July, or buying the latest box-office smash on DVD, or wearing jeans tailored to the latest trend. These things may, in fact, seem downright boring, but mainstream culture includes some of a society's most cherished traditions and widely shared values. Even in societies that have many different cultural traditions, products, ideas, values, and practices in mainstream culture can provide common touchstones that help everyone get along — and have something to talk about around the water cooler or over the backyard fence!

What's the difference between _mainstream culture_ and _structure_? It's a good question. After all, I said that _structure_ is also something everyone in a society shares. The difference is that mainstream culture is still _culture_ — it's not necessarily foundational to the way a society is organized, and like all culture (in the sociological sense), it sometimes changes quickly. Think about fashion: It sometimes seems like _everyone_ is wearing one brand of shoes one year, and _everyone_ is wearing another brand just the very next year. It would be a lot easier to get along having your own unique fashion (culture) than having your own unique currency (structure) — but still, most people tend to follow popular fashions. Even if they don't, they usually know what the popular fashions are. That's the power of mainstream culture.

Subculture

The word _subculture_ refers to a culture that is strikingly, often deliberately, different from mainstream culture. Values and practices associated with a subculture will often seem odd to people who aren't involved with that subculture, and they may even cause outrage. Subcultures that are especially critical of mainstream culture are often referred to as _countercultures_.

A good example of a subculture that caused outrage can be found in the 1970s punk subculture in England. As sociologist Dick Hebdige pointed out in a famous study of punks, members of that subculture adopted styles of dress that were designed to shock mainstream Brits. Punks pierced their lips with safety pins, spiked and dyed their hair, and — most offensively — used the British flag in subversive and disrespectful ways. By pinning Union Jacks to studded leather jackets and singing along to songs like the Sex Pistols' snarling, sarcastic "God Save the Queen," punks mocked the symbols of mainstream British culture.

Not all subcultures are so forthrightly political, but all subcultures depart from mainstream culture in some combination of ways. Subcultures are also coherent: People in a subculture are being different from the mainstream, but they're all being different in the same way, a way that they all share.

What makes a subculture a subculture (rather than just a different culture entirely) is that members of a subculture aren't ignorant of mainstream culture — they know exactly what mainstream culture is, and they deliberately reject it. Sometimes, in fact, people in subcultures are even _more_ acutely conscious of mainstream culture than are people in the mainstream. For example, some religious groups who disapprove of mainstream movies publish extremely comprehensive movie guides so that members of the sub-culture can be aware of which mainstream movies are considered acceptable to that subculture and which are not. Someone who's not in that subculture, on the other hand, could just walk into any cineplex and buy a ticket to any-thing that looks good.

Subcultures can even have subcultures of their own — groups of people who abide by some norms and practices of the subculture, but deliberately reject others. An example of this is the "straight edge" movement in punk rock: a group of punks who dress like punks and act like punks but who share a com-mitment not to use alcohol or drugs like punks do. This makes "straight edge" punks — are you ready for this? — a *sub-subculture.*

When subcultures reach a certain level of popularity, they may be absorbed into mainstream culture, thus ceasing to be different or shocking. Today you can walk into any London souvenir shop and buy a pair of thong underwear with the British flag printed on the crotch, and no one is likely to think you're very much of a rebel for doing so.

Microcultures

Subcultures reject mainstream culture, but there can't be such a thing as a subculture if there's no mainstream culture to reject!

Developments in communications technology — the invention of the printing press and, later, radio and television — have been responsible for the spread of mainstream culture, and further technological developments may be help-ing to bring it to an end. The Internet makes it easy for even relatively tiny groups to connect from anywhere around the world, thus making it easier to spend more and more time associating with people from your preferred subcultures. When there were only a few radio stations on the dial, almost everyone listened to the same music; now, Internet radio allows you to easily listen to any of thousands upon thousands of different radio stations. You can follow sports teams playing anywhere in the world, and you can order or download books published in any country.

Given these dramatic changes, sociologist Jason Kaufman has argued that it makes less and less sense to think of there even being anything like "main-stream culture." When you might have a completely different lifestyle than the woman living across the street or the guy sitting next to you at work, where is the mainstream? There may not necessarily be one. Kaufman says that we are increasingly living in a world of *microcultures,* where people can seek out small groups of like-minded people and spend nearly all their time interacting with them — rather than sharing the norms, values, and practices of people in their immediate surroundings. Birds of a feather have always flocked together, but now technology allows much smaller groups of birds to flock together from far-flung corners of the Earth.

Off to see *The Wizard*

When the movie *The Wizard of Oz* was screened on commercial television once a year in the 1960s, it used to be said that water pressure in big cities would suddenly drop during commercials because the toilets were flushing in nearly every house in town. Whether or not that was actually true, it seemed plausible because almost *everyone* would be watching the same movie. What else would they watch? There were only a few channels they could possibly watch. Now that most households have cable TV with dozens of channels — not to mention access to millions of videos on the Internet — every single person in every single house on the block could be watching something different.

Was life better back in the day when everyone watched the same shows and listened to the same music? Sociologist Robert Putnam believes that society used to have more "social capital" — more shared connections and understandings — whereas today people spend too much time in their own private worlds without caring what anyone else is doing. On the other hand, today's technology allows people to make new kinds of social connections: If you're not watching TV with your mom in the living room, you might be on the Internet connecting with friends across the country. Videos on the Internet can be seen by tens of millions of people around the world; that's still shared culture, even if they're not all coordinating their bathroom breaks.

If it's true that we're moving towards a world of microcultures, it will have important implications for everyone's lives. Even though mainstream culture sometimes seems dull or bland, it does give everyone in a society a way to connect, something to share despite all their other differences.

Socialization: Where You Connect in Culture

Despite all the different perspectives on culture, there's one thing everybody agrees on: Culture is not something you're born with, it's something you learn. *Socialization* refers to the process by which people learn the norms and values of their society as they grow up. Like all learning, socialization happens especially quickly when people are young, but it's a process that continues throughout life. As long as you're alive and interacting with other people, you're being socialized (and helping to socialize others).

Some socialization is very deliberate; for example, when companies have diversity training sessions meant to teach employees to value the fact that their coworkers come from different social backgrounds. Most socialization, however, happens by pure osmosis. Without even realizing it, you come to share the values and norms of the people around you. (See the beginning of this chapter for definitions of "values" and "norms.") As you grow up, you learn an entire way of life — often without even realizing it — that may be very different from what other people in other situations are learning.

Nature vs. nurture: Social psychology

The way people learn culture is by interacting with those around them. Normally sociologists are interested in large groups of people (that is, how human society works) while psychologists are interested in people as individuals (that is, how the human mind works). But the two disciplines meet in a field called *social psychology*, which is studied by both psychologists and sociologists. Social psychology is the study of how people as individuals learn from and interact with the people around them.

A perennial question in social psychology is the question of nature vs. nurture. *Nature*, in this formulation, stands for our genetic inheritance, the "programming" we were born with. *Nurture* stands for everything that happens to us as we grow and learn through interactions with other people. Our genetic inheritance definitively influences many of our physical characteristics and may have a profound influence on traits like personality, disposition, and sexuality. But even identical twins, who have exactly the same DNA, develop different personalities and interests.

Breaking from the norm

When I was in kindergarten and first grade, I attended a school where as soon as any kid finished eating lunch, he or she was allowed to stand up and run straight out to the playground for recess. Then I transferred to another school, and on the first day of second grade I finished my lunch and stood up, only to realize that *no one else was standing*. One of the nuns who taught at the school came over and explained: "At *this* school, we all go out to recess together." I blushed and sat back down.

Without even realizing what I was doing, I had breached a social norm: only when I did something differently than everyone else did I realize that I had been socialized into a different set of norms than the kids around me. A sociologist named Harold Garfinkel made a name for himself in the 1970s by instructing his students to go out and deliberately violate norms, just to see how people reacted. (For example, a student might board a city bus and try to negotiate with the driver about the fare.) Garfinkel's deliberate "breaching experiments," like my accidental one, demonstrated that we all live by rules that we've learned without even realizing that we've learned them.

There's no one right answer to the question of nature vs. nurture: in reality, people develop through an interaction of their genetic programming with the environment around them. Although it's not an inclusive list, Table 5-1 gives you some examples of how you grow and learn through nature, nurture, and the interaction of the two.

Table 5-1	Nature, Nurture, and Everything in Between	
Definitely nature	*Definitely nurture*	*Interaction between nature and nurture*
Eye color	Language spoken	Personality and disposition
Sex (male or female)	Social norms	Risk of disease and psychological disorder
Skin pigmentation	Specific knowledge about people, places, and so forth.	Skills and interests

You are who other people think you are

Through interpersonal socialization (see sidebar, "Not-so-secret agents") people learn the values and norms of the group they're born into, but they also learn who they are as individuals. This helps explain how even children born into the same family can develop very different personalities.

In *An Inconvenient Squirrel*, a children's play by Joseph Scrimshaw, the squirrel of the title is "inconvenient" because he refuses to accept a name like "Really Important Squirrel" or "Master Thespian Squirrel," a name that defines his identity. At one point, Evil Genius Squirrel explains to the inconvenient squirrel why having a public identity is so important: "You are," he says slyly, "who other people think you are."

Evil Genius Squirrel wasn't the first one to figure this out. A sociologist named Charles Cooley (a member of the Chicago School, described in Chapter 3) coined the term "the looking-glass self" to describe the way that each person develops an idea of himself or herself by noticing how people act towards him or her.

Cooley emphasized the importance of each person's "primary group" — the group of people with whom you interact most. Your family members, your very best friends, your closest coworkers: these are all members of your primary group. You implicitly learn norms and values from the members of your primary group, but you also notice how you're different from them.

If you're seen as "the quiet one" in your family, this becomes an important part of your identity, even if your family members generally are nonstop chatterboxes compared to the family next door.

Of course, some people break the looking glass, so to speak, and reject the way they are defined by their families. They may run away, rebel, or otherwise behave in a manner completely contrary to the way they were raised. It's hard to understand why people change identities and personalities through life, and I'm relieved to say that we sociologists have the luxury of not even *trying* to understand any one individual's behavior! It's with good reason that people who need personal counseling go to a psychologist, not a sociologist.

Not-so-secret agents

Sociologists use the term *agents of socialization* to refer to the various people and groups that socialize an individual into his or her culture(s). Here are a few different agents of socialization. Think about how they've affected the way you think about yourself and the world around you.

✔ Your *family* is a primary group that was responsible for your earliest and most important socialization. Your family has likely shaped everything from your habits to your moral values to your sense of humor and — most fundamentally — your sense of yourself. Who *are* you? What are the best and the worst things about you? Your parents and other close relatives have their own answers to those questions, and you can hardly have escaped being deeply affected by their views on the subject.

✔ A *church* (or sacred place generally) is a place where people go to connect with the spiritual world, but also — often very deliberately — to be socialized. Religious leaders and sacred texts often make strong prescriptions about everything ranging from when killing is acceptable to when wearing lipstick is acceptable. Religious services often include solemn rituals and have dress codes marking them as unusually important. People do sometimes switch religions, but they remain forever affected by the socialization they have received in communities of faith.

✔ *School* is another prime agent of socialization. Teachers and administrators typically make no bones about the fact that their socially-designated job is not just to transmit knowledge but to transmit culture. Government-run schools in many societies are limited to officially transmitting civic culture rather than religious or ethnic culture, but even then, schools drop a heap of socialization on every student every day — from a nation's founding ideals to which side of the hallway you're supposed to walk on. School is also a prime site of socialization by *peers*.

✔ The socializing power of the *media* is a matter of perennial debate. As I explained earlier in this chapter, people are active viewers, listeners, and readers who watch, listen to, and read media for many different reasons and learn different things from the same songs, shows, or books. That said, people certainly learn many important cultural lessons from media, sometimes as profound as the value of diversity, sometimes as mundane as the latest dance craze.

What sociologists seek to understand is how human groups behave in general, and what is true *in general* is that most people's individual identities are very strongly shaped by their primary groups. There's a real difference between the way most people relate to their families and closest friends (a personal, emotional connection) and the way they relate to their classmates and work colleagues (a friendly but more formal, less intimate connection).

Culture Paradox: Pulling Us Together and Pushing Us Apart

When people think about themselves in their social groups, they tend to notice cultural *differences* rather than cultural similarities. So one of the great contributions of sociology is calling attention to the many cultural values and norms that people *share,* that allow society to work as well as it does. When Garfinkel's students tried to negotiate bus fare, they made clear that despite all the many cultural differences among people riding on a city bus, they share at least one powerful norm: the norm of equality, that each person should pay the same amount for the same bus ride.

Understanding culture is about more than just figuring out how today's hottest recording artist sold all those millions of records. You have to understand culture if you want to understand society, and you have to understand culture if you want to understand yourself. You were born a unique individual because of your biological DNA, but also because of your social DNA. Think of all the social groups you're a member of: your family, your neighborhood, your peer group, your sports teams, your clubs. You're not the only member of any of them, but you are the only one who's a member of *all* of them. So socially as well as biologically, you're unique!

Uniting through culture

It's because of our shared culture that people are able to get along as well as they do. In Chapter 3, I explain how Emile Durkheim saw society as being akin to an animal, with different social "organs" working together but doing different jobs. In this view, culture is like the nervous system — it connects everything and makes sure that every part of the organism is working together. Durkheim was fascinated by this coordination, by the way that people in big, diverse societies manage to go about their daily activities with relatively few arguments about anything of real consequence.

Yes, there is tension in society — from international wars to interpersonal tiffs — but most people, most of the time, actually get along pretty well. They don't argue over bus fare, fight over whether they have to stop at red lights, or debate whether people should be allowed to have private property. People in democratic societies may argue over which candidate should be an elected leader, but except for societies in great turmoil, they don't argue over whether there should be an election or whether some people's votes ought to be counted more than others'.

It's thanks to all these shared values that people are able to build and maintain great cities, to work together to find cures for diseases, and to make and distribute movies and songs that are loved by millions. Think about how much harder it would be to accomplish these things if people didn't share cultural values and rituals.

Imagine having a business meeting where there was absolutely no small talk, where you felt absolutely no identification with the people you were meeting with. It would be excruciatingly awkward, perhaps to the point that it would be hard to accomplish anything—and what, exactly, would you be trying to accomplish anyway? Widely shared culture greases the wheels, sets the agenda, and sets helpful limits on what is and isn't acceptable. It's just about the most important thing we humans do with our relatively supersized brains, and it may be our crowning achievement as a species.

Dividing because of culture

Still, there are plenty of conflicts in society, and cultural differences are at the heart of many of them. Wars have erupted over differences of religion and tradition; in some neighborhoods, you might be shot for dressing a certain way or speaking a certain language.

Emile Durkheim likened society to an organism, but Karl Marx — who I introduce in Chapter 3 — would have thought that was far too optimistic. He would say that it's nice to think that people are all working together for the collective good, but in fact most people are working for the benefit of the few lucky ones who control what gets done and what doesn't. He called religion (an important part of culture) "the opiate of the people" because he believed that it just helped to lull people into a kind of snooze, making them feel warm and fuzzy while discouraging them from questioning the status quo. By this logic, all of mainstream culture might be considered an "opiate."

Other sociologists have pointed out that cultural differences can reinforce and even strengthen structural differences. Pierre Bourdieu pointed out that people with structural privileges — more wealth, better jobs — may use culture as a way to keep less fortunate people from claiming any of those privileges. No matter how qualified you are, you'll be at a disadvantage applying for many high-paying jobs if you show up speaking with a certain accent, or wearing the wrong brand of suit, or admitting that you know nothing about fine art. (See Chapter 8 for more on how *cultural capital* can contribute to social stratification.)

But cultural divisions aren't always class divisions. Sometimes cultural differences divide people despite the fact that they're in very similar structural situations. In some neighborhoods, different ethnic groups don't mix: they keep separate social groups and are suspicious of one another even though they live amongst each other, have very similar jobs, and face similar challenges that they could work together to solve if they weren't divided by cultural differences.

So culture in some ways unites us and in other ways divides us — the bottom line is that culture *matters*.

Chapter 6

Microsociology: If Life Is a Game, What Are the Rules?

In This Chapter

▶ Examining the paradox of society

▶ Making rational — and irrational — choices

▶ Taking the stage of life: symbolic interactionism

Sociologists study huge historical trends and conflicts among large groups, but many sociologists are also fascinated with the way individuals interact in society. This is called *microsociology* because it's the study of society at its "smallest" — as small as two people interacting.

The society you live in gives shape and purpose to your life, but it also imposes limits. How do you deal with the social rules that guide you, and how do you use them to your advantage? What do you do when you encounter someone who plays by different rules than you do?

Just as understanding society helps to understand the choices individuals face, so do sociologists need to have some idea of individual psychology to understand how society works. If people's actions and choices aren't to some extent predictable, then *nothing* in society is predictable. In general, sociologists find that people are fairly predictable on average — but that doesn't mean that their choices always "make sense." As you may have noticed in your own life, sometimes people are predictably confusing.

In this chapter, I explain how sociologists think about the individual person in society — how and why a person makes the choices he does, and what effect this has on his society. I start by laying out the fundamental problem: How can society be both outside you and inside you? I continue on to discuss the problem of people's unpredictability, and conclude with an explanation of how people "perform" in society like actors on a stage.

Within You and Without You: The Paradox of Society

Thinking about the individual in society forces sociologists to think about a very basic question: What *is* society? Are you "society"? Am I "society"? If we both live in the same society, we live by many of the same rules and understandings — but who made those up, and who's in charge of changing them? If it's not us, then who? From the perspective of any individual person, society is in many ways a paradox: Society is both within you (the norms, rules, and assumptions you take for granted; see Chapter 5 for more on norms and values) and without you (they've been taught by others, who continue to impose them on you whether you like it or not). In this section, I first explain how "social facts" are the sum of individual actions, and then discuss how your social knowledge can serve as a toolbox to help you do well in different contexts.

Social facts: The sum of our parts

In Chapter 3, I explain that Emile Durkheim urged sociologists to focus on *social facts:* facts about a society in general, not about any individual person within that society. By definition, a social fact is true of your society, but it doesn't say anything about *you* . . . or does it? You are part of your society, and your actions and beliefs are part of what defines that society. Your actions help make up the aggregate facts about your society, and your beliefs both influence and are influenced by your society's norms and values.

Aggregate facts: You don't have to be like everyone else . . . but it's a lot easier that way

An *aggregate* fact is a summary fact about a number of smaller things. When used in the context of sociology, the term "aggregate fact" usually refers to an overall description of what a large number of people are doing. An aggregate trend describes how an aggregate fact is changing over time.

The following aggregate facts are true of many societies in the world today, and they may be true of yours:

- **Marriages:** About half of all marriages end in divorce.
- **Jobs:** People typically hold several different jobs over the course of their working lives.
- **Musical Tastes:** Most people don't listen to classical music.

Knowing these facts about your society, however, tells me nothing about you as an individual. It doesn't tell me about your personal history or the choices you personally will make in life. Those social facts don't describe your life — but they do affect it! For better and for worse, those aggregate facts about your society heavily influence your own life, and make it different than it would be if you lived in a different society.

To understand how facts about society in general can affect your own personal life, think about these points:

- **Marriage:** When deciding whether to marry someone, you do so with the understanding that, however you may personally feel about marriage, in your society generally marriage is very often impermanent. That doesn't mean marriage is taken lightly, but it does mean that if the going gets rough and you or your partner decide to bail, you will be in the company of a large number of your friends and colleagues who have also experienced divorce. Consciously or unconsciously, the fact that divorce is socially acceptable may influence you to make a riskier marriage decision than you would in a society where divorce is not considered acceptable.

- **Job:** Similarly, when you take a job, you can't — and shouldn't — expect that it will be permanent. It may just be, but that would not be the norm. You can expect to have other job opportunities in the future, which would be very unusual for you to never take. This means that you probably won't look for a job that will last a lifetime — you'll look for a job that will serve you well over the next few years.

- **Music:** You can listen to whatever music you want, but if you choose to listen to Beethoven or Mozart, you won't be able to chat about it with most of the people around you — unless you happen to be a member of an orchestra. Everywhere from TV programs to dentists' offices to nightclubs, you're much more likely to hear pop, rock, or R&B than classical music. If you listen to mostly classical music, you are unusual, and it may cause people to make certain assumptions about your background and personality. For this reason, you may choose not to listen to classical music, or to listen to it only in private. On the other hand, you may very deliberately and openly choose to listen to classical music if you want to convey a certain impression.

Norms, values, and laws

In Chapter 5, I describe the continuum of social understandings and agreements, running from "structure" to "culture." All along that continuum there are norms and values that shape your life — the rules and repertoires of your society.

At the "structure" end of the continuum are rules that are hard and fast, relating to your economic system and the laws of the land. Laws are social norms that are seen as being so important that they're written down and made formal, so that if you break them you can be punished — with punishments ranging from a small fine to a death sentence. (For more on crime and deviance, see Chapter 11.) For example, you can't just

- Make up your own currency and expect it to buy you anything at the store.
- Give yourself a job or expect anyone else to give you one if they don't have one to give.
- Break the law and expect to not be punished.

At the "culture" end of the continuum are norms and values that are probably not written into law, but that are nonetheless real. For example:

- Current fashions and styles, such as whether or not it's acceptable to wear socks with sandals
- Religious principles and rituals, such as Bar Mitzvahs or the baptism of children
- Social traditions, such as shooting off fireworks on certain national holidays

You don't *have* to follow any of these social norms, but if you don't, people around you may find your behavior confusing or even rude.

It may seem unfair — you didn't *make* any of these rules. In fact, no single person did. Economic realities are beyond the control of even the largest companies; laws may be proposed by specific legislators but normally must meet with broad approval to be passed; and fashion trends may be started by popular people, but no one can single-handedly make something trendy.

No individual person makes social norms, but every single person helps perpetuate and enforce them. How? Simply by following them and by noticing when other people don't. You can try to buck the trend, but you'll almost certainly face resistance. (For more on movements directed at changing society, see Chapter 13.)

Use a tool (from your social repertoire) — don't be one

Your life as an individual in society is shaped by trends, norms, values, and laws, but what are you supposed to do when you don't *know* what to do? Societies today are diverse, and in the course of your daily life you may move through several different social circles, each with its own norms. For this reason, life in society can be very confusing, not to mention frustrating — even dangerous.

Sociologist Ann Swidler coined the term *cultural toolkit* to refer to all the cultural knowledge that you keep in your head. Your cultural knowledge is like a toolkit because you don't always use all of it — but it's ready for you when you want or need to use it. Whereas some social norms are so taken for granted that it might never even occur to you to do otherwise, some social norms vary dramatically from one place to the next; if you know the norms and values associated with different social contexts, you can act appropriately in a range of situations. For example:

- ✔ You might dress in a suit and watch your language at work — but then slip into jeans and a t-shirt for your after-work softball game, where you can freely drink beer and swear.

- ✔ You might know to accept a business card with one hand in the United States — but with two hands in China.

- ✔ You might know to clap and cheer after an impressive solo at a jazz show — but not at an orchestral performance.

The term *code switching* is often used to refer to this process of adapting to different social contexts. Prudence Carter, a sociologist of education, talked to inner-city teens and found that they were able to succeed at school and at home by knowing how to talk and dress in one way to impress their teachers in school, and in another way to impress their peers at home on the block.

Everyone does this kind of code-switching to some extent, but knowing how to do it well, and in many different situations, is a tremendous advantage. The trick is managing all those different roles.

This is part of the paradox of society: You have the freedom to choose how you will behave, but your own social background both determines what behaviors you are familiar with and influences which ones you'll choose. You've probably been advised to "just be yourself" — but who you are comes, in large part, from your society. Futhermore, "being yourself" varies from one social context to the next. If you wear a suit to work and do a job you're proud of, and then go home and sit on the couch watching TV in your sweats, in which context are you being most "yourself"? Some sociologists have gone so far as to say that the idea of "being yourself" only makes sense in a social context. When you think about "who you are," what you're really thinking about is how you're similar to, and different from, the people around you.

A friend of mine has a son who recently started playing with a team in the National Football League. The man is, of course, very proud of his son. The day his son was scheduled to play in the team's starting lineup for the first time, it happened to be an away game at the stadium of an opposing team. My friend and his brother-in-law flew out to the city where the game was being played and headed for the stadium wearing jerseys with his son's name and team on them.

As they approached the stadium, though, they began to be confronted by fans of the opposing team. Seeing the visitors' jerseys, the fans jeered and shouted threats at my friend — some even threw themselves in my friend's path and asked him what he thought he was doing. My friend's brother-in-law tried to make peace, yelling things like: "This man's son is starting in his first NFL game! You should buy him a drink!" The opposing team's fans didn't seem to care, and my friend came close to turning back and watching the game from the safety of his hotel room. The two pressed on, though, and finally made it safely to their seats.

This story shows how risky — even dangerous — it can be to violate certain social norms. It's not against the law to cheer for a visiting team; in fact, it would be illegal to try to stop someone from doing so. Still, my friend found himself walking into a situation where cheering for the visitors was such a violation of social norms that he could have been seriously hurt. He was free to ignore that norm — and he did — but it was at his own peril.

Rational — and Irrational — Choices

So at any given moment, you have choices — choices within, among, and outside of social norms. Understanding social norms is one of the things that sociologists do best. Collecting data about large groups and understanding aggregate decisions by hundreds or thousands of people . . . that's the meat and potatoes of sociology.

For Durkheim, that was *all* sociology needed to do. Other sociologists, though, have argued that a sociological theory is incomplete if it doesn't explain how social facts play out at the individual level. It may be convenient to imagine that one social fact (for example, a country's religious makeup) directly affects another (for example, that country's suicide rate) — but the actual fact of the matter is that social facts affect one another by affecting individual people. Spain doesn't "decide" to have a certain suicide rate; individual Spaniards decide for themselves whether or not to take their lives. Even Durkheim, for all his focus on social facts, offered theories about why a certain social fact (religion, the economy, war) might make an individual person more or less likely to commit suicide — thus affecting the country's suicide rate. Sociologists don't need to become psychologists, but they do need to have some idea of why people make the choices they do.

Making rational choices — *or, at least, trying to*

To understand how or why a person makes choices in society, it makes sense to begin with the assumption that everyone at least tries to be rational in his or her decision-making. After that, you can consider how and why people often seem to be *irrational* in the choices they make. In the following sections, I explain how what sociologists and economists refer to as *rational choice theory* (or, sometimes, *rational action theory*) works in situations from car shopping to date shopping.

Understanding rational choice theory

Besides sociology and psychology, another social science that seeks to scientifically understand human behavior is economics. For centuries, economists have operated under the basic assumption that people are rational creatures who will, in general, make the choices they feel are best for themselves. This is the principle of *rational choice,* which most economists and many sociologists believe is the best way to understand individual human behavior. They believe that even in cases where someone's actions seem inexplicable, there is probably a self-serving motive behind those actions. Understanding human behavior, in this view, means figuring out exactly how people believe they will benefit from the choices they make.

It's obvious what this means in economic terms: People will — or at least, they're *supposed* to — choose the savings account with the highest interest rate, or buy a product from the retailer who offers the lowest price. But real-life decisions, even decisions about relatively simple economic matters, are rarely that clear cut.

Say you're shopping for a car. You'd like to get a bargain, but of course you're not going to just buy the cheapest car you can possibly buy! There are some amenities you need and value in a car, and you understand that in general, more expensive cars are going to have more of these features.

Even then, a certain amount of money — say, $25,000 — might buy any of dozens or hundreds of different cars. There are several choices you need to make about what aspects of a car you value. For example, you might consider:

- How much is it worth to you to have a new car versus a used one?
- Would you rather have a very reliable car, or a very high-performing one?
- How much does it matter whether your car is fuel-efficient and environmentally friendly?

✔ Does it matter whether or not the car is made in your country? Would you pay more for a domestic car versus an imported car?

✔ Does it matter how the car looks? If so, what color or model do you want, and how much extra would you pay to get it?

It's a complicated decision — and you'll never find a car in any price range that has *all* the features you want — but social scientists who believe in the principle of rational choice argue that you do know the answers to all of the above questions, and when you go car shopping, you will buy the car that comes closest to meeting all your different needs.

Applying rational choice to non-financial decisions

What about decisions that fall outside the strictly economic realm, though? What about the decisions you make that have nothing to do with money as such? Are those decisions "rational," too? Indeed they are, many economists and sociologists believe.

Consider romantic relationships. In many ways it seems like you don't "choose" your partner; rather, a relationship just *happens.* People say things like, "when I met Darlene, I just *knew* it was right," or "all of a sudden it had been two years and bang! I found myself engaged."

The fact of the matter is, though, that unless you live in a society where marriages are 100 percent arranged by parents and family, you do have a choice in whom you marry. People even talk about it this way. "I've been looking for someone like you," someone will say, and the response may be, "I was hoping you would offer to take me out on a date, and I knew I would accept your offer."

Just as with cars, people may make a range of choices about what characteristics they're looking for in a romantic partner.

✔ Do you want someone who has a similar job to yours, or a different one?

✔ Does it matter to you how much money the person makes? (Be honest!)

✔ Does it matter to you how much education the person has, or what they studied?

✔ How much does physical attractiveness matter to you? (Again, be honest!) Are there certain characteristics, like hair color or height, that especially matter to you?

✔ Does it matter whether your partner shares your religious background, or comes from the same area you do?

✔ Does it matter whether your partner shares your race or ethnic background?

✔ Does it matter who your partner's friends and family are?

✔ Does it matter what your partner's leisure interests are? Is it important that they be similar to yours?

Art cars

If one challenge for rational choice theorists is understanding how people's personal decisions about things like love and relationships are "rational," another big challenge is understanding how and why people buy art. How do people even begin to place a value on a painted canvas that serves little purpose beyond hanging on the wall?

It turns out that they place a high degree of importance on knowing who the artist is. If the artist is someone well known, perhaps someone with an interesting personal story like Vincent van Gogh (who cut off his own ear) or Jackson Pollock (who tore his way through the New York art world, shocking and delighting people with his paint-splattered canvases), buyers will place a high value on almost *any* work bearing that artist's name.

Sociologists Joel Podolny and Marya Hill-Popper studied the market for cars, and they discovered that at the high end of the car market, buyers and sellers talk about cars less as though they were cars and more as though they were works of art. Much attention is given to the person who designed the car, the company that built it, and the context in which it was built and sold — just as would be the case for a work of art.

By contrast, if you're buying a relatively cheap car that will just get you from place to place, you probably won't be sitting around with the seller talking about the model's history and pedigree. My friend Paul was selling an old beat-up car for the appropriately low price of $500, and he received an e-mail from a prospective buyer asking him a number of complicated questions about the car. Paul's thought was to respond, "The answer to your first question is: five hundred dollars. The answer to every one of your other questions is: five hundred dollars."

Of course these things *do* matter, and online matchmaking sites take advantage of that fact to pair their members with one another. Some such sites boast surprisingly high success rates, suggesting that an algorithmic approach to romance might not be fundamentally incompatible with human happiness.

The rational choice theorists might seem to have it all sealed up: Even when it comes to something as intimate and personal as love and marriage, people are rational decision-makers who make choices that will give them maximum value.

Or are they? Sometimes people make choices that don't seem very rational. Can rational choice theory explain bad decisions?

D'oh! Making poor choices

Rational choice theory makes a world of sense when people are making choices that actually make sense — but what about when they aren't?

Often people make choices that just don't seem to be in their own self-interest. Isn't this a problem for economists and sociologists who believe people are rational choice makers?

When I was a teenager my parents often found themselves questioning my rationality — for example, when a friend and I tried to bicycle halfway across Minnesota on the shoulder of an interstate freeway — but they weren't the first ones to notice that people sometimes make inexplicable decisions. In this section, I go through four of the biggest challenges to rational choice theory. Do people's decisions make any sense at all?

Challenge #1: Sometimes people make sub-optimal choices

What does "sub-optimal" mean? It means that sometimes people make choices that aren't their *best* (that is, most optimal) choices. You might buy a car from one dealer when the dealer right next door has a much better car selling for the same amount of money. That's not very rational . . . is it? Well, maybe it is. This view of rationality is called *bounded rationality*: You make the best decisions you can, based on the information you have time to collect.

No one has all the time in the world, and it takes time to gather the information you need to make a good choice. One of the decisions you have to make when you're making a purchase, or a career choice, or a choice of spouse, is how much time you can afford to spend learning about all your options. Maybe you've just spent all weekend visiting several dealerships, and the car you chose to buy is the best bargain available at any of those dealerships. Sure, you may have found a better bargain if you visited the next dealer down . . . but then why not visit the next one as well, and the next and the next and the next? At some point you have to decide that you've spent enough time searching to make a reasonably well-informed choice. There is, after all, somewhere you want to actually *go* in your car!

Challenge #2: Sometimes people deliberately make irrational choices

What if you *know* you're being irrational?

Millions of people around the world gamble, putting billions of dollars at risk at casinos, in lotteries, and with bookies. They do this despite the fact that, on average, gambling is a losing proposition — governments run lotteries to make up budget shortfalls, and casino proprietors can reap fabulous profits. Sure, you *might* hit it big at the slots or in the lottery, but probably you'll lose. The house always makes sure that the odds are in its favor.

You know that, and you still choose to gamble. Why? You might choose to do so for entertainment value, knowing that your losses are essentially what you pay for an exciting night at the casino. Many people, though, don't see it that way — they play to win, even if they know that on average they won't. Why would they do this?

People are sometimes irrational in ways like this — but they're also *predictably* irrational. Social scientists have demonstrated a range of ways that people can predictably be tricked into making irrational decisions:

- Psychologists have discovered that people predictably respond to irregular reward patterns, so a slot machine is consistently much more addictive than, say, a change machine. You know that every time you put a dollar into a change machine you'll be rewarded with exactly four quarters. What fun is that?

- Economists have discovered that people consistently value near-term rewards over long-term rewards — so $20 now may be worth more to you than $25 next month. Credit card companies understand this principle, and they have great success offering huge amounts of immediate cash in exchange for long-term payments that may end up being over double the amount of the original loan.

- By creating associations, marketers know that they can influence people's purchasing decisions. If you see a celebrity you admire drinking a particular brand of soda, you place a greater value on that soda even if you wouldn't choose it over a competitor in a taste test.

These are irrationalities in human behavior — but at least they're *known* irrationalities. They can be incorporated into theories about human behavior; even when people are irrational, they're often still very predictable.

Head in the stars, feet on the ground

The writer Isaac Asimov was, by any account, a brilliant man: Besides penning some of the greatest science fiction stories of all time, he wrote hundreds of nonfiction books on everything from Shakespeare to biochemistry to the Bible. You would certainly think you could count on him to be rational.

And yet Asimov had an irrational fear of flying. He rode in airplanes twice when he was in the military during World War II, but after his discharge he never again flew anywhere. As his fame grew and he was in demand for speaking engagements in far-flung places, he and his wife would drive long distances — even though Asimov surely knew that on average, your chances of being killed in an accident are significantly greater if you drive across the country than if you fly the same distance.

Do people such as Isaac Asimov present a problem for social scientists? On the one hand, a story like this makes it seem like people are completely unfathomable — you can never predict human behavior. On the other hand, Asimov is an exception. Most people don't have a fear like Asimov's, and if they can afford to will choose to fly rather than drive long distances. Whether or not sociologists think of themselves as believers in "rational choice," all of sociology rests on the assumption that on average, people's behavior is at least somewhat predictable.

Challenge #3: Emotion

All this talk of "predictability" and "rational choice" makes people seem like computers — maybe computers with some programming quirks, but computers nonetheless. What about emotion? Don't people do things such as:

- Marry for love, even when it doesn't make "sense"?
- Strike out in anger without stopping to think about the consequences?
- Overeat to fill emotional needs?
- Respond to emotional appeals for money and other support?
- Have a hard time working because they're very sad about something that's happened to them?

How can anyone claim to understand human behavior without taking account of emotion?

An economist or a sociologist who believes in rational choice models of human behavior might respond to that challenge by pointing out that emotion actually plays less of a role in our decision-making than it might seem. For example, even if it seems to people like they're marrying for love, on average people are actually quite precise about marrying people who are similar to them. Stories about star-crossed lovers who pursue their romance against all odds make for great plays and movies, but most people, most of the time, don't fall helplessly into doomed love affairs — they conveniently fall in love with coworkers or classmates with whom they have a lot in common.

Emotion often follows rationality, rather than the other way around. (Oddly, this also works with beliefs and actions — people's beliefs often follow their actions rather than vice-versa. See Chapter 13 for more on this.) So although it certainly sometimes happens that people get carried away with emotion and commit self-destructive acts or do things that seem to make no sense, social scientists have observed that on average, people do in fact act rationally — or at least, predictably.

On a psychological level, extreme cases of irrationality caused by strong emotion may be associated with depression or schizophrenia: psychological disorders that occur for known reasons and are often treatable with medication and therapy. When people find that their emotions are tending to get the better of them, causing them to make choices that harm themselves or others, they often try to manage that irrationality and put themselves back on track.

Challenge #4: Altruism

Altruism refers, in a word, to generosity. When you offer a service or a gift with no thought of reward, that is pure altruism. When you offer something for a small reward (like a t-shirt or a hug), that's still generosity — even if it's not pure altruism. The existence of this kind of prosocial behavior may be the Achilles' heel of rational choice theory.

Of course, most people are not Mother Teresa. In many cases, when we give things away, we get other things in return. For example:

✔ A major donor to a museum or a college may be rewarded by having a building named after them, and may be given a seat on a board of directors, yielding valuable social and professional connections.

✔ When you give your boyfriend or girlfriend a birthday gift, you cause them to feel more attached to you and thus gain security in your relationship — plus, when it's your birthday they will probably turn right around and give you a gift of comparable value.

✔ When you volunteer your time to an organization, you are gaining potentially valuable experience and the social prestige of being seen to give your time away. Plus, you may be having fun and/or being directly rewarded with free services or products from that organization.

All this being true, it's still the case that often people do act altruistically in ways that are hard to understand from a rational-choice perspective. People make anonymous donations, stand by loved ones for years while they fight fatal diseases, and toil at services that few see or appreciate.

In fact, some sociologists argue that living peacefully and constructively in society requires constant acts of generosity on everyone's part. If everyone actually tried to get away with whatever they could, doing exactly what they pleased just so long as the reward eclipsed whatever punishment they might face, society would fall apart. Think about what it would be like if every storekeeper had to assume that every single customer would steal if given any opportunity, or if no one ever let anyone else merge into a crowded lane on the freeway. No police force could hold a society together if all its members were determined to act for their personal gain.

So why don't they? According to Durkheim, it's norms and shared values that hold society together. Society is not just about jumping on the back of the next guy so you can get higher; it's about cooperating to achieve goals together — and joining together to celebrate those achievements. People internalize the norms of society so deeply that they regularly act in ways that would seem to be contrary to any selfish motives . . . and fortunately, this leads to a working society that benefits everyone. To understand the decisions a person makes, you have to understand the society they come from.

This question is specifically relevant to people who want to design an effective government: What can you count on people to do for the good of society, and what do you need to force people to do? I cover that topic in more detail in Chapter 13.

Brother, can you spare a yam?

The yam exchanges of the Trobriand Islanders of the South Pacific, famously studied by anthropologist Bronislaw Malinowski, have become a classic example of how gift giving can knit a society together. At certain times, with great ceremony, men present their sisters and daughters with gifts of yams. The yams are stored in ceremonial yam houses, where they are preserved as symbols of social connection — in fact, the yams generally sit there until they rot because families will grow their own yams rather than eat the yams so generously presented to them by their relatives.

In other words, among the Trobrianders, a ceremonial gift of yams is purely a gift given for the sake of giving, in a ceremonial exchange that is virtually mandatory. It's a gift in the sense that it's not a payment for service, and it's altruistic in the sense that you're giving away actual yams that you could otherwise have eaten —

but though you know that the yams probably aren't actually going to be eaten, you'd better not keep them for yourself or you'll face serious social disapproval and life will become quite unpleasant.

So why, then, the yam exchange? Isn't it just a big waste of food? Regardless of how it came about, the yam exchange serves to make social ties visible and to remind everyone of their obligations to one another. Sometimes a gift is a gift of genuine value outside the exchange (like that $50 check you got for graduation), and other times a gift is just a gift (like that weird little ceramic figurine you also got). They both have a lot of importance in our society, and that's why your mother told you to say "thank you" for all your gifts. (Though unless you're a Trobriander exchanging yams, it's probably most appropriate to say "thank you" and "you're welcome" with words rather than ceremonial hip thrusts.)

Symbolic Interactionism: Life is a Stage

Symbolic interactionism is the term used to describe the study of individual human interaction in its social context. The word "symbolic" refers to the fact that as people interact with one another in society, they use a range of signs and symbols that have particular meanings in that society — everything from words to gestures to styles of dress. The fact that people don't always agree on the meanings of particular symbols makes life interesting, as each person tries to achieve their social goals by using the symbols to their advantage. Life is a stage, and each person may play a number of different characters.

That sounds complicated . . . and it is! The basic ideas behind the sociological study of individual interaction are not complicated, though. In the remainder of this chapter I explain how microsociologists understand individual interaction, what they pay attention to when they observe humans interacting face to face.

When you, or anyone else, use words, clothes, or other symbols to communicate, you know (or you should know) to take into consideration that different people will interpret them in different ways. A musician whose lyrics include a lot of profanity knows full well that the songs will offend some listeners and excite others.

Play ball! The rules of the game

As I explain in Chapter 3, microsociology was largely developed by early American sociologists, especially those in the Chicago School. They looked at people interacting in the busy, diverse metropolis and came up with some important ideas about how people negotiate complex social situations.

One of the most important thinkers in this tradition was George Herbert Mead, a Chicago philosopher who influenced many sociologists. Mead pointed out that social life is like a game, and argued that organized game playing among children was a crucial part of their socialization. (For more on socialization, see Chapter 5.)

In a baseball game, for example, there are several different positions — each with its own responsibilities and limits. Each position has a defined goal, which can be accomplished only through certain means. The batter's goal is to get the ball way into the outfield, ideally over the outfield wall; but they can't just grab the ball out of the catcher's mitt and run it out there, they have to hit it with the bat. Similarly, the pitcher's job is to keep the batter from hitting the ball, but the pitcher isn't allowed to hang onto the ball and make the batter try to steal it — it needs to be thrown over the plate so the batter has a fair chance.

Sociologists today talk about statuses and roles. Your *status* in society is similar to your position in a baseball game: It defines your relationship to other people and comes with certain freedoms and responsibilities. A *role* is the set of recommended and required behaviors that go with a status.

Why bother distinguishing between statuses and roles? Because they can both change from one situation to another. There are a different set of statuses in a company (president, vice president, manager, clerk) than there are in a family (mother, father, child, grandparent); and between social groups with similar statuses, those statuses may be associated with different roles. In one family, the father may have the role of disciplinarian, whereas in another he may have the role of nurturer. Your role in a social group gives you a certain set of goals and defines what you can, should, shouldn't, and can't do to achieve them.

But if there are different statuses in different social situations, what happens when they come into conflict — when you have to play multiple different positions at the same time? It's a frustrating situation, but you can try to avoid it by framing the situation to your benefit.

Frank Abagnale: A true player

The Steven Spielberg movie *Catch Me If You Can* stars Leonardo DiCaprio as Frank Abagnale, a crook and a fraud who repeatedly eludes capture by the authorities. It's a true story: Abagnale succeeded in convincing people that he was in turn an airline pilot, a doctor, and an attorney, also managing to cash tens of thousands of dollars in forged checks. (He even claims to have once posed as a sociology professor. The nerve!)

The movie shows how easily Abagnale was able to convince people that he owned statuses he actually had little or no qualification for, just by acting as though he did. He walked right onto planes wearing a stolen pilot's uniform, won the trust of doctors and nurses just by presenting himself as an authoritative physician, and easily cashed invalid checks because he so convincingly acted like a wealthy individual who would never need to forge a check.

Abagnale's story is an extreme example of a person using social cues such as dress and vocabulary to take advantage of others, but everyone tries, every day, to use social cues to their advantage. You may dress a certain way for work, to portray yourself as competent and respectable; or you may act falsely aloof when you're trying to impress a potential date, creating the impression that you're a highly sought-after partner who has no shortage of other romantic possibilities and will really need to be impressed if you're going to ask someone out. You may even surprise yourself at how often those tricks work!

Stop frontin': Switching roles, changing frames

As I mention in Chapter 5, the structure of a society defines the set of statuses that are available — and within a society, any given person may have a number of different statuses.

Most of the time, the roles associated with our various statuses are perfectly compatible. For example, my status as a Minnesotan does not conflict with my status as a teacher or my status as a brother. But once in a while, a person's statuses will come into conflict. What would happen if my sister enrolled in my sociology class? I'd be facing a potential conflict because my role as a brother requires me to pay special attention to my sister — but my role as a teacher requires me to pay the same amount of attention to each student. Anticipating this kind of possibility, many companies have rules preventing people from supervising anyone they have a family tie or close personal relationship with.

You can't make rules to prevent every role conflict, though — especially because social life is not like a baseball game where everyone wears a jersey with a number and team name. Roles are often ambiguous, and it's up to each person to remember and manage their roles appropriately. Unless they're very familiar with your identity and status(es), people around you are relying on you to communicate to them what your role is so they can respond appropriately. You can use this ambiguity to your advantage — in fact, to some extent everyone does.

The sociologist best known for writing about this is the late Erving Goffman, author of the 1956 book *The Presentation of Self in Everyday Life.* Like Mead, Goffman was interested in the ways that individuals manage their behavior in social situations — but instead of a game, Goffman preferred to use the analogy of a theatrical performance.

When a person behaves a certain way in a certain social setting, Goffman said, it's like wearing a mask: You're acting a certain way to convince the people around you that you occupy a certain social position and ought to be treated accordingly. The stage is the social setting you're in, which determines what "characters" are available to you.

Later, Goffman used the term *frame* to describe social situations — as in a frame that you put around a picture. Just as a picture frame influences people's interpretation of the picture that goes in it, so a social frame influences people's interpretation of a given interaction. Sometimes situations are naturally framed by the timing or location of an interaction, but in many cases frames are negotiated among people, with each person trying to apply the frame that most benefits him or her.

Here are some examples of how you can use social frames to your benefit:

- ✔ If you want to ask a stranger for money, you can start by making conversation about some neutral thing like the weather. After you've struck up a little chat, the situation is framed as an interaction between acquaintances rather than between strangers. The other person's role in your interaction is now that of an acquaintance, and the conventional rules of social interaction dictate that acquaintances should try to help each other when they can — whereas strangers have no obligation to do so.

- ✔ If you want to know whether a coworker might be interested in you romantically, you might ask one of their friends to accompany you on a coffee break. While you're walking to the coffee shop, you might share some personal piece of information like what you did the past weekend. This helps remove the interaction from the frame of the office — where only official business information is normally exchanged — and puts it in the frame of a social outing, where personal information is more readily exchanged. That makes it more likely that information about romantic attractions will be divulged.

> ✔ If you're operating a museum with free admission but want to encourage visitors to donate, you might require them to wait in line to get a ticket at a counter rather than simply letting them walk into the galleries. Even though they're not forced to donate, when they are at a counter taking a ticket, it's a situation so similar to situations where they'd be required to pay that it's likely they'll choose to donate much more often than if the situation was framed differently.

So people can choose to turn social situations to their benefit — but do they? As I explain in the previous section, often they do, but often they do not. That's the paradox of society: you control it . . . but it also controls you. The great insight of the symbolic interactionists is that society fundamentally exists inside people's heads; it's something they negotiate among themselves every day.

Chapter 7

Caught in the Web:
The Power of Networks

In This Chapter

▶ Seeing society as a network

▶ Examining the strength of weak ties

▶ Gaining insights from network sociology

*O*ne of the most important new ideas affecting sociology in the past few decades is the idea that society can be seen as a network, with each person being connected to a certain number of other people by professional or personal ties. Seeing society as a network has helped sociologists to understand everything from culture to power to markets.

In this chapter, I explain the basic insights of network sociology and describe some of the most important thinkers and studies in this tradition. I explain specifically how network sociology has changed the way sociologists think about the social world, and why network analysis is one of the most common tools used by sociologists today. Finally, I explain some of the specific ways network sociology might change the way you see your world — and how Web sites like Facebook and MySpace have made us all network sociologists.

The Global Village: Seeing Society as a Network

Seeing society as a network is not too difficult intuitively, but it has taken sociologists many years — in fact, almost a century — to appreciate the way that network analysis can lend new insights into problems that have concerned sociologists since the time of Comte and before. In this section, I explain how sociologists have learned to use the tools of network analysis.

It's all about you: Egocentric networks

In Chapter 6, I discuss some of the ways sociologists have studied individuals in their social world, While many sociologists continued — and continue — to focus on big-picture social facts, as Durkheim did, microsociologists have looked closely at individuals and how they negotiate a world of social symbols and norms, with its maze of rules to learn, remember, and use.

But that left a gap in sociologists' understanding of society: a gap between the level of societies overall — with their differing cultures and structures — and the level of the individual living in those cultures and structures. Network analysis, which grew out of the microsociological tradition, helps to connect the dots between the individual and society. What connects you to your society? The people you know.

Think about your personal network. It may include:

- ✔ Your family: your parents, your siblings, your spouse or partner, your children.
- ✔ Your friends, old and new.
- ✔ Your coworkers and all the people you are professionally connected with.
- ✔ The web of acquaintances you encounter in your day-to-day life: the mail carrier, your dentist, the barista at your favorite coffee shop, the guy at the bus stop.
- ✔ People you may not know personally but who you know of through your own network. People who know the people you know — especially people who are close to people you are also close to and who you might hear about through them — might be considered a part of your network as well.

These are the people you have some connection to, however slight it may be. These are the people who in effect define "society" for you. All of your meaningful social interactions are with these people — with your interactions being especially concentrated among the relatively few people who are closest to you.

Through mass media and other means, you may be able to collect information from — and spread it to — people beyond your social network, but it's the people in your personal network who constitute your most important conduits of information . . . and influence!

Your personal network is what sociologists refer to as an *egocentric* network. That doesn't necessarily mean you have a big head; it's a technical term referring to a social network as perceived from the standpoint of one individual. The first studies in network sociology were studies of egocentric networks because they're relatively easy to study. If you'd actually listed the people I referred to in the previous list, I'd have a map of your egocentric network. (See Figure 7-1.)

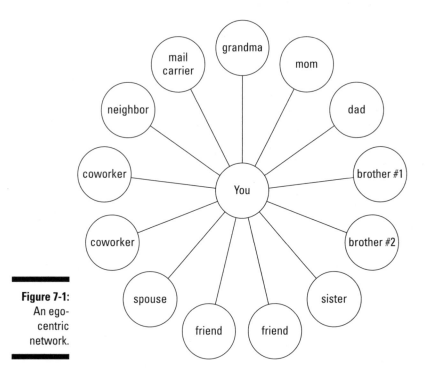

Figure 7-1:
An ego-
centric
network.

But what about the people your contacts are connected to — the people you don't know personally, but who you know through other contacts?

The game "Six Degrees of Kevin Bacon," in which players are challenged to connect Kevin Bacon to any given actor in Hollywood via chains of costars, is inspired by a longstanding conjecture that every person in the world is fewer than six degrees away from any other person, with each "degree" being a connection by personal acquaintance. Whomever I might name in the world, goes the theory, you at least know someone who knows someone who knows someone who knows someone who knows someone who knows her. It's a tough theory to test, but a number of different studies have found that it's at least roughly accurate.

In other words, you're connected through chains of acquaintance to almost every person on Earth. But does it matter?

Yes and no. Certainly, in some cases multi-degree social connections can be valuable and meaningful (see the several examples elsewhere in this chapter) — but even a first-degree social connection is of limited use if it's not very close. When I was applying to graduate school at Harvard, I asked an acquaintance who is a Harvard alumnus whether he would be willing to write me a letter of recommendation. "Um . . . sure," he replied. "What we're going to have to finesse, though, is the fact that I've only met you once."

Social networks and social manners: A rude awakening

David Gibson is a sociologist who is combining the insights of network analysis with the kind of microsociological observation that Erving Goffman and members of the Chicago School would appreciate.

In a study of a large banking corporation, Gibson first surveyed the bank's employees to map the various social connections among them. He then sat in a series of meetings, quietly observing how the different employees in the meeting interacted with one another. You might expect that the people who knew each other best would feel most free talking with one another and would exchange the most information, but Gibson found that in fact that was not the case: A lot of conversation went on among people who were not closely connected. After all, the point of a meeting is to create a social situation where information is shared, and the people who worked most closely together had already shared a lot of information outside the meeting.

A good way of predicting which employees knew one another best, Gibson found, was to see which employees took one another's turns in conversation. People who knew one another well might even seem to be rude to each other, answering questions asked of the other person and interrupting him or her when she was talking.

You can observe this effect at parties. Watch people who are close friends or romantic partners; they'll often stand beside one another in conversational circles and field questions together, interrupting each other in a (hopefully) friendly fashion to clarify details or add anecdotes. They've become so close that they're essentially functioning as a single conversational unit. If one of them interrupted someone *else*, though . . . now *that* would be rude!

Sociologists often study networks of individual people, but network analysis can also be applied to networks of groups or organizations. For certain studies it may be useful to think of your family as being part of a network of families who live in the same neighborhood or attend the same church, or to think of your company as being part of a network of companies that do business with one another. The tools and strategies used to study networks of individuals can also be applied to networks of groups.

A web of relationships

Your network is large — it probably contains hundreds of people you could list offhand if you thought about it carefully and systematically, plus hundreds more you wouldn't even think to list (which is a problem for studies of egocentric networks), but it doesn't include all the people in the world. In fact, it probably doesn't even include everyone in your company or school, in your neighborhood or apartment building, or all the people you're related to beyond first or second cousins.

Imagine drawing a network map of your school or the company where you work. There would be a dot for each individual, and each individual would be connected to each individual they know personally. You can imagine that there would be clusters of tight-knit groups — cliques of friends or coworkers who all know one another well — and that each person in a cluster would share some number of connections to people outside the cluster. If you could actually draw every personal connection in your school or company, you would have a complete network map of that organization. (See Figure 7-2.)

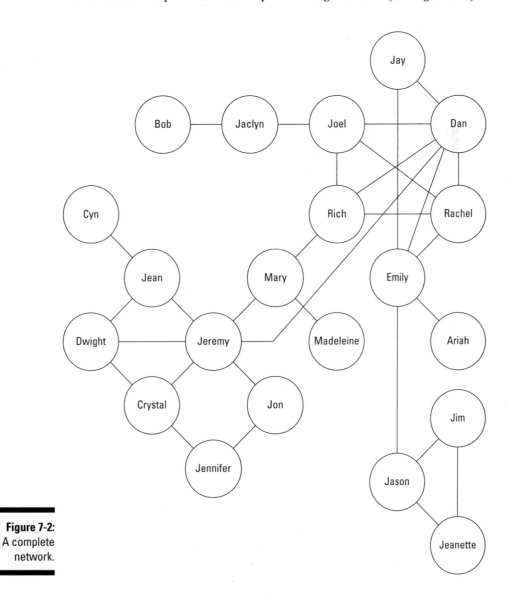

Figure 7-2:
A complete
network.

And then, of course, each individual in that organization maintains a large number of connections outside the organization: family, friends, former coworkers. Those connections link your organization to many more organizations, and ultimately to every other company or school on Earth.

It's exciting to think that you're probably somehow linked to almost every other person on earth, but of course so is everyone else (see sidebar). Your position in a network is a limitation as well as an asset. A social network isn't like the Internet, where information can freely whip from one end of the network to the next . . . and actually, it doesn't always work that way on the Internet, either.

You can only maintain so many meaningful social connections; there are probably no more than several hundred people you would recognize and greet by name if you passed them on the street, and there are many fewer people who you actually see regularly and have substantial interactions with. One of the most important insights of network analysis is that it's that small circle of people, rather than the total number of people who belong to the social groups you're nominally a part of, who really define your social situation.

The Strength of Weak Ties

When you look at a social group as a network of connected individual nodes, it changes the way you think about both the group and the individual. You can see any given individual's place in the social structure, and you can see exactly where their lines of information and influence are arranged. Information and influence normally don't flash through a group like wildfire; they flow like water trickling through a series of streams.

In this section, I describe some important discoveries sociologists have made about social networks; and the discoveries' implications for individuals who want to strategically position themselves in their own social networks.

Why your acquaintances are more valuable than your best friends

This section takes its title from a 1973 article by sociologist Mark Granovetter, which has become one of the most influential publications in all of sociology. Granovetter was studying the process of job seeking: How do people find jobs? It's a natural subject for network analysis because jobs are very often found through personal connections.

In Chapter 6 I explain the concept of *bounded rationality* in markets: You don't have perfect information about all the products available for purchase, so you need to decide how much time it's worth taking to gather information. Job seeking works under the same principle, even more so than buying a car or another consumer product.

Many jobs are publicly listed online or in newspapers, but many are publicized to only a limited audience, so there are a large number of jobs you're not going to find out about by surfing Craigslist. Further, when you do find a job you're interested in and qualified for, it helps tremendously to have a personal connection with someone at the company where you would like to work. That person can both supply you with detailed information about the job and, often, increase your chances of being hired by recommending you to the hiring committee.

In mapping network ties, Granovetter made the crucial decision to distinguish between strong ties and weak ties.

- ✔ **Strong ties** are your most intense personal connections: your connections to your closest family members and friends. People with whom you share strong ties are people you know very well; you may live with them or talk with them daily.

- ✔ **Weak ties** are all your other social connections: your connections to people you *know*, but don't know particularly well. Coworkers, classmates, neighbors, most friends — you might not talk to or see these people very often, but you know them and they know you.

Granovetter's finding — which, like many important sociological discoveries, was surprising at the time but seemed like common sense after it was established — was that for job-seeking purposes, your strong ties are actually not all that valuable to you.

Why? Because your closeness to them means that you already know everything — and just about every*one* — they know. If there's a job opening they know about, you probably know about it already. If they have a good "in" with a particular company, you probably know that person, too.

From a network perspective, your strong ties are *redundant.* That is, by and large they connect you with people you have other connections to. For example, your spouse may have introduced you to all their friends and family when you first met, but after years of marriage, you've formed your own connections with those people. If your spouse were to die, devastating as that would be from an emotional standpoint, from a social network perspective your network would not be much changed despite the fact that you've lost your strongest tie.

From a network perspective, it might be worse to lose your socialite friend, with whom you have only a weak tie but who connects you to many people you might never encounter otherwise. It's your weak ties that help you out when you look for a job because they are connected to many people you have no acquaintance with and they can, therefore, supply you with much more information. Plus, there are many more of them: you can maintain only a few strong ties, but you may have hundreds of weak ties, each of whom represents an entire world of potentially useful connections.

Think, for example, of a cousin who lives in another neighborhood and whom you see only once a year at the annual family reunion. From a network perspective, that cousin is essentially spending all the other 364 days of the year working for you — meeting new people with whom you're not acquainted, learning new information that you don't know. When you're looking for a job, you can call on them to help you out. So, in this way, your acquaintances may be more valuable than your best friends.

Of course, just because information *can* flow through a network tie doesn't mean that it *does*. Sociologists today appreciate that even where weak ties exist, they're no good unless they're activated. People may have a reason to hide information from you — they may have a stake in keeping that information to themselves — but more likely, they just don't think to tell you. You don't share much knowledge with most of your weak ties ... that's exactly what makes them weak ties. If you want to activate your network of weak ties, you're probably going to have to put some effort into it.

Companies are well aware of this, which is one reason they pay their employees for successful job candidate referrals. It may seem odd to think that anyone would need an incentive to tell a job-seeking friend about a good opportunity, but in fact there are several reasons you might fail to spread information about job openings at your own company.

> You may worry that suggesting a job opening will offend your friend by making it seem like they need help.

> Most people have hundreds of acquaintances that they rarely speak to; if you haven't talked with someone in a couple of years, it may be awkward to pick up the phone and suggest that they apply for a job at your company.

> You may just forget.

This is why companies feel the need to offer incentives to help motivate their employees to pick up the phone and let their friends know about job openings.

But how *much* should a company pay for a successful referral? Sociologist Alexandra Marin studied the pay-for-referral process at a large company, and in the end she found that companies should save their highest referral bonuses for the least specific positions. Why? Because a position with very specific qualifications (say, someone familiar with a specific programming language) requires a very specific type of applicant. If you happen to know one who's looking for a job, you're likely to pass the information on, but a job with very general qualifications (say, a "project manager") is less likely to fire any immediate light bulbs in your head, and you may need a little more incentive to reach out to potential candidates for that job.

This is an example of how different kinds of information flow through different kinds of network connections. You may see your neighbor every day and be acutely aware of when she gets a new haircut or buys a new car, but have no idea of what her job qualifications may be — whereas you may be familiar with a former coworker's job qualifications but have no idea whether he has a new haircut, a new spouse, or even whether he's living or dead. Separating "strong ties" from "weak ties" makes sense, but it doesn't do justice to the complexity of human relationships.

Find a structural hole and jump in!

You're probably already starting to see the tremendous value of network analysis for businesspeople. In the business world, information is money: a tip about anything from a cheap supplier to a competitor's marketing campaign to an under-the-table merger discussion can inform strategic decisions that might yield millions of dollars in profits. Where does this information come from? You might catch it on TV or in the newspaper, but that's information everyone knows. The most profitable information likely comes through network connections that provide "inside" information.

And it isn't just information that travels through network connections — it's influence as well. If you have a connection at another company, you can possibly ask your connection to prod that company to do business with yours, to shun a competitor, or to hold off on the launch of a product.

So clearly, any businessperson wants to increase their personal network . . . but it doesn't make sense to just add contacts willy-nilly. For one thing, you can't productively maintain an overly large number of social ties (even weak ones), so you have to pick and choose. For another thing, everyone wants to feel special, and if you're "friends" with everyone, well, everyone is likely to know that and will not consider you a particularly special friend. Good luck exercising influence in that situation!

The question, then, becomes *which* network ties you want to build and maintain. Sociologist Ronald Burt's research suggests that you pay particular attention to building ties across "structural holes."

What's a structural hole? Think about a network map, with dense clusters of people who know one another well and just a relatively few ties connecting those clusters. Between some clusters, there may be no ties at all. For Burt, these places where not many ties exist are *structural holes* — gaps in the network structure. The best-positioned people in a network, says Burt, are not the people at the center of dense clusters but rather the people who fill the structural holes.

Inside information: It's a good thing

In December 2001, homemaking maven Martha Stewart sold all her shares of stock in a drug company called ImClone. Her timing was extremely good because shortly after Stewart's divestment it was announced that a key product ImClone was developing had not been approved by the U.S. Food and Drug Administration (FDA) — news that caused the stock price to plummet. Had she not sold the stock, Stewart would have lost nearly $50,000. Stewart's decision later attracted scrutiny because her friend Sam Waksal, ImClone's CEO, had known about the FDA decision before it was made public. Stewart was found guilty of lying to the government in a subsequent investigation and spent time in jail, though she continued to maintain that she had not received any inside information from Waksal.

Why would it be a problem if she *had* received a tip from her friend? Because in the United States and most other countries, it is illegal to exchange certain kinds of information about publicly held companies. That law exists to even the playing field between the Martha Stewarts of the world, who know many powerful people, and the rest of us, who don't.

The law against "insider trading" is, in effect, the government's official acknowledgement that network ties can be a source of profit. There is supposed to be one official bridge — the corporate spokesperson — between the cluster of people who know what's happening in a company and the many people who invest in that company. Through her friend Sam, Martha Stewart had a network tie bridging that structural hole: a tie that she allegedly cashed in on to the tune of about $50,000 at the expense of the people she sold the stock to, people who didn't have access to the information she did.

This is an extreme case of a valuable network tie, but *all* your network ties are potentially valuable . . . especially the ones you keep to yourself.

The people at the center of dense clusters may know a lot of people well, but if it's a close-knit group — say, a small company — all those other people know each other well, too, and don't have to rely on any one person for information. You don't actually need to know that many people, Burt's work suggests, or even know them very well, just so long as *they don't know each other*. When that's the case, each group relies on you for information about the other group. You have information both groups want, and you can sell that information at a profit.

This may sound nefarious, like being a double agent spying for two different countries. A double-agent superspy is certainly filling a structural hole . . . but then, so are all these people:

- ✔ **Movie producers:** connecting filmmakers with actors, studios, financial backers, and other groups necessary to make a movie.
- ✔ **Realtors:** connecting house buyers and house sellers.
- ✔ **High school counselors:** connecting students and college admission officers.

> ✔ **Political lobbyists:** connecting legislators and groups who want to influence them. (This is why so many former legislators become lobbyists — they're essentially selling their personal connections to sitting legislators.)

People in all these professions, and many more, earn a lot of their salary simply by knowing people who have an interest in knowing one another — or at least knowing *about* one another. You pay them to bridge network holes that you want to cross.

This principle of filling structural holes doesn't only work in business, though — it works in personal life as well. Say you're a teenager looking for a party. There are probably one or two parties this weekend that a lot of people at your school are going to — but that's also probably true of every other school in town. To find the best parties, you'd rather have five acquaintances at five different schools than ten close friends at your own school.

Insights from Network Analysis

Now you have a basic sense of what network analysis is and how it works. The connections among people in a social group form a structure, along which information and influence can be traced. How does thinking about society in this way change the way sociologists think about social life? What specific insights has this approach yielded?

In this section, I explain how network analysis has changed the way sociologists think about the spread of behaviors and the spread of information, and concludes with a discussion of sites like Facebook and MySpace that make social networks visible — to the endless fascination of their millions of users.

The difference between "your society" and your society

Network analysis has been an important tool for sociologists in recent decades because it opens up a whole world of inquiry that didn't previously exist. Before network analysis became widely used, there were two main ways of studying society.

> ✔ **Top-down,** or macrosociological, analysis is the study of social groups considered as entire units. For example, Karl Marx's argument about the historical rise of capitalism and Max Weber's argument about increasing rationalization across all of society are macrosociological arguments. When Emile Durkheim said sociologists needed to focus on "social facts," he was saying that they should pay attention to the big picture rather than individuals in society. (See Chapter 3 for more on these ideas.)

✔ **Bottom-up**, or microsociological, analysis is the study of individuals in their social worlds. The Chicago School studies of people from different groups interacting on the street were studies in microsociology, and when Erving Goffman wrote about the different "masks" we wear in different social contexts, that was a microsociological argument. (See Chapter 6 for more on microsociology.)

Network analysis allows sociologists to focus on the connective tissue between individuals and society. To talk about "your society" is to say that there's some social group that you are "a member of" and are somehow influenced by. That's pretty vague! Where does this influence come from? Do you somehow inhale it, or get psychic vibes from the fifth dimension?

It's true that there are some forms of social influence that affect people across an entire society (for example, mass media), but the most important influence comes from the people you know personally and directly encounter. In this way, network analysis helps sociologists appreciate that your *actual* society — that is, the people you actually interact with and are influenced by — can be quite different than "your society."

Here's an example of how this insight has been put into practice. It's well-known that obesity is a growing problem in the United States, and for obvious reasons, medical professionals would like to know why. There are a couple of society-wide (no pun intended) culprits that are probably involved: Unhealthy food is becoming ever cheaper and more available relative to healthy food, and advertising campaigns for unhealthy food downplay the risk of obesity. Still, can those factors entirely explain the rise in obesity? Why is the risk especially high among certain groups?

Nicholas Christakis, a sociologist who's also a physician, worked with network analysis expert James Fowler to study the spread of obesity in a Massachusetts town over three decades. Christakis and Fowler discovered that obesity could be observed to spread through social networks. In effect, it seems, you can "catch" obesity by befriending people who are overweight. As more and more people become overweight, obesity spreads through their networks to become a growing epidemic.

What the researchers' obesity study (among other network studies over many years) has proved is that social networks can be conduits for the spread of everything from information to influence to behavior, influencing people's lives at every level. If you're trying to stay fit, it doesn't help that your grocery store will sell you a box of cookies for less than the price of an apple, that you see ads everywhere for unhealthy foods, or that your job probably involves you sitting still at a desk for eight hours a day — but what's really devastating is when the people around you are practicing unhealthy behaviors, overeating, and under-exercising. That makes it seem normal and, in fact, good for you to do the same thing.

Think about the implications of this finding for other important behaviors that might be socially influenced:

- **Drug use:** Do your friends abuse drugs, or do they stay clear of dangerous substances?

- **Sexual health:** Do your friends have casual sex — and if they do, do they use protection?

- **Economic stability:** Do your friends gamble? Do they make risky investments? Do they max out their credit cards?

- **Study habits:** Do your friends devote time and attention to their schoolwork, or do they blow it off?

These are just a few examples of potentially hazardous behaviors that are probably spread through social networks.

The significance of social networks in this respect is in some respects an inconvenient truth. If there were one or two factors that caused a social problem by affecting everyone equally, the problem could be solved by taking those factors away. If a problem is spread through social networks, though, you'd have to cut the network off to keep the problem from spreading — like digging a trench around a forest fire. Not only is that unethical, it's probably impossible.

It's also important to remember, though, that just because one person — or even many people — you're connected to behaves a certain way, you'll automatically "get the message" and act on it. You may be getting different messages from different people.

In a study of teenagers in Boston, sociologist David Harding found that it was true that teens who made risky decisions were getting messages consistent with those decisions — for example, their friends might be telling them that staying in school wasn't worth it — but they were *also* often getting "the right messages" from their teachers, their parents, and even many of their friends, who encouraged them to graduate and get jobs or go to college.

The problem wasn't that troubled teens were getting only "the wrong messages." The problem was that they were getting *mixed* messages, giving them different scripts to follow (as Goffman might say) in challenging situations. Sometimes they chose the "wrong" script — have risky sex, drop out of school — and sometimes they chose the "right" script. Kids who weren't getting those mixed signals had a much easier time sticking to one course of action.

Harding's study wasn't a study of social networks in the technical sense, but it did incorporate the basic insight of network analysis: that our social connections are important influences on our behavior. What happens when our social connections send us mixed signals? It's an empirical question that sociologists conducting network analyses may be paying a lot more attention to in the future.

Opening the channels of communication

If information and influence spread through social networks, is there a way to spread messages more efficiently?

In the great sociologist Emile Durkheim's classic study of suicide (see Chapter 3), he basically took for granted that all members of a given society shared a set of norms and values. If you live in a Protestant-majority society, then he assumed that you probably have Protestant-majority values.

Durkheim has been criticized for committing the *ecological fallacy*, which is to assume that because something is true of a system it's true of all that system's members. Durkheim observed that Protestant-majority countries had higher suicide rates than Catholic-majority countries, which he took to mean that Protestants were more likely than Catholics to commit suicide. But those data didn't actually tell him that: How did he know that it wasn't the minority-group Catholics committing suicide — maybe as a result of persecution by the majority-group Protestants? He didn't. He just assumed, and he may have assumed incorrectly. (We'll never know.) Durkheim's study remains an influential landmark in sociology, but a sociologist today would be much less likely to make that kind of assumption.

The German sociologist Georg Simmel, whose most important work came shortly after Durkheim's, was a big influence on microsociology and has come to be regarded as one of the fathers of network analysis. Simmel focused closely on individual interaction and argued that there are different forms of social interaction, with different rules and norms and through which different types of information are spread.

The moral for those with a message to spread is that it may be a waste of energy to try to broadcast it over an entire social group. What you want to do is make sure your message is heard — and passed on — by the right people in the right settings.

This implication of network analysis has been appreciated not only by sociologists studying the spread of ideas and behavior (see previous section), but by marketers looking to sell their products. Here are some marketing strategies you've probably come across; each is inspired by the idea of society as a network:

- ✔ Distributing free samples of products. If you play a free CD and enjoy it, you may play it for your friends and introduce them to the artist as well.

- ✔ Sponsoring events where influential people are likely to gather. Many companies sponsor parties or concerts for young people, in the belief that young people can influence older people to use a product — but not vice-versa.

✔ Using social media (for example, networking tools such as Facebook or Twitter) to encourage individuals to willingly spread marketing messages. Distributing — often online — a video, song, or game that advertises your product but is also entertaining enough that it might be willingly passed on to friends is a practice called "viral marketing."

These techniques can obviously be used to make profits, but they've also become popular with nonprofit organizations promoting health, environmental awareness, charity, and other good causes. Going through social networks is often an extremely effective way to spread a message, and both sociologists and marketers have taken note.

In journalist Malcolm Gladwell's popular book *The Tipping Point*, he writes about the phenomenon by which an idea or behavior (like, say, wearing Hush Puppy loafers) quickly goes from being relatively rare to being wildly popular. Gladwell argues that a few key types of people — people he refers to as *mavens*, *salesmen*, and *connectors* — need to get hold of an idea and help to spread it.

Gladwell's book isn't a sociological study, and he provides only examples (rather than systematically analyzed data) to make his point, but sociologists have read and appreciated Gladwell's book for its compelling argument that social networks are profoundly important in the spread of everything from clothing fads to musical tastes to business practices.

Gladwell's idea of a "connector" is similar to Ronald Burt's idea of a person filling a structural hole (discussed earlier in this chapter). A connector is a person who knows many different people from many different groups, so they are in a position to spread ideas or trends from one group to the other.

Just as biological epidemics caused by dangerous viruses can spread by way of people who move freely from one group to the next, so can social epidemics spread through social connectors — people who can "catch" an idea in one group and then spread it to the next group. When an idea or behavior spreads to multiple different social groups, it's become a social epidemic. This may be a good thing or a bad thing — depending on, say, whether you think Hush Puppies are attractive shoes — but it is the way the social world works.

Social networking online: Making the invisible visible

If you're a member of a social networking site like Facebook or MySpace, you've probably thought about it multiple times while reading this chapter — and, in fact, while reading this entire book. Social networking sites are a subject of fascination for sociologists and for just about everyone who participates on them.

These sites normally allow each user to create an online profile, which they can then link to their friends' profiles. The result is a visible display of something that's normally invisible: a social network. These sites' incredible draw — they now involve hundreds of millions of users around the world — is evidence of how important social networks are in people's lives.

Next time you're on your favorite social networking site — whichever it may be — consider how people's behavior on the site illustrates these sociological ideas.

The presentation of self

As I describe in Chapter 6, sociologists observe how we play roles in society — like actors on a stage, as Erving Goffman would put it. A user's profile is a perfect example of this. Unlike in face-to-face interaction, a user has perfect control over the "face" they present on a social networking site. They can choose which pictures to display, what information to divulge, and which acquaintances to acknowledge.

A lot of the most stressful moments on social networking sites come from tension and cracks in this careful presentation of self. A friend might post something on your profile that you would prefer not be visible, your mom might post an embarrassing photo from when you were an awkward teenager, or your boss may see pictures of you doing something, oh . . . let's just say *unprofessional*. All of these things get in the way of your attempt to filter the information about you that is known by the world.

The diversity of social ties

Social networking sites clearly demonstrate a principle that network sociologists have been trying for decades to grapple with: There are as many different kinds of relationships as there are pairs of people in the world, and no matter how many different options a networking site offers you, there will be a lot of relationships that are awkward to manage.

On Facebook, for example, as of this writing you can be a "fan" of a public figure, can specify that you're a son or daughter or mother or father of one of your family members, and can be in one of several flavors of involvement ("In a relationship," "Engaged," "Married," "It's complicated") with one significant other — but beyond that, everyone you're connected to is just a "friend." So your "friends" might include:

> Your best friend
>
> Your boss
>
> Your grandpa

Someone you have a huge crush on

Your ex-boyfriend

Your ex-boyfriend's sister

Your best friend from kindergarten who you haven't talked to in 15 years

In reality you have very different relationships with all those people, but on Facebook they're all your "friends." If a distant relative keeps making inappropriate comments on your profile, you're going to have to confront her or de-friend her. You can't publicly note that your relationship to her is not "friend" but rather "crazy second cousin once removed."

The transitivity of social ties

"Transitivity" is a technical word that basically means "transferability." In other words, if you have a close social tie, your other close friends are liable to "catch" that tie. Mark Granovetter writes about what he calls "the forbidden triad" — a situation where one person has close ties to each of two other people, who don't know one another. (See Figure 7-3.) He calls it "forbidden" not because it's actually forbidden, but because it's just so unlikely to happen.

Social networking sites can speed the "healing" of forbidden triads. If you have two good friends who both often comment on your profile, they're apt to come to know one another and even start a conversation — maybe about you! If that feels weird . . . well, maybe it's your own fault for not introducing your friends to one another.

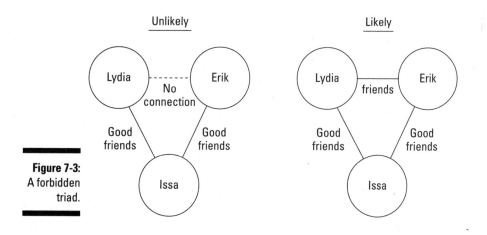

Figure 7-3:
A forbidden triad.

The spread of information through social networks

As if gossip didn't spread quickly enough before the Internet, it spreads like wildfire now. If one of your friends posts a picture of you making out with someone you met at a party, *all* your friends will know about it, more or less immediately. This is true of other information as well, including information on breaking national and international news, information about funny videos, and even false information about supposed scams and other urban legends.

The principle that most information spreads most efficiently and effectively through social networks was true before the development of the Internet; although the Internet has made it theoretically easier to broadcast something to a mass audience (everyone in the world could read your personal blog *right now* if they wanted to), it's also made social networks more important because it's increased the efficiency of spreading information through them. People still trade information over the backyard fence and around the water cooler, as they always have, but now the backyard fence and the water cooler are online, and you don't need to wait until you're thirsty to get the latest scoop. All you have to do is log on.

Online friendships: Trading quality for quantity?

As technologies such as cell phones, laptops, and wireless networks have proliferated, many people have voiced concerns about the effect those technologies are having on "real world" relationships. Ever since the telephone was invented, people have been concerned that technologies that make it easier to connect with people far away will distract from people's relationships with others who are nearby.

Although it may seem like your little brother is always chatting online and never wants to talk with his actual family, the fact of the matter is that he probably wouldn't be much more enthused about talking with his family even if the alternative was sitting out on the stoop and watching traffic go by. Historical and sociological evidence from the past century suggests that as technology makes communication easier, what happens is that there's simply *more* communication . . . with everyone.

Think about your own life. Who do you talk with most on the phone, trade the most texts with, chat with most online, and trade the most Facebook wall posts with? Chances are, it's your girlfriend or roommate or best buddy: someone you often see in person. You probably also communicate quite often with people far away, and you probably do a lot more of that than people did before the development of cell phones and the Internet — but that doesn't necessarily mean you're neglecting your close relationships with people you actually encounter in person on a daily basis. You're probably just supplementing them with far-flung friends.

Sociologists and psychologists are still gathering data on how social networking sites and related technologies *affect* people's relationships, rather than merely *reflecting* them . . . but in general, people seem to use those technologies to grow closer to a wide range of people they value. It's not an either/or proposition.

Part III
Equality and Inequality in Our Diverse World

The 5th Wave   By Rich Tennant

"I always assumed elves just naturally dressed like this. I never imagined it was a condition of employment."

In this part . . .

Any society is made up of many parts — and which "part" you belong to isn't always obvious. Do I belong to the middle-class part of American society? The white part? The male part? The Catholic part? The law-abiding part? In this section, I explain how sociologists understand the lines that divide a society.

Chapter 8

Social Stratification: We're All Equal, But Some of Us Are More Equal Than Others

*T*he title of this chapter refers to George Orwell's *Animal Farm*, a novel that is an allegory meant to show how difficult it is to create a society where everyone's truly equal. In the book, animals in a barnyard drive the farmer out and try to create a social order where all animals are equal. Eventually, the pigs start taking advantage of their leadership position and justify their special privileges by the dictum: "All animals are equal, but some animals are more equal than others."

The story rings true because no society, ever, has been completely equal. Social inequality is a topic at the heart of sociology, and in this chapter I explain why.

First, I explain how sociologists think, in general, about inequality — and why it may be a necessary feature of society. Next, I go through the many different means of inequality: all the different ways people manage to draw social boundaries that privilege some at the expense of others. Finally, I look at how inequality changes over time — both for individuals (social mobility) and for entire societies.

Excavating the Social Strata

The word "stratification" is a geological term referring to the way that layers of earth and rock are stacked on top of one another. *Social stratification* refers to social groups being similarly stacked on top of one another. In this section, I discuss how sociologists think about social inequality in general, and then explain the debate over whether inequality is necessary.

Understanding social inequality

What does it mean to be "unequal" in society? From a sociological perspective, it means *having unequal access to social resources.* In other words, you and I are unequal if one of us has, or is able to get, more of some desirable resource than the other one has. These resources might include:

- ✔ **Material possessions:** Anything from food to shelter to luxury items.
- ✔ **Money:** Currency or credit that can be exchanged for goods.
- ✔ **Power:** The ability to influence others to do as you want.
- ✔ **Prestige:** Interested and respectful treatment by others.
- ✔ **Relationships:** Access, whether personal or professional, to people of value.

These are resources that you might reasonably want in society, but that you probably have less access to than others. Just how *many* others have more access than you to these things depends on where you stack up in the stratification order of your society.

As it happens, having more of these resources puts you in a better position to *get* more of them — in most societies, advantages are multiplicative, meaning that if you're relatively high in the stratification order, you have access to a lot of resources that will help you stay there. If you're relatively low in the stratification order, on the other hand, you may have a hard time climbing up. People with a lot of money, for example, are able to invest in business ventures that can earn them even more money; people without money have to work for pay and take whatever their employers pay them.

But there isn't just a single dimension of stratification: You can't just add up all the different resources you have and come up with a single score or a number or even a category that completely sums up where you stand in the stratification order. There are many different bases of social inequality — people are where they are in the stratification order for a number of different reasons that may persist no matter how much power or money they have. If, for example, you are a racial minority in a society that discriminates against racial minorities, you're going to have an obstacle to face no matter what you achieve in life. (See sidebar, "Locking the Gates.")

In the next section of this chapter, I discuss several different common bases of social stratification: money, occupation, ability, motivation, connections, credentials, specialized knowledge, race, sex, caste, and age. These are all ways people may be different from one another that may lead to having different positions in a society's stratification order — but not *all* differences among people lead to differences in stratification. I have a birthmark on my chest; that makes me unique, but in my society that difference is not apt to lead to either an advantage *or* a disadvantage in the stratification order. Some people may find it ugly and some people may find it attractive, but either way it's probably not going to make it any easier or more difficult for me to find a job or to influence others.

It's conceivable that there might be a society where it *would* matter: societies differ, sometimes dramatically, in how the stratification system works. Some of these differences are formal differences (that is, differences written into the legal system and organizational rules, like whether or not slavery is legal) and others are informal differences (that is, rules that are not written down but are nonetheless meaningful, like whether or not racism pervades a society). The bottom line is that each society has its own system of social stratification, and those systems vary over time.

Sociologists divide bases of stratification into two categories.

> **Ascribed** bases of stratification are attributes that you're born with, and that society judges you upon — for example, your physical appearance (including your race), your place of origin, and your caste, if you live in a caste system.

> **Achieved** bases of stratification are attributes over which you have at least some control: your job, your social connections, your education, your wealth. These attributes may change over the course of your life.

To make things even more complicated, different bases may matter in different places and at different times, and they may interact with one another to determine your place in the stratification system. For example, some jobs may be more advantageous for women than for men, and vice-versa. Social stratification is quite complex, but it's worth taking the time to understand because it's so very important to everyone — in *any* society.

It's easy to be confused when talking about "social class." The word "class" is typically used to refer to differences in a society's stratification order, whatever that may be. If you're "upper class," you are relatively privileged. If you're "lower class," you're relatively unprivileged. When people use these terms in reference to modern capitalist society, they're generally referring to money matters. "Upper-class" people have more money than "lower-class" people.

But class is about more than money, even in industrial capitalist societies. A librarian and a steelworker may make about the same amount of money, but does that mean they're in the same class? A lot of people would say no, which is why many sociologists prefer to link "class" with occupation rather than with income alone.

Even more factors could be considered. It gets so complicated, in fact, that people don't even know their own class; if you define "middle class" as being in the middle third of a society by income level, many more people consider themselves "middle class" than actually are. The fact of the matter is that in most societies there's no hard-and-fast definition of the social order that everyone can agree on, so the question of what "classes" are — and which people belong in which class — will always be a matter of some debate.

The perennial debate: Is inequality necessary?

Orwell's animals aren't the only ones to wonder whether social inequality is necessary. Wouldn't it be nice to have a society where everyone is equal — where no one is privileged over anyone else?

Among sociologists, Karl Marx most famously called for the creation of a society where everyone would be equal. In Marx's communist utopia, people might do different jobs, but no one would be locked into a job that made them miserable. People would receive the resources they needed to meet their basic needs and have whatever luxuries might be available, but no one would reap rewards on the backs of others. "From each according to his ability," wrote Marx, and "to each according to his needs."

But how would the dirty work get done? It would ideally be like in a family: when you see something that needs doing, you do it and then no one else will get stuck with the job. Other family members would turn around and do the same for you.

Anyone who's ever lived in a family, though, knows that's not always how it works . . . could that system ever work on the scale of an entire society? Most sociologists think not. Not only is it questionable in theory, what empirical evidence exists suggests that it's untenable. (See sidebar, "Misadventures in socialism.")

Locking the Gates

Henry Louis Gates Jr., a black man, is one of the most respected academics in the world: chair of Harvard's Department of Afro-American Studies, he is the author of many books and is often seen on television speaking about the black experience in America. He draws an appropriately handsome salary, and he owns a house in a wealthy neighborhood in Cambridge, Massachusetts.

One night in summer 2009, Prof. Gates came home to find that he'd accidentally been locked out of his house. He and a friend opened a window to crawl in, and a neighbor who could see only that two men were climbing through the window of the house called the police. When the police arrived, they asked Gates to provide identification proving that he owned the house. He became indignant, and was ultimately placed under arrest, though he was later released and no charges were filed against him.

Gates accused the white police officer who arrested him of racism, igniting a national debate. In the 21st century, was America still a place where a man — even a wealthy, famous man like Prof. Gates — could get arrested just for being black? It's impossible to know if the incident would have gone differently had it been a white man breaking into his own house, but in the wake of the incident many African-Americans came forward to cite examples of racial discrimination they faced every day. The discussion about the incident made clear to the entire country that in the United States — just as in every other country — social stratification is not just a matter of what job you have, or how much money you make, *or* the color of your skin. All of those attributes matter, though just how *much* they matter varies from one situation to the next.

The most notorious sociological argument for the necessity of social stratification — that is, inequality — was made in 1945 by functionalists Kingsley Davis and Wilbert E. Moore. Davis and Moore were frank about the fact that people are of differing abilities, and that society has an interest in matching the most-able people with the most-important jobs. If someone has a brilliant mind and an exceptionally steady hand, it might benefit thousands of people for that person to become a surgeon . . . but what if she doesn't *want* to be a surgeon? If surgeons are paid significantly more than people in less critical jobs, that provides people with an incentive to compete for jobs as surgeons; that way, the most able can be chosen rather than the job just going to whomever wants it.

Further, Davis and Moore pointed out, after a person is in a job, they need to be motivated to work hard — and there's no motivation like the threat of losing your job and ending up on the street. If people are allowed to do whatever they want, whenever they want, they'll be too tempted to be lazy and very little will actually get done.

Misadventures in socialism

As I explain in Chapter 4, one of the challenges of sociology is that you normally can't experiment on society — put one group of people in one situation and another group in another situation — and see what happens. You have to observe whatever situations happen to occur, and do your best to figure out why and how things turned out the way they did.

Fortunately for sociologists studying stratification, over the past century quite a few countries have created a natural experiment by organizing themselves along socialist lines inspired by Marx's ideas. No country has ever become the kind of perfect communist society that Marx imagined, but many have tried to hew to Marx's values by strictly limiting the amount of money any one person can earn while guaranteeing certain things — food, shelter, employment — to all. How has the experiment turned out?

In some respects, it's turned out pretty well. Communist China is a world superpower, and many countries — for example, the Scandinavian nations — have had great success levying high taxes and guaranteeing many benefits, thus limiting social inequality even though they remain essentially capitalist.

In other respects, the experiment hasn't turned out that well. The Soviet Union fell, and its constituent republics have largely become capitalist democratic countries rather than remaining communist. Sociologist Gerhard Lenski, after close study, has come to believe that the failure of many socialist societies shows a fundamental flaw in Marx's theory. "Freed from the fear of unemployment and lacking adequate material incentives," writes Lenski, workers didn't willingly pitch in as Marx thought they would. "Worker performance deteriorated and production stagnated or declined in Marxist societies everywhere." In other words, maybe people do need some financial incentive such as the threat of losing their jobs to do everything that needs to be done in a society.

So, to sum up Davis and Moore's argument:

> People need to be motivated to work hard and to take the jobs they're best suited for.

> *Motivation* means *reward* . . . and the real possibility of having significantly more or less reward.

> Because there need to be people who are rewarded more than others, there needs to be inequality.

It seems to make a lot of sense, but Davis and Moore's article has become one of the most-criticized in all of sociology. Why? Many sociologists believe Davis and Moore's argument justifies the status quo. (The same criticism was leveled at their colleague Talcott Parsons; see Chapter 3.)

Just because people may need *some* motivation to work hard doesn't mean that the amount of inequality present in most societies is necessary or humane. Plus, the system of financial reward as it actually exists doesn't necessarily do much to reward effort rather than dumb luck: the biggest financial disparities are not disparities of income but rather disparities of wealth (that is, money in the bank), which is largely inherited and has nothing to do with how hard you're working at your job. There are also vast inequalities by ascribed attributes (see the section "Understanding social inequality" for a definition of ascribed attributes) — it doesn't make any sense to reward someone simply for having been born a white male.

Today, most sociologists believe that at least some inequality is inevitable — whether or not it's "necessary" — but that a lot of the inequality in society is excessive, hurtful, and unproductive.

The Many Means of Inequality

When some people end up near the top of the social ladder and others end up near the bottom, there are many reasons for the disparity. The first thing that comes to mind when you think of social inequality is probably inequality based on money; absolutely, that form of inequality is very real and very consequential. However, there are many other reasons that some people end up privileged over others in any given society.

In this section, I'll discuss several of the most important bases for social stratification — that is, several of the most important variables that can be different among people and can lead to social inequality. This, though, isn't a complete list; *any* difference among people can result in social stratification.

Income and wealth

In societies that use money — that is, almost all currently existing societies — the distribution of money is one of the most important factors in social stratification. The fact that it's relatively easy to measure (the amount of money you have is a number that is usually beyond dispute) is another of the reasons it's often used by social scientists. *Income* refers to the amount of money you earn at your job; *wealth* refers to the amount of money (and/or assets worth money, like a house or a car) you have in your possession.

In advanced capitalist societies, money is almost like magic: you can turn it into just about anything you want, from cars to houses to food to drugs to sex. Money can't buy you love, but it can buy you attractive clothes and meals at nice restaurants. Crucially, it also buys security and freedom. The more money you have, the more freedom you have — it's as simple as that.

Further, as I previously mentioned, with discipline and patience, money can be turned into more money. Savings can be invested for interest, or can be risked in ventures that may result in vast profits. If you don't have savings, you're bound to live paycheck to paycheck, trading your time for the highest wage you can negotiate.

Whether or not Marx was right that money and wealth constitute the fundamental basis of social inequality, he was absolutely right that people with more money can exercise direct power over people with less money. If I have a lot of money and you have very little, you may be forced to do just about anything I say if I'm willing to give you some of my money in return. Many people in capitalist societies find themselves with many job options to choose from, but people with no money and few specialized skills (see section, "Specialized knowledge") may have to consider themselves lucky to get *any* job. In the most dire cases, people may be forced into extremely risky and unpleasant actions that may include theft, drug dealing, or prostitution.

Yet even beyond this "magical" power to buy anything, money has a second important influence: people with lots of money are typically treated better — and thought better of — than people with just a little money, even in situations where money isn't directly involved. Max Weber believed that one of the most important factors in the rise of capitalism was a religious belief that wealthy people were smiled upon by God; in capitalist societies today, most people believe that people with more wealth have worked harder and are more deserving than people with less wealth. This means that people with more money can exercise power and influence without having to spend a dime.

For all these reasons, money is at the heart of social stratification in almost all societies that exist today.

Occupation

If money is important, then jobs are important — if for no other reason than the fact that jobs produce income. But the job you do is an important basis of social stratification in and of itself.

It's a little rude to start a conversation at a party by asking someone what they do — but people often do exactly that because knowing what someone does for a living tells you so much about them. It tells you about how much money they make, it tells you about how much education they have, and it's a decent indication of what they are probably interested in and have knowledge of.

The simplest way to measure "social class" (see section, "Understanding social inequality") is to consider income or wealth, but another way many sociologists measure social class is by measures of occupational prestige.

Sociologists have surveyed people in different countries to determine what occupations they find most prestigious; people in the occupations considered most prestigious may be considered at the top of the stratification order, and people in the least-prestigious occupations may be considered to be at the bottom.

What makes an occupation prestigious? It turns out to be a combination of factors. The amount of income a particular occupation yields is important, but so is the amount of education and training needed to work in that occupation. Further, people tend to respect occupations seen as caring or doing good in the world. For this reason, a job as a teacher may be about as prestigious as an occupation in banking, even though the banker probably makes more money. Similarly, despite the multi-millions made by some professional athletes — and the adoration lavished on a few high-performing stars — the general occupation of "athlete" is about as prestigious as the occupation of "computer programmer." The occupations considered most prestigious tend to be jobs that pay well, that require considerable education and skill, *and* that involve working in areas seen as important: Doctors, lawyers, corporate executives, and college professors all have highly prestigious occupations.

Besides yielding money and respect, your occupation also may equip you with important social connections and specialized knowledge that may come in handy down the line.

Innate ability

Without delving too deeply into psychology's nature/nurture debate — the debate over whether your genetic makeup or your environment is more important in shaping who you become — it's safe to say that some people are born with skills that can help them climb a society's stratification ladder. Exactly *what* skills are useful may vary from society to society, but most societies have some way for people to turn inborn gifts into money, influence, and respect.

Some people may be born with a talent for doing math; others may have a talent for reading or using language. Athletic skills can be advantageous, and instinctive social skills can be tremendously useful. All of these skills, and more, probably have at least some genetic component — so it's possible to be born equipped to succeed in some task important in your society. That doesn't mean that you *will* succeed; you'll need support, education, and opportunity to make the best use of your skills. Still, everyone has some inborn dispositions and talents, and it would be naïve to deny that those make a difference as you earn or are assigned (in most cases, it's actually some of both) a place in your society's stratification order.

It's important to make clear, though, that there is no convincing evidence that innate ability co-varies with any other basis of social stratification — that is, a person who is relatively wealthy or well-connected or well-educated was not necessarily born with some special gift. All of those qualities derive from a number of different causes, so you shouldn't assume that someone who is particularly successful or esteemed in society was somehow born with a genetic silver spoon in their mouth; or, conversely, that someone who has relatively little money or prestige was somehow born to fail.

Motivation

Motivation is a complex topic, and psychologists have spent careers trying to understand why people are motivated to do the things they do — and not to do the things they don't do.

To some extent, the causes of any individual's motivation are unknowable. Why is one kid motivated to do her homework whereas her brother is content to sit and watch TV? Why are some people go-getters at work, whereas others sit back and do only the minimum that's required of them? Why do some people take initiative and start new projects whereas others prefer routine and predictability, disliking the risk or effort associated with being a pathbreaker? It's hard to say.

In some ways, though, behavior that might be called "motivation" varies among people from different backgrounds, for predictable reasons. Sociologists who study childhood have found that parents who are relatively well-educated and well-off financially tend to teach their children from an early age that they should exercise initiative and express their opinions and desires, even if they're contrary to what an authority figure — such as a schoolteacher or employer — seems to want. On the other hand, parents who are less well-to-do tend to teach their children to be obedient and respectful, and not to rock the boat. (See Chapter 15 for more on childhood and the life course.)

Each attitude will serve children well in some situations and not in others; in that case, it's not a question of how *much* motivation a person has but rather what *kind* of motivation. In any given social situation, a certain type of behavior is likely to earn a certain type of reward (or punishment). If it's not clear what behavior is best, people can only guess at what will be rewarded, based on what they've been taught. If two different people have been taught differently about how to behave, they may behave differently in the same situation. You'll only ask for a raise, for example, if you think the possibility of getting one outweighs the possible annoyance or embarrassment of asking and not getting one. It may depend on how you think your boss expects you to behave, and that may depend on how your parents expected you to behave.

I is for initiative . . . take some!

When I was in college, a member of the dorm staff made a sign reading i is for initiative...take some! and hung it on the wall by the elevator. My friends and I made fun of the sign because we thought it was highly unlikely that a goofy sign on the wall would motivate an under-achieving student. That may be true, but it's also true that the expectations and encourage-ment (or lack thereof) we get from the people around us can play a very big role in determin-ing what we achieve or don't achieve in life.

William I. Thomas, a sociologist who was a member of the Chicago School, pointed out that a situation defined as real is real in its con-sequences. For example, if it is believed that someone is incompetent, that person won't even be given the *chance* to succeed. If people from a certain social background are believed not to be "college material," they'll be discour-aged from applying to college and will have no opportunity to disprove what may be a very mis-taken assumption about their academic ability.

They won't be placed in college-prep classes or challenged to join academic honor societies. Thus, a situation defined as real (they're "not college material") becomes real in its conse-quences (without college-prep classes, they are in fact unprepared for college). This danger is one reason for the widespread institution of affirmative-action policies, which are designed to ensure that everyone is given a chance to succeed.

That said, it's also true that often people do succeed despite being discouraged by all sides. When I was a teenager and told my dad that I was going to bicycle across the state of Minnesota, his skeptical response only made me more determined to do it. (I did it as part of a ride to raise money for multiple sclerosis research.) To say that the encouragement and expectations of influential others are important is not to say that any one person — or any mil-lions of people — can determine the choices you will make in life.

Connections

As I explain in detail in Chapter 7, social connections are a form of power in society. The better-placed you are to get information from and exercise influence on people in your society, the more power you have. As I note in that chapter, there are some powerful and prestigious occupations that rely almost entirely on people's ability to bridge social gaps — but the right con-nections are helpful in *any* social situation.

You may be a naturally social person who has a knack for making the right connections, but the number, nature, and strength of your social connections is also a function of how you stack up on the other variables listed in this sec-tion. Consider:

✔ If you are wealthy, you can buy or will be offered admission to situations where you can meet other wealthy and influential people. If you have little money, it will be relatively difficult for you to meet people who have a lot of money.

✔ You may make a large number of social connections through your job; these will continue to be valuable to you even if you lose your job or switch jobs.

✔ You are likely to meet many people through your schooling, and being an alumnus of a certain institution may open doors with fellow alumni you haven't even met. (The importance of classmate connections is demonstrated by the very fact that you're reading this — it was through a friend from graduate school that I learned of the opportunity to write this book!)

The critical importance of social connections for an individual's place in a stratification order has only been recognized relatively recently by sociologists, and it's one of the reasons research into social networks has received so much attention over the last few decades. The importance of social connections can be deeply frustrating when you're on the losing end — for example, when a job you want goes to someone who's friends with the boss — but the fact of the matter is that social connections are an important part of the stratification system everywhere you go.

Credentials

A *credential* is certification by some known body that you have a skill, an experience, or another valued attribute. Credentials may be revoked, but they're typically yours to keep when you've earned them. Examples of credentials include:

✔ A school degree

✔ An award

✔ Membership in an organization

✔ Employment for a company, whether past or present

Credentials are typically earned by the performance of some feat at some point in time, so they're typically meaningful with respect to a person's abilities or experiences — but they can also be misleading or outdated. If you graduate from college and then proceed to spend the next thirty years leading a life of crime and corruption . . . well, you're still a college graduate!

Given this fact, why do credentials matter so much? In large part, it's because they're relatively easy to communicate. A one-page résumé gives you a quick summary of a person's credentials, and you can glance over it in just a few seconds; interviewing that person to learn more about their skills and experiences would take much longer. Jobs typically aren't granted on the strength of credentials alone, but an impressive credential may earn you an interview; on the other hand, a lack of impressive credentials may disqualify you before the interview process even begins.

Education

The process referred to as "education" is actually many things. Going to school means earning a diploma (a credential), making connections, and . . . oh yeah! . . . actually learning things. These are all reasons that people benefit from going to school.

On the other hand, education costs money. It's generally a good investment — that's why most countries force children to attend school and strongly encourage adults to attend college — but one of the reasons education is such a thorny political and social issue is that it's far from clear exactly how much the education system should try to accomplish, and by extension how much it should cost. College can cost tens of thousands of dollars each year, but that cost likely includes room and board, access to world-class researchers, and amenities ranging from workout facilities to mental health counseling to private security. This is all part of a college "education" — but should it be? There are similar debates over education at every level.

In most societies education is one of the most important determinants of who gets ahead. but it's important to remember that being "educated" means many different things, not all of which have to happen at a school. My father, for example, doesn't have the credential of a college degree, but after decades of work he has certainly earned an "education" through on-the-job training. "I have a Ph.D.," he likes to say, "in O.J.T.!"

Specialized knowledge

"Knowledge is power," wrote the philosopher Francis Bacon. You've probably heard that from your parents, teachers, and educational programs on TV; it's certainly true, but to paraphrase George Orwell, a sociologist might prefer to say, "All knowledge is power, but some knowledge is more powerful than other knowledge."

What's the difference? The most powerful knowledge in society is knowledge about topics that are regarded as useful or important. Knowledge that may be very powerful in one society may be virtually useless in another. Sociologists distinguish between two kinds of specialized knowledge that may give a person a leg up in a stratification system, and refer to them both as "capital" — because like financial capital, they're valuable assets.

Human capital

The term *human capital* refers to useful skills that a person has learned. Examples of skills and knowledge that might count as human capital include:

- ✔ Knowledge about how to use a computer program.
- ✔ The ability to fix a car.
- ✔ Knowledge of medical treatments.
- ✔ Understanding of a country, state, or city's legal system.
- ✔ Knowledge of sociology.

These are skills that might be learned through schooling, through job experience, or through self-education. All of these skills are potentially valuable on the job market, and in some cases can allow you to perform services for yourself and your family that you'd otherwise need to pay for.

Cultural capital

The term *cultural capital* was coined by the sociologist Pierre Bourdieu (see Chapter 5). It refers to the knowledge of, and a liking for, high-status culture. What counts as "high-status culture" varies from one society to the next, but Bourdieu emphasized that the most consequential forms of cultural capital involve specialized knowledge that is you're not likely to be convincingly conversant in unless you were raised in an environment where that knowledge was taught and valued.

Examples of what Bourdieu considered cultural capital include:

- ✔ Knowledge of classical music; being able to identify compositions with their composers.
- ✔ An interest in art that may look ugly to most people (for example, a photograph of a car wreck) but is considered fine art by museum curators and their wealthy patrons.
- ✔ Knowledge of fine wine and gourmet food.

None of this knowledge has much practical value — if your car breaks down, knowing who wrote the *Eroica* symphony is not going to help you fix it — but it's all evidence that you were likely raised by relatively wealthy, well-educated parents. Bourdieu pointed out that if you have this knowledge, other privileged people are likely to see you as one of their own and are likely to treat you with special favor.

Race/sex/caste discrimination

Discrimination on the basis of race, sex, or caste is a prime example of *ascribed* stratification, (mentioned earlier in this chapter): stratification that depends on a characteristic that you were born with and is virtually impossible to change.

In this context, *race* refers to the aspects of your physical appearance that identify you with a particular group recognized by your society; *sex* refers to whether you're a man or a woman; and *caste* refers to your social status in societies where your family of birth is permanently associated with one status or another.

This is a central topic in sociology, and it has its own chapter — Chapter 9 — in this book. Much more on this topic appears in that chapter, but it appears here as well because it's simply impossible to talk about social stratification without considering this kind of discrimination. In societies around the world, throughout history, people's sex and the color of their skin have been social statuses that have had vastly determinative effects. At worst, race and gender have been the bases for explicit or implicit slavery, depriving millions of people of freedoms enjoyed by others.

Today, explicit slavery (that is, slavery openly identified as such) is virtually extinct, and discrimination by race and gender is happily on the wane in most societies. That said, racism and sexism are extremely stubborn forms of discrimination, and no one should pretend that there's a place on earth where race and sex don't matter in determining people's life chances. Another means of ascribed stratification, and one being hotly debated around the world today, is sexual orientation — whether a person is sexually attracted to members of the opposite sex, the same sex, or both. All of these characteristics (race, sex, sexual orientation, and caste) continue to be very important parts of societies' stratification orders.

Age discrimination

Age discrimination is another means of ascribed stratification — but unlike race, sex, or caste, age does obviously change over a person's lifetime. Your actual or perceived age has real consequences for how people perceive you and what opportunities you may or may not be given in society.

The role of age in social stratification can be difficult to sort out because unlike race or caste, age does correspond to real differences in a person's experience and abilities. People are obviously too immature to do most paying jobs until they've grown out of childhood, and as they progress through adulthood and into old age, people gain skills and experience but eventually lose physical and, possibly, mental endurance and agility. So when assessing a person's fitness for a job, age is not irrelevant in the same way race and sex normally are. (I say "normally" because although race and sex do not correspond to differences in ability, they may be relevant characteristics for certain specialized jobs.)

That said, age can also be the basis for unfair discrimination — people may be treated poorly because they're seen as being "too young" or "too old," or may be esteemed just for being a certain age. This has become an increasing issue in contemporary society as people's work lives have become longer and jobs have become less stable: A person who is middle-aged or older may find themselves losing a job to a younger person who is no better qualified. Further, this treatment may vary with other ascribed characteristics: Women may face harsher age discrimination than men for some jobs, and vice-versa for others.

Comparing inequality internationally

If different societies vary in the ways that their members are stratified, it only makes sense that some societies would actually be more equal than others — that inequality would be more severe in some societies than in others. In fact, this is the case, and sociologists have learned some important facts about how different societies are stratified, and how stratification has changed over time.

It's not just the degree of inequality that varies among societies, though. David B. Grusky, a leading expert on inequality, notes that social stratification systems vary along a number of dimensions, including:

- **Type of assets.** What is the main attribute that people high in the stratification order have more of than others? In some cases it's money, in others it's human capital, in others it's political power or cultural prestige.

- **Classes.** What are the major classes in society? In "classic" capitalist society, it's the bourgeois and the proletariat as Marx said; in other societies, it's slaves and slave-owners or nobles and commoners.

- **Degree of inequality.** How much inequality is there between the people in the highest classes and those in the lowest classes? In medieval feudal society, inequality was very high; in prehistoric tribal society, inequality was relatively low. In our advanced industrial society, says Grusky, the degree of inequality is in between those two extremes.

- **Rigidity.** How much social mobility does a society allow? A traditional caste society, where people are born into inflexible social classes, allows virtually no mobility; hard as it sometimes seems to "get ahead" in modern capitalism, it does happen. (So, to the dismay of many overambitious financiers, does "going broke.")

Thinking about stratification this way makes clear that even if modern industrial capitalism is no bed of roses — especially for people on the bottom of the social hierarchy — it's far more open than most societies, for most of human history, have been.

Furthermore, almost all societies around the world are increasingly similar in the way their stratification systems are organized. Globalization and international development has made the industrial capitalist model near-universal around the world; few countries today are dominated by the kind of rigid stratification systems that were previously common. Advanced industrial countries like those in Europe and North America have seen the emergence of a large, basically happy middle class. (See Chapter 16 for more on social change.)

Members of the middle class aren't particularly wealthy, but they have enough income to comfortably provide for their families and buy a few luxuries to boot. Their jobs may be wearying, but their fingers aren't worked to the bone, and they likely even have some managerial responsibilities and freedoms. Compared to the lives of most people at most times in history, middle-class life is good.

Some sociologists, though — especially those who tend to agree with Marx that capitalism leads to exploitation — have observed that the prosperity of the developed world is built on the back of the developing world. The luxuries that middle-class Americans, Europeans, and Japanese enjoy are so affordable because they're built by workers in China, Mexico, and other developing countries who earn a small fraction of what their counterparts in the developed world earn. A factory worker in Michigan can afford a lifestyle that's absolutely prince-like compared to what a factory worker in rural China can afford. This disparity in living standards has fueled two developments:

- ✔ **Waves of immigration** into the developed world from the developing world, as workers move in search of better wages and, often, greater personal freedom. The difference in earning power, even for undocumented immigrants without the legal right to work, can be so much greater that men and women will leave their families for months or years at a time so they can send a portion of their earnings back home. (See Chapter 9 for more on immigration.)

- ✔ **Outsourcing** of industrial production and, increasingly, skilled labor to the developing world. Things can be built and done so much more cheaply in the developing world that it's all but irresistible for companies interested in making a profit (and what company isn't?) to hire workers in the developing world to do any work they're capable of doing. Because more and more work is able to be done in the developing world, more and more work is being outsourced — despite the fact that it's led to the loss of millions of jobs in the countries doing the outsourcing.

Some sociologists, collectively called "world-system theorists" — a term inspired by the work of the sociologist Immanuel Wallerstein — believe that the bourgeois have only managed to stave off worldwide revolution by outsourcing the worst, most exploitative jobs. They believe that eventually, the worldwide proletariat will get wise to this system and will prove Marx right by revolting and changing the rules of the game.

Will that happen? It's impossible to say for sure. The rules of the stratification game have changed many times before, and it's only reasonable to think that — one way or another — they're likely to change again.

Chapter 9

Gender and Ethnicity: I Know My Race, But Where's the Finish Line?

*R*ace and sex: everyone's got 'em. They're not "supposed" to matter any more, but of course they still do. People in societies around the world still pay close attention to the color of your skin and to whether you're a man or a woman. What they make of that information varies from place to place — and has of course varied dramatically through history — but there's no getting around the fact that race and sex still matter, and they're going to keep on mattering for the rest of your life and the rest of mine.

Along with social stratification (see Chapter 8), this is one of the core areas of sociology. Sociologists also study all the other subjects in this book — religion, education, politics, business, and the economy — but if you're a journalist or a policymaker, sociologists are most likely to be filed in your Rolodex of experts under the subject race and sex discrimination.

In this chapter, I start by explaining the general idea of bias and discrimination as they are studied by sociologists. I then explain what sociologists have learned about race specifically, and then what sociologists have learned about sex. (Along the way, I'll explain what the differences are between "race" and "ethnicity," and between "sex" and "gender.") Finally, I explain why even in the post-feminist, post-Civil-Rights era, race and sex still matter — very much so.

Bias and Discrimination: A Two-Sided Coin

You're special. You're unique. You know this because your mom probably told you so, and umpteen children's TV shows certainly told you so. It's absolutely true — there's no one exactly like you. There *are*, however, millions or billions of other people who are the same race as you are, and even more people who are the same sex that you are. When someone uses race, sex, or any other of your personal attributes to make assumptions about your other characteristics, that is *bias*. When those assumptions affect the decisions they make regarding you, that is *discrimination*.

First off, let me get one thing out of the way: You are biased regarding other people, and you practice social discrimination every day. So do I. Maybe you'd like to believe that's not the case, but accepting the universality of bias and discrimination is the first step towards understanding them — and figuring out how to minimize their most harmful effects.

Do you think I'm wrong about you? Aren't you biased? Don't you discriminate? Okay, maybe you don't . . . but have you ever done any of these things?

> Guessed that someone with a certain skin color, in a certain neighborhood, is "not from around here"?

> Guessed that a young child is a boy because he's wearing blue, or a girl because she's wearing pink?

> Taken account of race or sex in assessing someone's job performance — whether or not they work for you?

Whether or not it's morally right, empirically it's not unreasonable to consider race or sex in these ways. If you're an English-speaker in Shanghai looking for directions and you see only one person on a crowded street who doesn't have Asian features, it makes sense to pick that person to ask directions. It doesn't necessarily make you a backward-thinking traditionalist to dress your baby daughter in pink or your young son in a gender-neutral color rather than in blue overalls and a baseball cap. The millions of African-Americans who were especially supportive of the presidential campaign of Barack Obama because he's black probably don't think of themselves as having been inappropriately "racist."

Race and sex are examples of ascribed statuses: statuses that are assigned to us because of factors beyond our control. You had no control over the color of skin and the sex you were born with, and yet people routinely judge you on the basis of those characteristics. It's not fair, but it happens. The previous examples show that the subject gets complicated when identities become involved — when people take ownership of those characteristics.

In those cases, these ascribed statuses become points of pride. In that case, is it still best to ignore those statuses? You of course have your own opinion on the matter, but most people would say not.

The subjects of race and sex are very complicated, and it does no one a favor to simplify them. On the one hand, racism and sexism have fueled some of the most horrible episodes in the history of the human race:

- ✔ The slavery of millions, from ancient Rome to the present day

- ✔ The Holocaust and other episodes of genocide

- ✔ The widespread — in some eras, nearly universal — refusal to allow women the right to vote, the right to own property, or even the right to choose where, when, and with whom they will share their bodies

- ✔ People being institutionalized, imprisoned, or even killed for consensual intimacy with a person of the same sex

This awful history has given rise, in recent decades, to the widespread passage of laws that prohibit depriving anyone of equal rights because of the color of their skin or whether they are a man or a woman. These laws are far from universal, and far from universally effective in areas where they exist, but they've gone a long way towards eliminating the most heinous abuses and inequities.

Somewhat paradoxically, though — yes, you can add this to the long list of social paradoxes — it's precisely this history that has led to pride and solidarity among members of racial and ethnic groups, among women and among men, among lesbians, gays, and the transgendered. Most people are proud of their race and proud of their ethnicity, and many are proud of their sex and their sexual orientation. They want you to know that they're Mexican, or Lithuanian, or American Indian, or African-European. Thousands parade down city streets in celebration of women's rights or queer pride. None of these people would want it denied that they are who they are — but they don't want that to limit their freedom to make choices about what to do with their lives.

Making things more complicated is the fact that members of each of these groups disagree — sometimes violently — about what being a member of a particular race or sex means. There are as many different ways of being Asian-American as there are Asian-Americans, as many different ways of being female as there are women, and as many ways of being straight or gay as there are people in the world. There may be leaders within these communities, but it's not for any one person to determine what it is to *be* Asian-American or female or gay.

This is the complex landscape of the social world today: a world where race and sex matter, but where they matter in different ways for different people at different times.

Race and Ethnicity

In this section, I describe the sociological study of race and ethnicity, a subject at the heart of just about everything sociologists care about: equality (and inequality), identity (and lack thereof), social change, and (for better and for worse), social stability.

You can choose your ethnicity, but you can't choose your race

In sociological terms, *race* refers to an ascribed status: something determined by others based on the physical characteristics you were born with. *Ethnicity*, on the other hand, generally refers to an achieved status: a status you choose for yourself by the identity you assume, the groups you associate yourself with, and the behaviors you practice.

Race

Every society has its own set of racial groups that its members understand and react to. In some societies, there are dramatic differences in physical features: Some people, for example, have very light skin whereas others have very dark skin. In other societies, the differences may not be so dramatic to an outsider but are easy to recognize for those who are raised in those societies: Relatively subtle differences in skin shades or facial features can lead to just as much bias and discrimination as differences that are objectively much more marked.

In fact, the exact same physical appearance can mean different things in different societies. As an example of this, consider what it means to be "black." That's a widely-understood racial category in the United States, the West Indies, and many other areas; it's associated with having particularly dark-pigmented skin, and in both the United States and the Dominican Republic has been (in fact, often still is) associated with negative discrimination.

In the United States, though, "black" people have historically been people of African descent, their families often brought unwillingly to America as slaves. Many Americans assume that an individual with dark skin is of this heritage. If they discover that a "black" person is actually an immigrant from the West Indies, Americans often treat that person differently.

Sociologist Mary Waters has described the frustrations of dark-skinned American immigrants from the West Indies, who can find themselves excluded by both non-black Americans — who regard the newcomers as "black" and discriminate against them on that basis — and by African-Americans, who regard the immigrants as outsiders who are — despite the color of their skin — not "really" black. Some of these immigrants, in some contexts, consciously adopt the dress and speaking styles of African-Americans to fit in with that group; others, in other situations, emphasize their West Indian heritage through their accent and their dress to avoid the discrimination faced by African-Americans.

This example shows the complexities of race, and the frustration that can be experienced by both racial minorities and members of a racial majority as they try to gain acceptance and avoid discrimination.

Ethnicity

I explained at the beginning of this section that sociologists use the term "ethnicity" to describe a status that a person chooses for himself or herself, an identification with a group of people. In common usage, the term "ethnicity" is often used to refer to a national or cultural heritage that isn't necessarily associated with distinctive physical features. It's worth remembering, though, that in the English language some social categories that are today called ethnicities — for example, *Italian* or *German* or *Russian* — were often called "races" 100 years ago, when they were generally seen as being more fundamental and were more often used as the basis of discrimination. (American newspapers from the turn of the 20th century are full of derogatory references to, for example, "the Irish race.")

Even if the terms "race" and "ethnicity" are sometimes used interchangeably by non-sociologists, in sociological terms they refer to very different types of social groups. As I noted earlier in this chapter, your race is something others decide for you, whether you like it or not. It mainly describes your physical features. Your ethnicity, on the other hand, refers to the cultural group with which you consciously identify. A person's ethnicity often includes the following features:

- ✔ A historical narrative, generally associated with a place of origin. When I say that my ethnicity is "German-American," that means that I identify with a group of people who lived in one area in Europe for many generations, then crossed the Atlantic to the United States.

- ✔ Cultural customs, such as food, holiday celebrations, a language. My grandmother grew up in New Ulm, Minnesota, speaking German, eating German food, and celebrating German-Catholic holidays. I've never learned German, but I've eaten more than my share of sauerkraut and dumplings.

- ✔ Symbols and distinctive styles of dress. Ethnicities are often associated with flags and colors, and especially at times of celebration, unmistakable outfits. (No, I've never worn lederhosen — but if you saw me in a pair, you'd certainly know what my ethnicity is!)

Although ethnicities are often associated with races, they are by definition more free-floating — spouses often adopt one another's ethnic practices, and people may embrace ethnicities that have nothing to do with their parentage or biological characteristics, becoming indistinguishable from someone who grew up in a particular ethnic culture. In cases where ethnicities are not closely associated with a set of obvious physical characteristics, or where a certain physical appearance might plausibly be associated with any of a number of ethnicities, ethnicity may become almost entirely elective.

Mary Waters — the same sociologist mentioned earlier for her study of West Indian immigrants — wrote a book about European-Americans called *Ethnic Options*. The title refers to the fact that although African-Americans or Asian-Americans or Hispanic-Americans are typically obviously identifiable as such, Irish-Americans, Italian-Americans, or Norwegian-Americans are not. Their ethnicity is something they can choose to play up with flags and anthems, or completely ignore if that's what they prefer.

Ethnicity is so flexible, in fact, that in the modern world, people might choose to identify with groups and traditions that you wouldn't necessarily think of as "ethnic" but are used that way. Think of alumni of certain universities who wear their college shirts and proudly declare their membership in that college community, or people who grew up in a certain state or city or neighborhood and take that fact as an essential aspect of their identity. In this way, being "a Domer" (an alumnus of the University of Notre Dame, which has a building with a golden dome), a Californian, or a New Yorker can be a person's primary "ethnicity."

Racial discrimination: Conscious and unconscious

Race remains relevant around the world for many reasons, but first and foremost because in virtually every society, the color of your skin and other physical features — the color of your eyes, whether your hair is curly, you name it — are likely to affect the way people perceive you and the way they treat you.

Obviously this is illogical in the sense that a person's physical features tell you nothing about their abilities, personality, or background. People know better than to judge the quality of a car's engine by the color it's painted, and similarly they should know better than to judge a person's mind or heart by the color of their skin. And yet, they do — and they do, and they do, and they do, again and again and again.

It isn't right, and in most countries today discrimination by race is illegal . . . but it happens, consciously and unconsciously. In this section, I explain these two types of racial discrimination.

Caste in stone?

"Caste" is not a concept that most people today are very familiar with, but it's something that has virtually defined the lives of many millions of people throughout history. A *caste* is an inherited class status, one you're born into if you live in a society that subscribes to the idea of caste. Other ascribed class statuses — including race and sex — are also inherited, but in societies with caste systems, caste transcends race and sex, and is associated with cultural practices as an ethnicity might be.

Societies around the world have had castes of one sort or another. Many societies have had priestly castes, where people seen as especially holy or having important spiritual roles descend from one another. An inherited monarchy or aristocracy is another form of caste, with ruling power being passed on from mothers and fathers to sons and daughters. Some societies — for example, traditional societies in India — are divided up into many inherited castes, sometimes including an "untouchable" caste at the bottom of the social ladder.

Castes share some features of races and ethnicities: Biological inheritance is central to caste membership, as it is to membership in all racial groups and many ethnic groups. Castes are different, though, in that they're explicitly tied to a society's power structure. Because a caste system means that power (or lack thereof) is inherited rather than earned, most people today see strict caste systems as unfair and undesirable. Around the world, caste systems have been challenged and have lost a great deal of their influence — the queen of England, for example, still nominally has power over all of Great Britain, but as a practical matter the position is largely symbolic. (You wouldn't normally hear the term "caste" used to describe the British aristocracy, but in a sociological sense it is indeed a caste: Like any other caste status, royalty is a class position one is born into and cannot lose.)

Still, caste systems are far from gone or forgotten: Hundreds of millions of people in the world today have faced discrimination based on the caste that they were born into.

Conscious

Through the course of human history, many — in fact, probably most — people have consciously discriminated by race. That is, they have deliberately chosen to treat people differently based on skin color or other attributes. This has been so widespread that the unfortunate tendency to interpret physical appearance as being a significant predictor of a person's abilities and personality seems to be a basic feature of human nature. Look at kids in a schoolyard: Whether they're in a big multicultural city or a homogeneous rural community, they always find *something* about each other's appearance to pay attention to, and in many cases make fun of or ostracize each other based on appearance. It's not pretty, but there it is — there's no mystery about why racism started in the first place.

Over time, ideas about race become institutionalized and formalized: they're written down and sometimes passed into law. Today, biological anthropologists understand that there's really no such thing as "race" in the sense of an objective set of biological categories into which humans might be placed (yes, there are differences in skin color and other features, but they fall along a continuum and have no relevance for people's intellect or abilities). For centuries, though, it was widely believed — and documented in highly questionable texts — that there were fundamental differences among the "races of man," and that those differences made it only logical to treat different races differently. At worst, these completely mistaken ideas justified slavery and genocide.

Without excusing the millions of people who have actively participated in outright and unapologetic racial discrimination around the world, it's worth pointing out that the example of racism illustrates the power of society to influence people's beliefs and actions. When you grow up in a society where racial discrimination is completely embedded in the social fabric, it can be very difficult to see beyond what you're taught from early childhood and what is taken for granted by everyone around you. And, of course, if you're a member of a group that benefits from racial discrimination, it can be very convenient not to question this received wisdom.

Unconscious

If all racial discrimination was conscious, it wouldn't be nearly as much of a problem today as it continues to be. In societies where racism has been scientifically debunked and socially deplored, it should end . . . right? Well, yes, it *should* . . . but it doesn't.

For one thing, there are people who continue, despite all evidence, to consciously believe that there are fundamental differences among races — and they're not just the few extremists who praise Hitler and burn crosses. When I was growing up as a middle-class kid in St. Paul, Minnesota, I knew people who genuinely believed (though they would say so only privately) that interracial love affairs were improper.

Beyond that, though, *unconscious* racism continues to be widespread. This is when someone takes another person's race into consideration without even knowing it. This continues to happen for at least three different reasons: the weight of history, the self-fulfilling prophecy, and basic human nature.

The weight of history

Even someone born in the 21st century in one of the world's most progressive societies is going to come across a huge amount of explicitly or implicitly racist material. The world's history of racism is too vast to be completely wiped out — and in fact most people would say that the past must be remembered to avoid repeating it.

Books, movies, art, and stories that propagate racist stereotypes are still widely available, and no one can completely escape the influence of this material. In some cases, these influences and others may lead people to act or think in a racist manner without even realizing it.

The self-fulfilling prophecy

In Chapter 8, I cite the sociologist W.I. Thomas, who said that a situation defined as real is real in its consequences. When a group of people face systematic discrimination based on their physical appearance, the hurtful effects of that discrimination add up over time and can't be easily erased.

In the United States, for example, African-Americans were initially enslaved and then subjected to many decades of explicitly discriminatory practices and policies. That meant lost opportunities for education and employment experience, and today black Americans are still catching up to white Americans in these areas. There is a persistent gap between the average academic achievement of African-Americans and white Americans, and blacks — especially black men — are incarcerated at a significantly higher rate than are white Americans.

The fact that these actual disparities say nothing about differences of ability does not stop many white Americans from unconsciously discriminating against blacks, every day across the country. This is one reason for the widespread adoption of pro-diversity policies: Undoing centuries of conscious discrimination may require an equally conscious effort.

The unpleasant truth is that people seem to need no excuse to treat one another differently based on appearance. This doesn't make it okay, but it does mean that fighting racism is probably going to require constant vigilance as long as people are people.

The myth of the "model minority"

One of sociologists' most important contributions to the understanding of race and racism has been to debunk the myth of the "model minority."

The "model minority" is an idea that's been used to underplay or dismiss the continuing significance of racism. The proponents of this idea point to the fact that some racial minority groups have been exceptionally successful at quickly achieving equality — or better than equality — with a majority group in terms of education and career success. The example most often mentioned is Asian-Americans, a racial minority in the United States who, despite the fact that many families initially arrived as immigrants with few resources, are now on average as comfortably situated financially as are white Americans — and are, on average, now better educated.

Some observers have looked at the achievements of Asian-Americans and called them a "model minority," a group that proves racism isn't really a deterrent for people who are willing to work hard and try to get ahead. If Asian-Americans did it, they say, so can African-Americans and Hispanic-Americans.

Sociologists, though, have pointed out that there are vast differences among minority groups, and though there are some patterns and similarities in minority groups' experiences, in no way is it accurate to say that one group can be a "model" for another. As much credit as Asian-Americans deserve for their success in the United States, it's wrong to say that they can serve as "models" for other minority groups in the sense that a "model student" can inspire other students to study harder. Here are a few specific reasons the "model minority" concept is misguided:

- **Not all racism is the same.** It is absolutely true that Asian-Americans have faced, and continue to face, racism and discrimination. Immigrants from East Asia have had to fight hateful stereotypes and have been denied jobs, housing, and schooling on the basis of their physical appearance. It does Asian-Americans no discredit, though, to say that not all racism is the same, and that other racial groups may have faced and may continue to face discrimination that is even *more* hurtful, based on different sets of (equally misguided) ideas about differences in ability or intellect.

- **Different groups come from different circumstances.** Although all immigrants face challenges acclimating to a new country (see next section), people don't arrive as blank slates. Compared to, say, African-Americans, Asian-Americans are on average relatively recent and relatively well-educated arrivals to the United States. Further, upon arrival they were often able to live in communities of similar immigrants who were able to support each other. Not all immigrant groups have had these advantages.

- **Any "minority group" is actually many minority groups.** Asian-Americans come from many different countries, and came for many different reasons; this is true of any racial or ethnic minority group. It's difficult, and is often misleading, to make any general statement about "Asian-Americans" as a group. Hmong-Americans, for example, are by and large recent arrivals who fled their homelands in the wake of violent conflicts. They've faced tremendous challenges immigrating to the United States, including some discrimination from *all* racial groups, fellow Asian-Americans included. To sweep Hmong-Americans under the "model minority" rug and deny that their circumstances are exceptional and might require exceptional support would be to do them a serious injustice.

The achievements of Asian-Americans and members of other groups that might be characterized as "model minorities" are very real and very hard-earned, but it's simply not the case that they've figured out some secret trick that other racial minority groups just need to learn in order to overcome the harmful effects of racism.

Immigration and "assimilation" (or not)

Not all ethnic groups are immigrant groups — most societies have a number of indigenous ethnic groups as well as ethnic groups that have come from elsewhere, plus there are ethnic groups not associated with a place of origin. Still, almost all sociologists interested in race and ethnicity find themselves looking closely at the experiences of immigrants.

The members of the Chicago School were among the first sociologists to really look closely at immigration. The turn of the 20th century saw a wave of immigration to the United States that transformed America's social landscape, and that transformation was most visible in big cities like Chicago, where the new arrivals went looking for work.

Initially, sociologists thought immigration could be understood in terms of "assimilation." The word *assimilation* means to be absorbed into, to become one of. America was seen as a great "melting pot" where people from all different places arrived to be incorporated into one big whole.

The theory of assimilation has it that people arrive speaking their native languages, wearing their native styles of dress, and otherwise practicing the traditions of their home countries; over time, they are "assimilated" into their new community, adopting that country's language and traditions. If that's the way it works, the study of immigration is just the study of why some groups assimilate more quickly and peacefully than others.

As sociologists have spent more time studying immigration, though, they've come to understand that it's just not that simple. It's certainly true that all immigrants choose to, or are forced to, adapt to the ways of their new homes to at least some extent — but it's not a linear path where they go from being 0 percent assimilated to 100 percent assimilated. Sociologists of immigration today appreciate that there are at least three things wrong with the basic "assimilation" theory:

✔ **Assimilate to what?** If immigrants are assimilating to something, to what, exactly, are they assimilating? The United States and other countries do have mainstream cultures (see Chapter 5) containing some quintessential features, but modern societies are so diverse that it's impossible to even describe what a fully "assimilated" person would look like. You've heard the phrase "as American as apple pie," but does that mean that if I don't like apple pie, I'm not completely assimilated to American culture?

✔ **"Assimilation" means many things.** Imagine three immigrants to the United States from China. One learns to love hot dogs and Elvis Presley but never learns a word of English. Another learns perfect English but continues to dress and eat as she did in China. Another makes several Mexican-American friends and learns fluent Spanish. Which of these three is most "assimilated"? This example shows how absurd the question is. Joining a new society can mean a number of different things, and they don't necessarily all go together.

✔ **Why assimilate?** Immigrants vary widely in how much they *want* to trade their native cultures for the lifestyle of the country they move to. Some immigrants enthusiastically do anything they can to adopt the ways of their new country, but others prefer to keep doing things as much as possible the way they always have. There are many factors — including age, location, and reason for immigrating — that go into these choices, and sociologists have learned not to assume that it's in any given individual's interest to "assimilate" to a new way of life. Many immigrants live in ethnic enclaves where they are able to continue speaking their native language and associating with fellow immigrants from their country, and they are perfectly and justifiably happy with that choice.

Does speaking Spanish mean you're a Latino?

It's easy to rattle off a list of ethnic and racial groups, and one of them is likely to be "Latino" or "Hispanic." You have a general idea of what a "Latino" is — they probably are descended from Spanish-speaking people, and may have the skin colors or facial features associated with residents of Mexico or Central America — but you probably don't know *exactly* what a Latino is, even if you are one yourself!

That's because there's no universal definition of who counts as a Latino. It's a term of convenience used to describe people with either of the characteristics I mentioned, or who are descended from residents of Latin American countries. Like any term for an ethnicity or race, "Latino" includes a wide range of different people; even wider than most. A man living in Brazil, a woman in Alaska whose grandmother was born in Mexico, a Spaniard whose father came from the Dominican Republic . . . all of these might be considered "Latinos."

Sociologist Wendy Roth studied Latinos in the United States, in the Dominican Republic, and in Puerto Rico, and found that many of the people she talked with didn't identify themselves as "Latinos;" they considered themselves "Dominicans" or "Puerto Ricans." And, if they immigrated to America, they found that they were often regarded as "black" or "white" simply because of the color of their skin. For all of these reasons, "Latino" would hardly seem to make any sense as a category.

And yet it does, and it's become widely used and adopted — in part, says Roth, because of international television stations like Univision that promote the idea of a common identity among Spanish speakers. Binding together under one big "ethnicity" also helps Latinos gain visibility and political clout, even if it has little to do with how they actually see themselves. This example illustrates the complexity of race and ethnicity. You may "be" a certain race because people see you that way, and you may "be" a certain ethnicity because you identify with a group of people, but ethnicities and races are always in flux as people and societies change.

Every society is diverse, and to assume there's one way to "properly" be a member of that society is not fair to either longtime residents or to new arrivals.

Sex and Gender

Just as "race" and "ethnicity" are often used interchangeably but mean different things from a sociological standpoint, such is the case with the terms "sex" and "gender." As used by sociologists, the word *sex* refers to a person's biological sex; with a few exceptions, this is unambiguously male or female. *Gender* is a more complicated term that refers, like "ethnicity," to a role that a person identifies with; it may or may not correspond to a person's biological sex.

In this section, I describe the history of sex and gender from a sociological standpoint and explain how sociologists are trying to keep up with the rapid recent social changes in how sex, gender, and sexual orientation are viewed.

"You've come a long way, baby"?: The women's movement and its discontents

Women can have babies. Men can't. After the babies are born, women can nurse them. Men can't. The basic biological differences between men and women have always led to them having different roles in societies. As societies grew and institutionalized — that is, created social institutions such as businesses and governments, with elaborate codes of law — these differences became formalized in specific rules about what men and women could do.

This played out differently in each society, but in most societies around the world, it was made difficult or impossible for women to take formal leadership roles. In many societies women were for a long time unable to own property or vote.

As with racial discrimination, sex discrimination came under increasing challenge as the principle of equality that fueled the revolutions of the 18th and 19th centuries (see Chapter 3) spread, and as science made increasingly clear that there were no significant differences between men and women in intellect or ability. An international suffrage movement around the turn of the 20th century earned women the right to vote in most countries around the world, and other legal barriers to women's equality began quickly to drop away.

But even as formal distinctions between men and women fell away, many informal distinctions remained. In the postwar "Baby Boom," women were still typically expected to stay at home and care for the children and the home while their husbands went off to bring home the bacon. This theoretical ideal was never actually as widespread as it seemed (see Chapter 15), but many women felt suffocated by the expectation that they would inevitably find a life of domesticity more rewarding than any alternative.

A wave of influential thinkers — Betty Friedan, Gloria Steinem, and others — called for a complete rethinking of the roles of women in society, and millions of women around the world actively resisted being pigeonholed in the role of passive nurturer. In part because of this cultural shift and in part because of an economic recession, women entered the workforce in record numbers, and today it's normal for women in many, if not most, societies around the world to have independent careers in addition to, or instead of, raising children.

Today, many young women prefer not to identify themselves as "feminists." The term is often associated with a strident political stance, and some women believe that the success of the women's movement created challenges for women who freely choose, for example, to leave their jobs to raise children. Some feel that the new challenge for feminists is to advocate for woman-friendly and family-friendly laws and corporate policies that make it easier to take time off work for childbearing or family responsibilities.

Still, for all the success of the women's movement, the fact of the matter is that women continue to face negative discrimination in almost every society. Women's earnings are still not as high as those of men with comparable experience, and women are still underrepresented in executive suites.

There are several reasons for the continuing disparity in career achievement between men and women. A few of the most important include:

- **Direct discrimination.** In many cases, women face direct discrimination by men (or even other women) who decline to hire them for high-paying positions or to pay them as much as a man might earn in the same position. This discrimination continues to happen for many of the same reasons that racial discrimination continues to happen (see previous section).

- **Different career timing.** Though parental leave is today widely available for fathers as well as mothers, women remain more likely than men to take time off for childbearing — and to take more time off when they do. This time off can put them at a disadvantage when competing for raises and promotions with colleagues who have been working continuously, even if their total experience is comparable.

- **A segmented labor market.** Among careers, some are especially dominated by women (nursing, teaching, library work) and others are especially dominated by men (construction jobs, computing, engineering). On average, male-dominated fields are higher-paying. This means that women are — whether by choice or for other reasons — concentrated in relatively low-paying careers, and when they try to enter higher-paying careers, they are especially vulnerable to discrimination.

Should gender matter on the job market?

I did a lot of babysitting when I was in high school, so when I arrived at college in another city, one of the first things I did was to go to the college employment office and submit my résumé for possible employment in child care. The woman at the desk was thrilled to get my application — they almost never, she said, received child care applications from men. "But I have to tell you," she warned me, "you won't be hired." Why? "Because when a parent calls me, I'll give them three names: yours, and the names of two women. They'll call the women first." She was right; I never did get a call from any parent who was given my name through that service.

Was I the victim of sex discrimination? Absolutely, and it would be illegal for the owners of a public child care facility to selectively interview only females for employment. Why would the parents — likely, professors who considered themselves open-minded people — act that way?

When it comes to their children, any parent is likely to be very risk-averse: There's nothing in the world that's more important than the happiness and safety of one's children. On average, women will be more experienced at child care than men; children who have never had a male babysitter will likely be more startled and upset at a new male babysitter than at a new female babysitter; and it's an undisputed fact that the large majority of sex offenders are male. From the standpoint of an individual parent, it makes all the sense in the world not to take a chance on a man when you have qualified women who might babysit your children.

When large numbers of parents act this way, though, you can see the pattern that will inevitably emerge: Qualified men will be unable to find employment in child care, and in many cases will probably seek employment in another field, perpetuating the gender division in child care. This is an illustration of Thomas's maxim that a situation defined as real (men are unsuitable for child care) becomes real in its consequences (few men seek or find employment in child care). You can see how this effect might work the other way around when it comes to construction work or other male-dominated occupations.

This being true, women are quickly catching up with men; in education, they have already surpassed men in most of the developed world. Increasingly, attention is turning to the challenges boys face in school, which may be related to challenges some men face in the workplace. Just as surely as women, men find themselves with a stereotypical role to play, and may be punished in the form of scorn or discrimination if they fail to play the role as they're "supposed" to. For both men and women, gender roles still very much matter — in *all* societies.

If someone chooses a role or lifestyle that's considered "traditional" for their gender doesn't necessarily mean that they've been brainwashed. It's typical for mothers to work outside the home in many societies today, but choosing not to work outside the home is a choice that many mothers are proud to make.

GBLTQ rights and the deconstruction of gender

"GBLTQ" is an alphabet soup of a term; it stands for *gay, bisexual, lesbian, transgender,* and *queer.* Some members of the GBLTQ community identify with one of these terms, some identify with multiple of them. Some people who identify with the term "gay" find the term "queer" to be derogatory and inappropriate, while others who identify with a "queer" identity consider terms like "gay" and "lesbian" to be restrictive and outmoded. So the term "GBLTQ" (or, sometimes, simply "GBLT") is used to include everyone whose sexual orientation is other than — or at least *broader* than — heterosexual.

The term is a little awkward — it doesn't exactly roll off the tongue, and it unites people who don't necessarily always want to be united. But it's become necessary as societies around the world have increasingly come to see sexual orientation as something that individuals are free to determine for themselves. Whether that means "straight," whether it means "queer," whether it means "lesbian," or whether it means something else is for each individual to say.

The widespread recognition of sexual orientations other than heterosexual as valid and healthy is relatively new — it wasn't that long ago that most psychologists considered homosexuality to be a mental disorder — and it's still unclear where laws and customs regarding sexual orientation will go in the future. Many consider the debate over sexual orientation to be a moral debate, and you may be among them; but remember that sociology is about looking at the big picture and setting aside your personal views so that you can understand society objectively. From a sociological standpoint, the debate over GBLTQ rights can be seen as the next step in the overall debate over sex and gender.

If you're allowed to decide whether you work, where you work, and whom and when you marry despite your biological sex, it follows logically that many people will want to decide for themselves who they have sex with and when — and whether that other person is a man or a woman. However you feel personally about the matter, the fact that sexual orientation is increasingly regarded as a matter of personal choice is consistent with what sociologists would expect given many of the other sociological ideas in this book. (By "personal choice," I don't mean to say that people aren't born with one sexual orientation or another. I mean to say that from a social and legal standpoint, people are increasingly allowed to say for themselves what their sexual orientation is rather than being told by someone else what it is.)

✔ Sociologists of culture (see Chapter 5) are seeing a transition to "micro-cultures," where groups of people who identify with one another are able to come together from across a range of social backgrounds. This means that people who consider themselves, say, queer can share a common culture that may be different than mainstream cultures.

✔ Sociologists of race and ethnicity (see earlier sections in this chapter) have seen that "race" is losing legitimacy as a category people are born into and that determines what they can or should do with their lives. Sex is changing in the same way — it's increasingly seen as something individuals can and should express for themselves.

✔ Sociologists studying social change (see Chapter 16), from Durkheim to Weber, have all observed that individuals are increasingly seen as having the right to say for themselves what they'll do and with whom they'll associate. There's no reason that association in bed should prove to be an exception to that rule.

It's often said that governments are getting "out of the bedroom," but sociologist David John Frank, who has studied international changes in sex laws, says that that's not exactly true. On the one hand, it is true that some sexual activities that were once forbidden by law — for example, gay sex — have increasingly been permitted by law in countries around the world. On the other hand, some sexual activities that were once permitted — for example, a husband forcing his wife to have sex with him — have been increasingly made illegal. The common theme is that laws around the world have been changing, for decades, in favor of allowing individuals to decide for themselves what intimate activities they are going to participate in, and when, and with whom.

Race, Ethnicity, Sex, and Gender: Why They Still Matter

If it's true — and it is — that in societies around the world, all individuals increasingly have the right to choose for themselves what they will do, with whom they will do it, and what identities they will choose, are ideas like race, ethnicity, sex, and gender outdated? Does it even *matter* what race or ethnicity or sex or gender you are? Why even bother having an ethnicity or a gender, or a particular sexual orientation? Some people feel this way; in fact, there are people who identify their sexual orientation as "omnisexual," claiming complete freedom to be intimate with anyone they happen to be attracted to. As people from different races and ethnicities mix more and more, maybe "omniracial" and "omniethnic" identities will also increasingly be adopted.

That probably will happen, but sociologists believe that race, ethnicity, sex, and gender aren't "going away" any time soon. Those concepts are grounded deep in the fabric of every society, and saying that they don't matter any more is simply false. No matter where you live, your physical features and biological sex are going to influence how the people around you see you, and they're going to influence how you see yourself.

Ethnicity may be an "option" for some people, but although ethnicity (unlike race) is not determined by how others see you, that doesn't mean it's easy to renounce the ethnicity you were raised in — even if you want to. Novels like *The House on Mango Street* (by Sandra Cisneros) and *Portnoy's Complaint* (by Philip Roth), films like Ang Lee's *Brokeback Mountain* and Tyler Perry's *The Family That Preys*, and plays like *Fences* (by August Wilson) and *Angels in America* (by Tony Kushner) movingly depict people's struggles to reconcile their personal hopes and dreams with the strengths and limitations of the ethnic communities to which they belong.

Similarly, sex and gender are increasingly complicated categories that remain just as meaningful to individuals as they were when they were simpler. Your sex, your gender, and your sexual orientation are part of who you are, and though societies increasingly allow you to decide how and when you will express your gender and your sexual orientation — and, also increasingly, forbid others to judge you by them — that doesn't mean that your sex and your gender don't matter profoundly to you, and to others.

If you're confused or frustrated trying to understand your own race, ethnicity, sex, or gender, you're not alone! Many groups exist to help people find support and advice about their identity, no matter what it is. A visit to a counselor, a trip to the library, a quick Web search, or even a conversation with a caring listener can help connect you with other people who are wrestling with the same concerns you are.

Chapter 10

Getting Religion: Faith in the Modern World

*A*fter 13 years in Catholic school, when I arrived at my first comparative religion course in college, I wondered how the professor was going to handle the fact that not all religions could be *right*. I wasn't sure that Catholicism was entirely "right," but I figured they couldn't *all* be right. Members of different religions have very different beliefs about the spiritual world; I wasn't sure how you could study religion without taking a position on which set of beliefs were "correct."

I soon realized that my professor was not going to tell us which religion was right; whatever her personal religious beliefs, they weren't the point. When social scientists — sociologists, anthropologists, psychologists — study religion, they are not studying God (or gods), they are studying *people*. It's the job of theologians and philosophers to study the hereafter; social scientists study the here and now.

And religion is indeed very much here and now. Every day, billions of people around the world pray and gather to share their faith, whatever that might be. Religious practices and organizations have always been at the heart of the social world, and for a sociologist to ignore religion would be like a physician ignoring the nose on your face. So sociologists have studied religion, just as they've studied every other major feature of society.

In this chapter, I first outline the important early sociologists' ideas about religion. Then, I explain the difference between religious beliefs or values and the organizations that support people's religious practices. Finally, I encourage you to think about the relationship between religious belief and social action in the world today.

Understanding Religion in History

When sociologists first set out to understand how society works, they immediately appreciated that their theories had to account for religion. Karl Marx, Emile Durkheim, and Max Weber all had ideas about the role of religion in society. In this section, I explain each of their theories in turn. (For more on Marx, Durkheim, and Weber, see Chapter 3.)

Marx: Opiate of the people

Many people see religion as being at the core of their lives, at the heart of what makes them happy. Most sociologists believe that religion is mostly, if not always, a constructive force in society. There are, however, some sociologists who believe that religion has an impact on society that is by and large negative, even destructive. The most famous of those sociologists is Karl Marx.

Marx believed that understanding society was fundamentally about understanding power, and that power was fundamentally tied to what he called "the means of production." If I own the field that you need to grow food, or the machinery you need to build a home, or the company you need to work at to earn money, I have power over you. It doesn't particularly matter what you *believe* about the situation; what matters is the material reality of the situation, which is that you will starve unless you do as I want.

Marx was personally a skeptic, and his social theory reflected his belief that any promise of divine reward for hard work and a "good life" was empty; that people without power in the here and now should not count on justice being done in the hereafter.

Many theologians and people of faith believe that earthly suffering happens for a reason, whether or not that reason can be understood by those who are suffering; Marx believed that whether or not that was the case, the affect of religion in the societies he could observe was largely to distract people from fighting for fair treatment.

If a person is barely getting by, working hard all day and being given only a fraction of the profit their work is earning for their employer, that is wrong, thought Marx — and if a person's religious belief that they would reap rewards in heaven deterred that person from fighting for fair treatment on earth, that would be bad. Religion, thought Marx, tends to get in the way of human happiness. It lulls people to sleep and keeps them from recognizing the injustice of their surroundings; that's why he called it "the opiate of the people."

Most sociologists today find Marx's views extreme, and you might too — but his ideas are important to think about. Marx was skeptical of not only religion, but of anything that kept people from questioning the status quo. That could include all or any of these phenomena:

- ✔ Advertisements for expensive products that you "need to have"

- ✔ Politicians who say that people who have different policy ideas than they do are "unpatriotic"

- ✔ Traditions that keep members of a certain sex or race in a subservient position because "it's always been that way"

Whether or not they agree with Marx, sociologists do agree that it's hard to understand the social world if you approach it with a set of preconceptions about how things are "supposed" to be. At the heart of Marx's criticism of religion is a rejection of anything that keeps people from working towards a society that is fair for everyone.

Some communist governments based on Marx's ideas have tried to eradicate religion altogether, but they haven't been entirely successful. A man who would not be surprised at that is Emile Durkheim, who believed that religion is an essential feature of a healthy society.

Emile Durkheim: A metaphor for society

Emile Durkheim didn't agree with Marx that religion was a destructive force in society. Why, asked Durkheim, would something destructive be at the center of virtually every society ever known? It just didn't make sense. Durkheim believed that religion must serve a function in society, must do something to help people work together happily and productively.

Marx thought that religion was an "opiate," something that put people to sleep and kept them from standing up for themselves. Durkheim agreed that religion helped encourage people to trust others, but unlike Marx, Durkheim believed that this was by and large a good thing. If every man and woman just looked out for themselves, believed Durkheim, society would fall apart. Sharing religious beliefs, values, and practices helps people recognize what they have in common, and helps encourage them to set aside their differences and make personal sacrifices for the good of society. Religion, said Durkheim, is one of the essential institutions in any society.

Durkheim's ideas about religion are especially interesting with respect to social change. Societies change over time, Durkheim observed — from Africa to Asia to America to Europe, societies tend to follow a general path of evolution from relatively simple tribal societies to complex industrial societies, even if they don't follow that path at the same pace. Further, Durkheim noticed, the religious beliefs and practices of those societies tended to change as well — which only makes sense. If a society is changing, and religion is at the heart of that society, then religion needs to change too!

Durkheim believed that religion helped societies maintain their *solidarity* . . . but what kind of solidarity a society needs, thought Durkheim, changes over the course of its history. In this way, religion is a metaphor for society itself.

Mechanical solidarity

Early on in any society's history, people's lives are similar and it's useful for them to follow very specific rules: rules about where to go and when, rules about what responsibilities are associated with various social statuses, rules about specific rituals and practices. Durkheim called this *mechanical solidarity* because people need to "mechanically" follow very specific rules, or the society could be in danger. The society's needs are too specific, and too pressing, for individuals to decide for themselves what practices they're going to follow.

Sure enough, noticed Durkheim, religious beliefs in simple societies tend to be very specific and ritualistic. Members of these societies tend to believe in divinities who make specific demands on people and who have human-like personalities. There may be a rain god who will be angered unless a specific ritual is followed, or a war god who has clear ideas about how territorial incursions ought to be dealt with. The Judeo-Christian God of the Old Testament fairly micromanages His people, showing up in a column of smoke or a burning bush to have conversations with mortals and hand down precise edicts. For Durkheim, this was the essence of mechanical solidarity.

Organic solidarity

As societies grow and become more complex, noticed Durkheim, it's less workable for everyone in a society to follow the same specific rules and practices. People's lives become much more diverse, and if everyone followed the same very precise set of rules and rituals, the social system would grind to a halt. What's more useful is for people to follow a general set of common principles that can be applied to diverse situations. Durkheim called this *organic solidarity* because people in complex societies need to organically adapt their behavior to the particular situations they're in.

As societies move toward organic solidarity, Durkheim pointed out, their religious beliefs tend to become more diffuse and general. Members of these societies are less likely to believe in gods with human-like personalities making concrete demands on mortals; instead, members of big, complex societies are likely to believe in gods who are at a greater remove from humanity. People have general ideas about what kind of behavior these divinities want, but they are less likely to go through their days attending to specific rituals. In general,

Christians today decreasingly identify with the personal God of the Old Testament; rather, they identify with the God of the New Testament, who loves His children and wants them to care for one another but is unlikely to show up on Earth to tell them exactly what to do in any given situation. This, for Durkheim, is what organic solidarity is all about.

The bottom line

Durkheim's theory is challenging, and may seem hard to understand, but here's the bottom line about what Durkheim believed:

✔ Religion is an essential feature of society. It encourages cooperation and mutual respect.

✔ Because of this, as society changes, religion needs to change also — and it does.

To understand how this works, consider the separation of church and state, which was a core belief of the founders of the United States. No church, they believed, had any business directly influencing a country's laws. To this day, citizens of the United States are free to practice any religion without interference from the government; government leaders are not allowed to make laws that favor one religion over another. This is also the case in most other countries around the world . . . but it hasn't always been that way.

For most of human history, church leaders have had official influence on laws and social structure. In many cases, religious leaders essentially *were* the leaders of governments. People whose religious beliefs were contrary to those of the leaders could be punished, even killed, for their beliefs. Horrible though this was, Durkheim would say that in societies bound by mechanical solidarity it made sense. If you believe that there's a divinity who has very specific ideas about what you should do and when, that divinity might well have ideas that conflict with others'. In this kind of society, it's hard for people of different faiths to live and work together.

In societies bound by organic solidarity, on the other hand, people tend to believe in divinities who have relatively general notions of acceptable behavior: Treat others as you would want to be treated. Don't kill. Don't steal. Be honest. People today don't tend to believe in divinities who prescribe specific styles of dress or specific hard-and-fast social roles for people of different sexes, races, or families of birth. People with this kind of religious belief have a much easier time living and working together, and it makes sense for governments to allow them to do so without following the exact same religious traditions.

Where things get hairy in these situations is when people need to follow specific religious practices that conflict with civic laws. That's a relatively rare situation, but it does happen — you can probably think of some examples — and it can cause a flurry of debate, even violent debate. Social solidarity isn't always easy!

Max Weber, the last of the "big three" early sociologists, agreed with Durkheim that religion changes along with society — but he didn't think there was necessarily anything "mechanical" or "organic" about it.

Weber: A switchman on the tracks

Max Weber agreed with Durkheim that religion was a fundamentally important part of society, but Weber also noticed that religion didn't always lead to peace, love, and understanding. There's no question, agreed Weber, that religious beliefs and values fundamentally affect the way that people lead their lives — but whereas Durkheim believed that changes in the social structure would more or less inevitably lead to changes in religious beliefs, Weber believed that it often worked the other way around: that religious beliefs and values led to widespread social change.

In Chapter 3, I mention Weber's view of religion as a "switchman on the tracks." Specifically, Weber wrote about the importance of the Protestant values of hard work and thrift in the development of modern capitalist society. If theologians like Martin Luther and John Calvin hadn't promoted these values, believed Weber, modern capitalism would probably never have succeeded. It's not that Luther and Calvin exactly *wanted* to bring about a capitalist society, but the values they preached nonetheless led to that outcome, said Weber. Both Marx and Durkheim, on the other hand, believed that the arrival of capitalism was basically inevitable and would have happened with or without "the Protestant Ethic."

Weber used the "switchman on the tracks" metaphor to acknowledge that not *all* outcomes are possible in society — there are distinct sets of "tracks" that a society might follow, depending on how things turn out. Which set they choose, though, may be determined by religious or cultural values. (See Chapter 5 for more on culture.)

Many sociologists today lean towards Weber's view of religion rather than Marx's or Durkheim's because Weber's view makes room for *both* cohesion and conflict:

- ✔ Like Durkheim, Weber appreciated that religious values, beliefs, and traditions can serve as a powerful form of social glue holding people together and helping them cooperate to achieve shared goals.

- ✔ Like Marx, though, Weber also understood that religious values don't always line up with social realities — and that they can lead to unnecessary conflict.

Marx believed that religion leads to conflict and exploitation while Durkheim believed that religion leads to cooperation and unity. Weber understood that *both* of those perspectives might be correct.

As much peace and happiness as religion has brought to people, as much as religious ceremonies and rituals are among the most treasured moments in people's lives, it's also true that (sincerely held, if distorted) religious values have served as the basis for some of the worst atrocities in human history — from the 15th-century Inquisition to 21st-century suicide bombers.

Religion in Theory . . . and in Practice

When studying religion, sociologists distinguish between the religious beliefs that people hold and the organizations that they form to facilitate their religious practices. In this section, I first explain how sociologists think about religious beliefs, then I explain how sociologists study religious organizations.

Religious ideas, ideology, and values

For any one individual, personal religious beliefs are often at the core of their religious experience — often, indeed, at the very core of everything that's important to them. They may feel a deep and true connection to a larger world than that which we can see here on Earth. This is true of sociologists as well, most of whom are people of faith and practice some form of worship with their families in private.

When they put on their sociological lab coats, though, they must acknowledge that questions about the hereafter can't be answered empirically. That's what separates religious beliefs from other beliefs: they are matters of faith or philosophy rather than matters that can be tested with empirical observations. (See Chapter 4 for more on sociological research and empirical observations.) To study religion from a sociological standpoint, you need to focus on aspects of religion that can be observed in the here and now.

You can't, of course, directly observe someone's mind — or, if you prefer, soul. What you *can* observe is what they say, what they write, what they read, and what they do. Early sociologists like Marx, Durkheim, and Weber were interested in history and anthropology; they spent a great deal of time studying how religious beliefs had changed over time and varied across different societies in their own times.

What they found — and what many other sociologists, anthropologists, historians, and other scholars of religion have found — is that religious beliefs and values, intensely personal as they feel to any given individual, are generally shared by people in particular times and places. Further, they change over time in a way that doesn't seem to be random. So *why* do they change over time? *Why* do they vary among different societies?

Though they disagree about specifically why religious beliefs and values vary over time and among different societies, sociologists agree that those changes are typically related to changes in society.

> **Marx** believed that religious values change to suit the interests of the powerful.
>
> **Durkheim** believed that religious values change naturally as societies grow and become more complex.
>
> **Weber** believed that religious values, as propagated by charismatic religious leaders, both influence and are influenced by social change.

It might be disorienting to think that religious belief and values have *anything* to do with society. After all, many people of faith believe that religious belief is a kind of antidote to social change, providing a compass for the faithful to sail by regardless of which way the prevailing cultural winds are blowing.

That belief is not inconsistent with a sociological view of faith. After all, the essential reason sociologists are interested in religious values is precisely because they *do* influence action. If religious belief were an entirely personal matter that had no affect whatsoever on anyone's actions, it would clearly be beyond the scope of sociological study.

What makes religious belief a matter of interest to sociologists is the fact that people's religious values do — or, at least, *can* — influence their actions. For many people, religious beliefs do provide a compass that acts like, to use Weber's terms, a "switchman on the tracks" that influences what they will do in a given situation.

In Weber's example of the "Protestant Ethic," this meant that people who might have worked only as hard as they needed to get by day to day decided, instead, to work as hard as they could, to scrimp and save and to amass wealth. In your life, a religious belief that stealing is wrong may influence your decision not to take advantage of a situation where you could steal something and get away with it.

So for this reason (plus out of simple curiosity), sociologists are interested in why and how religious values change — and they have discovered that religious values *do* change, and change in ways related to changes in society.

You may believe it *should* not be the case that religious values change; you may believe that there is a single truth — whether it be found in the Bible, the Koran, the Torah, or elsewhere — that applies to all people, in all times. That may well be the case, but sociology studies the world as it is, not as anyone believes it should be, and the empirical reality is that religious beliefs are not constant.

Open the church: Religious organizations

When you were a kid, someone might have taught you the game where you clasp your hands together and recite the rhyme, "Here is the church, here is the steeple, open the doors and see all the people," wiggling your fingers to represent the congregation. Although religion is for many people a purely personal experience, most people — whatever their religious beliefs — gather with others for worship, mutual support, and perhaps to work together for goals consistent with their faith.

This means that in large part, the sociological study of religion is the study of religious organizations. Whereas members of religious organizations are united by faith rather than by the desire to make a profit, play a sport, or save the whales, religious organizations share many of the characteristics of organizations like corporations, teams, and nonprofits. (In fact, in most countries they *are* considered nonprofit organizations.) They have rules and bylaws, they set goals, create budgets, raise revenue, and elect or otherwise choose leaders.

As I mention earlier in this chapter, in centuries past (and in many societies today) religious organizations essentially *were* governments, taking direct responsibility for not just holding worship services but also managing the economic system, waging war, and enforcing laws. In most societies today religious organizations are separate from governments, and the primary task of many religious organizations is simply to maintain places of worship and offer religious services every day or week.

Many, though, set more ambitious goals. Churches and religious groups have been, and continue to be, directly instrumental in many aspects of society.

- Martin Luther King, Jr. was a minister, and churches were deeply involved in the American Civil Rights Movement.

- In almost every country, religious groups are among the most important groups offering aid to the needy through shelters, food shelves, and economic assistance.

- Many religious groups run schools that offer secular instruction in reading, writing, and 'rithmatic along with religious education.

- It's common for religious groups to advocate for one side or another of a civic political issue — anything from health care to international relations — and to mobilize support for that position.

This important role that religious groups play in society is yet another reason sociologists appreciate that religion is an integral part of society.

Cops, churches, and the "Boston Miracle"

In the 1990s, violence — especially youth violence — in the city of Boston plummeted. In 1990, there were 152 murders in Boston, but in 1999 there were just 31; for a period of two and a half years in the late 90s, there were exactly zero teenage homicide victims in Boston. This amazing development became known as the "Boston Miracle."

Why did this happen? The Boston Police Department points with justifiable pride to a unique program that began in the early 1990s, where cops joined forces with African-American religious leaders to fight youth violence. Inner-city churches held community meetings where ministers and police officers stood side by side to form a united front, telling young gang members that their behavior was destructive and had to stop. Many of the kids got the message, and many of those who didn't were apprehended and imprisoned — with the cooperation of people in the communities they were terrorizing.

Sociologist Christopher Winship has been studying crime and policing in Boston neighborhoods for decades, and he agrees that the cop-church partnership played an important role in reducing violence in Boston — though he points out that violent crime dropped in many U.S. cities in the 1990s, suggesting that in some ways Boston was simply part of a national trend. What Winship thinks may be most impressive about the Boston partnership is the way that it's helped to minimize specifically racial violence in a city that saw terrible racial tension the 1970s and 1980s. The fact that black ministers have been seen publicly working with the police, Winship believes, has helped the entire community focus on fighting crime rather than pointing fingers at people because of the color of their skin.

The success of the Boston partnership — which continues, successfully, to this day — shows the continuing importance of religious organizations, especially in communities where other civic organizations are mistrusted. Because the Boston ministers had the trust and respect of their communities, they were able to help the police make those communities safer.

In the lives of believers, religious organizations may play a role well beyond facilitating worship. It's common for religious communities to host meals and social gatherings, as well as to provide opportunities for members to engage in public service or recreation together. Recent decades have seen the rise of suburban "megachurches," massive structures housing huge congregations. Members of these congregations may visit church every day whether to worship, study the Bible, relax at the coffee shop, watch a movie, or even work out on the church's exercise equipment. Especially for people who feel that their values aren't reflected in mainstream culture, it can be very satisfying to have a place to gather where they know they will be surrounded by people who share their beliefs.

Even when religious organizations don't have an official role in governance, they can virtually define neighborhood communities. My father grew up in St. Paul, Minnesota, and he still talks about the city not in terms of neighborhoods but in terms of Catholic parishes, which is how he grew up thinking about the city's geography. "They live in St. Marks," he'll say, or "she bought a house down there in Nativity." In communities where religious organizations and civic life are closely intertwined, religion can even function like race or ethnicity. ("People say we didn't have any minorities in St. Paul when I was growing up," jokes my dad. "Of course we did . . . we had Lutherans!")

Although they're like other social organizations in many ways, religious organizations have a unique relationship with their members because believers see them as representing a here-and-now connection to the spiritual world, the eternal realm that, for many believers, is much more important than anything in this world. This gives religious organizations a special power that can be tremendously constructive — as with organizations that help hold communities together in times of war or strife — or tremendously destructive — as in the case of corrupt cults that exploit their members financially and otherwise. For billions of people, religious organizations are among the most important social organizations in their lives.

Faith and Freedom in the World Today

In today's world, where most societies maintain a separation between church and state and where immigration and other factors are leading to increasing religious diversity everywhere, religion is an especially complicated subject. Faith remains central to billions of people's lives, but what implications does that have for their actions? In this section, I describe trends in religious participation and look at the circumstances under which faith translates into action.

Shopping for God

Sociologists distinguish between *faith* (or beliefs, or values) and *action*. A high proportion of people in the world today attend religious services, but an even greater proportion express a belief in a higher power. These are both important indexes of religiosity, but they measure different things.

The distinction is particularly important in today's world, where people in many societies have considerable freedom to express whatever beliefs they like and whether or not to act on them. In the United States, for example, a large majority of people say they believe in a higher power, and nearly half say they regularly attend religious services; this has declined in recent decades (especially if you look at whether people *actually* attend services and not whether they *say* they do), but not as quickly as in Europe, where the rate of belief is falling and the rate of attendance is falling faster.

Conservative Christian culture: A world apart

One of the most striking developments on the religious landscape over the past several decades has been the emergence of a coordinated, well-defined coalition of conservative Christians. Particularly in the United States, where it's known as "the religious right," this movement — under the leadership of massively influential leaders like James Dobson — has played an important role in defining and influencing the national debate over issues ranging from abortion to capital punishment to taxation and budgeting.

The movement is controversial not just because of its strong policy views, but because of its unapologetic insistence that religion belongs at the heart of any political or social debate. Members of the movement have argued that removing religious symbols from government buildings and forbidding judges and lawmakers to invoke religious beliefs in their deliberations has potentially disastrous consequences for American public life.

The movement is also distinctive for having given birth to a vast array of consumer products aimed at those who don't feel mainstream products reflect their values. From music to literature to TV to movies, there's an entire alternate universe of explicitly Christian products aimed at the faithful; some of these, like the *Left Behind* novels, sell as well as or better than their mainstream counterparts. Even on the Internet, there are Christian search engines, Christian social networking sites, and a Christian video site called "GodTube."

In some ways, this movement is a textbook example of a *subculture* (see Chapter 5): a culture formed in conscious opposition to a mainstream culture. In other ways, though, the movement embraces the realities of mainstream politics and entertainment; its members are enthusiastically using the freedom contemporary society affords them to choose their own faith, their own entertainment, their own social world.

In many respects, religion in the contemporary world is becoming a consumer good: something you choose to "buy" because it satisfies a need you have. This may seem like a heretical, or even offensive, way to look at something so profoundly personal, but it does describe the behavior religious organizations have been demonstrating — and, in fact, the way many people think about religion.

People in free societies do have the ability to choose for themselves whether or not they'll participate in a religious organization — and if so, which organization they'll participate in. Most religious organizations welcome converts, and they realize that people may be swayed by many factors when choosing a religious orientation generally and a particular community specifically. People may consider:

- Their personal sense of the supernatural world, preferring organizations that resonate with their most deeply-felt beliefs.

- The family and tradition in which they were raised, possibly preferring an organization with beliefs, rituals, and a structure that mirror the ones they grew up with.

✔ The social values of a denomination or a congregation, preferring to worship among people who share their commitment to a set of social policies or public service interests.

✔ The other members of a congregation, looking — for example — for a congregation with many young families, or many active seniors.

✔ Geography, preferring to attend service in their own neighborhoods.

✔ Other services offered by a congregation: schooling for children, classes or workshops for adults, outings, and other features of life in that community.

Religious organizations recognize that people have a choice in their religious affiliations, and the organizations often respond by advertising themselves in ways ranging from flyers at the back of the sanctuary to billboards or even radio and TV ads. Churches in neighborhoods with many gay or lesbian residents may display rainbow banners, and churches looking to attract families with young children may advertise their daycare centers or Sunday School offerings.

Do people actually think about religion this way? Do they actually think about faith as something to be shopped for, like cereal or a winter coat?

In some ways, of course not. Faith is a deeply personal, sometimes highly sensitive subject, and many of the faithful would rightly bristle at any suggestion that they would treat a church like a vacation destination.

That said, it is true that in societies where people do have the freedom to choose their faith and the ways in which they practice it, they tend to exercise that freedom. A 2009 Pew survey showed that 44 percent of American adults do not belong to the faith in which they were raised — some have switched affiliations, some have simply stopped practicing. Another 9 percent switched faiths at some point before returning to their childhood faith.

Of course, people convert for many reasons. As network sociologists (see Chapter 7) and those studying social movements (Chapter 13) have discovered, it's rare that people change their behaviors out of thin air. In many cases, religious conversion is the result of an interfaith friendship or romance; a new work situation; or a move from one place to another. Often, action follows belief . . . but often, it's the other way around.

Belief, action, and everything in between

So, again, why do sociologists care about religion? What business of theirs is it to whom people pray, or where people expect to go after they die? It's because religion is *not* something that exists merely in your head or your soul; it's also, typically, something you *do*.

✔ You might join a religious organization, which may be of pivotal importance in your community.

✔ Your faith might affect the votes you cast in polling places (that is, influence your political views) and the votes you cast in shopping malls (that is, influence the things you buy).

✔ Religion can affect your social networks, which in turn affects everything else you do.

These are all reasons that religion is important for sociologists, political scientists, and economists to consider when studying the social world. But does faith directly affect people's actions? From a sociological standpoint, does it matter *what* you believe, beyond it simply mattering *that* you believe?

Of course it does. The question is *when* and *how*.

All the major sociological theories about religion emphasize that faith somehow influences people's actions — not just by influencing them to build buildings and form organizations and buy books, but by influencing them to take specific actions in *this* world consistent with their beliefs about the *next* world.

Marx believed religion was relatively unimportant; however, he argued that in some circumstances religion could serve the interests of the powerful, by discouraging people from challenging the status quo. Marx was particularly wary of faiths that offered the promise of heavenly rewards because he believed that people who expected to be rewarded in heaven might be less likely to demand their just desserts on Earth.

Durkheim believed that religion was key to social solidarity. He believed that religious teachings and ceremonies teach people how to get along in society, and make it less likely that people will pursue personal goals that are at odds with larger social goals. In earlier societies, this meant that they were often encouraged to be intolerant of diversity (because diversity can be dangerous when there are a few very specific tasks that need to be accomplished); today, this means that they are often encouraged to welcome diversity (because intolerance can be dangerous when many different kinds of people need to get along despite having very different tasks to accomplish).

Weber believed that religious values could influence people's actions in any number of ways. He believed that religious values consistent with capitalism helped that economic system get off the ground. Religious values, for Weber, don't completely determine the direction a society will take; nor do they necessarily change to match a social structure. There's always a back-and-forth interaction between religious values and other social forces.

In all these theories, specific religious beliefs and values directly influence people's actions beyond the walls of the church or the synagogue. Most sociologists of religion today lean more toward the perspective of Weber than towards the perspectives of Marx or Durkheim because Weber has more appreciation for the complex interactions among religious institutions and other social institutions. Religion matters, but the specific *way* it matters will depend on the structure of any given society as well as the nature of religious beliefs.

Religion can be profoundly important in people's lives, influencing all the actions they take. It can also, at least in today's world, be completely absent from a person's life. A person can claim no religious affiliation, and have personal beliefs about the hereafter (or lack thereof) that have no bearing on their actions in the here and now. What's more, the place of religion in the structure of a society can vary: In some societies, even today, religious institutions are synonymous with the state, and religious practices are closely monitored and enforced. In other societies, religious institutions are completely separate from the state, and have little political clout.

Compared to most places and times in the past, religious beliefs and practices in the world today are incredibly diverse — and people with diverse religious beliefs and practices are increasingly rubbing elbows in societies around the world. That makes it harder to generalize about the role of religion in social life, but it doesn't make religion any less important.

Today, religion brings people together as it always has. Every week, billions of people around the world gather in living rooms, public squares, and private houses of worship to share their faith and share their community. Whether their faith is the only one they've ever known or whether they've converted from another creed, whether they live in places where everyone has the same religious affiliation or whether their neighbors all subscribe to different religious views, religion offers them solace and support. It links them to a larger social world and, according to their beliefs, to a spiritual world as well.

Religion also, however, sometimes inspires, fuels, and justifies terrible conflict and violence. In some cases, this violence is a direct extension of faith — some people genuinely believe that they have a divine imperative to act in a hostile manner towards those who do not share their beliefs — but in most cases, religious distinctions merely serve to highlight and exacerbate other divisions. When religious differences happen to coincide with differences of ethnicity or class, conflicts along those lines can take on an especially bitter character. Social activists interested in working towards a just world have always seen it as downright tragic that distinctions of religion and race can divide people who might otherwise find common cause in a shared economic or political situation.

A popular graphic seen on t-shirts and bumper stickers is the word coexist, with Christian, Jewish, and Islamic symbols standing in for certain letters. The suggestion is one that it's hard to argue with: that people of different faiths should learn to get along and tolerate the differences among themselves. It's a noble goal, and one that many people are successfully working towards every day — but sociologists of religion understand that it's not always that easy.

Religion: The remix

Over time, religious life changes in many ways. There's change in the extent of people's religiosity, in the distribution of religious beliefs, and in the beliefs and practices of particular faiths. Another way that religious life changes — and, like almost all forms of social change, it's happening more quickly now than ever before — is in the way that religious traditions interact with and influence one another.

Anthropologists and historians have traced the tremendous spread, change, fragmenting, and consolidation of religious traditions. Christianity, Judaism, and Islam are today regarded as three different faiths, but they share common roots — and within each of those faiths, there are any number of different divisions. Among Christians alone, there are the Catholics, the Eastern Orthodox Catholics, the Lutherans, the Methodists, the Baptists, the Mennonites . . . the list goes on.

Besides the fragmentation of religious traditions into new and separate faiths, there are new faiths that are created by the intermixing of different traditions. Haitian voudou incorporates elements of European Christianity with elements of the beliefs and practices immigrants brought to Haiti by African immigrants. The Liberal Catholic Church blends Catholic theology with the insights of mystics and seers. One branch of Judaism unites the traditions and practices of that faith with the secular philosophy of Humanism; another, "Jews for Jesus," blends Jewish cultural and religious traditions with Christian beliefs.

This intermixing happens as people seek to find or create religious practices that both soothe their souls and speak to the circumstances of their lives. When couples from different traditions marry, they may blend their beliefs in their family lives — perhaps lighting the Menorah *and* plugging in the Christmas tree. Religious change is not just something decided by groups of spiritual leaders meeting in solemn congress; it's something that happens in every city, in every country, every day.

Religious traditions do include distinctive symbols and styles of dress, but a religion isn't just a hijab or a turban or a skullcap, it's an entire philosophy about the fundamental nature of reality. Your religious affiliation is a social status like your race or your sex or your class, but it's different than any of those because it corresponds to a whole set of values and beliefs that you may believe are dictated or influenced by a force higher, more powerful, and more important than any human being or social institution. The fact that religious beliefs and practices are almost always intertwined with ethnic traditions and family ties makes them even more profoundly important.

From this perspective, it may be disappointing that religious differences are behind some of today's most bitter, brutal conflicts — but it shouldn't be a surprise. Religion is, as it has always been, a deeply important part of people's social lives. Managing the transition to a society of increasingly diverse religious beliefs, for all its obvious benefits, is not an easy thing to do.

Chapter 11

Crime and Deviance: I Fought the Law . . . and I Won!

Crime has always been a subject of intense interest for sociologists. On the one hand, it's obviously a very practical thing to understand. There aren't many higher priorities for society than fighting crime, and any insights sociologists are able to contribute might help. For this reason, sociologists often receive funding to collaborate with other scholars and with law enforcement authorities to investigate why crime occurs and how it might be minimized or prevented.

On the other hand, though, crime is an interesting phenomenon for sociologists to study because it represents the absolute edge of what is socially acceptable. Societies may be incredibly diverse and tolerant of a wide range of behavior, but those behaviors defined as crimes are where societies draw a line in the sand and say *you may not*. Different societies draw that line in different places, and they have different strategies for keeping people from crossing it — as well as punishing them when they do. Understanding how and why those lines are drawn can tell you a lot about how a society works in general.

In this chapter, I look at how crime is defined and fought in society. First, I explain the difference between "deviance" and "crime"; then, I go through different explanations of why criminals commit crimes. I then explain how crime is defined — both in the courts and on the streets — and how societies today are fighting crime. Finally, I look at teenage drinking as a case study in crime.

All Crime is Deviance, but Not All Deviance is a Crime

Every social group has its norms. Some of those norms are *informal*, meaning rules that are not written down and not officially defined as rules. There's no official agreement about what's supposed to happen to you if you stray from these norms, but if you do, people will probably notice and might well punish you in one way or another for failing to heed them. Some examples of informal norms include:

- Having good manners, such as saying *please* and *thank you*, holding the door for others, not eating with your mouth open.
- Keeping secrets among friends.
- Dressing according to generally accepted standards when you're interacting with other people.
- Getting married in your twenties and having kids in your thirties.
- Walking on the right (or, in some places, left) side of the hallway.

When you violate any social norm, sociologists call it *deviance*. If you don't behave in the way you're expected to behave, you are acting in a deviant manner. That sounds harsh, but it's okay — you're a deviant, and so am I. No one person behaves in a manner exactly like they're supposed to. Sometimes you feel bad about this (for example, if you're rude to a friend), sometimes you feel proud of this (for example, if you violate a social norm against having friends who are gay), but deviance is just part of social life.

Deviance may have benefits. You may impress a fellow "deviant" (for example, someone who agrees with you that a particular unusual style of dress is attractive), you may save time or money (for example, by waiting until the last second to merge on the freeway, saving you time but slowing everyone else down), and you may inspire social change (for example, a girl who tries out for a football team may make it easier for other girls who are interested in playing football).

It's also apt to have costs, though. You will draw attention to yourself, and people may avoid you, make fun of you, or even attack you for being different. Whether or not it's worth it for you to deal with that depends on the benefits you expect to earn, and what you think of the norm itself. Everyone makes these calculations every day when they consider the social consequences of their actions.

Some norms are stronger: these are called *formal* norms. These are norms that are publicly stated (usually put in writing), and that may have an officially determined consequence. Some examples of formal norms include:

- ✔ A family rule that you have to do your chores before going outside to play.
- ✔ A school rule that students have to wear a certain uniform.
- ✔ A company policy that you need to ask your supervisor before scheduling a vacation.
- ✔ A state law that you can't exceed posted speed limits on the highway.

When formal norms are made by units of government and backed with the threat of force, they're called *laws*. Breaking a law is deviant — and it's also a crime.

Because crime is just a specific type of social deviance, everything that's true of deviance is also true of crime. There may be benefits to crime (money, power, thrills), but there are also obviously costs — costs that may include fines, imprisonment, or even death. What's important to understand is that crime is just one particular subset of deviance. What counts as "deviant" may vary from one social group to another, and within that general category of deviance, what counts as a "crime" is something that has to be sorted out by government agencies. Those decisions are what distinguishes deviance from crime, and deviants from criminals.

Criminals in Society

So who are these criminals? Why do people commit crimes? In his book *Sociological Insight*, Randall Collins looks at different reasons why a person might think criminals fall on the wrong side of the law; in this section, I discuss the two main theories Collins offers — they're just bad people, and they're driven to it — before explaining why sociologists think some crime is simply normal.

Some criminals are just bad people (but . . .)

When you see the word "criminal," the images that may come to mind are pictures of brutal men and women: cold-blooded murderers, street thugs, and furtive child molesters. When these crimes come to light, the perpetrators don't look good. In fact, they often look downright evil. Their grainy mug shots are put on TV next to the smiling faces of their innocent victims, and the news anchors somberly tell viewers about their horrible crimes. Are people like this just plain evil? Isn't that why people are criminals — there's just something wrong with them?

There's no doubt that in many cases, there's something deeply wrong with people who commit serious crimes. They may have severe psychological disorders, or just a flat lack of regard for the feelings of others. It's hard to explain their actions any other way.

But that can't possibly work as a satisfactory explanation for all crimes. Of course people choose their actions freely and must be held accountable for their decisions, but it's just too simple to say that all criminals are bad people — period, end of story.

For one thing, there is a wide range of crimes, from those that involve grievous harm to others (murder, rape, assault) to those that involve milder forms of harm (theft, libel, disturbing the peace) to "victimless crimes" that involve harm, if any, only to oneself — illegal drug use, or failing to fasten one's own seatbelt. A murderer may be a "bad person," but is someone who plays his stereo too loud also a "bad person"? Is someone who smokes marijuana in a place where it's illegal a "bad person"? There are many different kinds of crimes with many different consequences and motivations, and it's clearly too simplistic to say that there is a single psychological or moral factor that binds all people defined as criminals.

Further, crimes are committed in different circumstances. Some people murder in self-defense whereas some murder in cold blood. Some people steal to feed their families whereas others steal to feed their taste for expensive clothes. In neighborhoods where government-appointed law enforcement officers are corrupt or unfair, can a person be blamed for throwing their lot in with a street gang? Social and political revolutionaries such as George Washington and Harriet Tubman were technically criminals in the eyes of the appointed authorities — were they fundamentally bad people?

Though it is certainly the case that many criminals can be fairly judged to be sick or immoral, sociologists don't believe that black-and-white moral judgment is the best way to understand why and when people commit crimes. The world just isn't that simple, and the law just isn't that infallible.

Some criminals are "driven to it" (but . . .)

If it's not adequate to understand crime simply in moral terms (criminals are bad, law-abiding citizens are good), then maybe it makes more sense to think about it in rational terms. That is, maybe the best way to think about crime is as something people are forced into. Setting aside the people who choose to commit crimes because they have a psychological disorder or have completely renounced any sense of obligation to others, maybe the rest of the criminals are reluctant ones. They don't *want* to be criminals, but for some reason or other they're *forced* to be.

Certainly, this describes a large proportion of criminals. It would have been very convenient for George Washington if Britain had recognized America's sovereignty and the American Revolution hadn't had to be fought, and beyond question Harriet Tubman would have rejoiced if the government Washington helped to found had in turn outlawed slavery rather than forcing her to conspire with fellow abolitionists in the creation of an Underground Railroad. Kids who join gangs to get the protection law enforcement can't offer them, or people who steal to feed their families when they can't find work to earn a proper living are clearly reluctant criminals.

This is a rational choice view of crime (see Chapter 6): It assumes that people weigh the costs and benefits of every action they take, and if they make the choice to commit a crime it must be because they've decided that the benefits of crime outweigh the risks or consequences. Rational choice explanations are popular among economists, and in fact there have been many economic studies of crime demonstrating that "criminal" acts and transactions — from drug trafficking to prostitution — are an important part of the global economy.

Even people working at legal jobs are not infrequently on the wrong side of the law; millions of immigrants are working without legal permission in countries around the world, an arrangement that technically makes them criminals but in which they participate because the pay and employment prospects in their native countries are often very limited, and because jobs are available with employers who benefit from the relatively cheap labor. A person who generally respects the rule of law may still choose to break specific laws because their circumstances otherwise would be dire.

This explanation, though helpful, is also incomplete. In most cases, committing a crime somehow makes sense to the criminal — that is, it's not completely irrational or illogical — but it's hard to understand why people feel "driven to" break the law in very different circumstances. Some people will die of starvation before they'll steal, whereas other people are fabulously wealthy and still embezzle money from their companies. Other people commit crimes where they don't stand to make any personal gain: vandalism or assault. To say that crime is something criminals are "forced into" is something that is accurate in many cases — and *feels* accurate to the criminals in many more cases — but leaves a lot of crimes unexplained.

Some crime is simply normal

Some criminals are just bad people . . . that's hard to argue with. Many criminals feel driven to it . . . yes, absolutely. But neither of those explanations is really a satisfactory explanation for all the various crimes committed in every society, everywhere, since the beginning of history.

Emile Durkheim, as I explain in Chapter 3, believed in the survival of the fittest societies; as among plants and animals, he said, if a given feature is observed in many societies across a range of situations, there must be a reason for it. It must serve some kind of function for society, or at least be a necessary byproduct of some other function.

Crime occurs, without exception, in every society. Hence, Durkheim argued, it makes sense to see crime as normal. It's just going to be there, whether you like it or not. Further, crime may actually be *useful* to a society. In this section, I first explain why crime is virtually inevitable, and possibly even useful.

Crime is inevitable

To call something "normal" isn't necessarily to call it good, or nice. It's normal for people to accidentally stub their toes every now and then; it's normal for hurricanes, tornadoes, and tsunamis to occur; and it's normal for some people to step outside the bounds drawn by their society. Even in a community of saints living in a monastery, said Durkheim, there will be laws — and even in that community, every once in a while someone will break a law. That might mean a very minor offense — say, being late for prayers or letting a few weeds grow in the garden — but nonetheless, it will count as a "crime" in that particular society.

The whole point of laws, after all, is to force people to not do something that they may otherwise be tempted to do. It would obviously be a serious problem if every single person in a country decided to take one particular day off work, but there are no laws forcing people not to all take the same day off because it's so extremely unlikely that it would occur. It's much more likely that someone would cheat on their taxes, so there *are* laws against that.

At the same time, laws are written to cover situations where there is actually some chance where the laws will be enforced. It would be nice if everyone in a country said "please" and "thank you" at the dinner table, but cops have more important things to worry about than enforcing table manners . . . so there are no laws against simple rudeness.

Because laws are written to apply in situations where people are likely to break them, it's more or less guaranteed that any given law will be broken sometimes — which means that it's almost guaranteed that a society will have "criminals." It's not necessarily guaranteed that a society will have murderers or embezzlers (think of Durkheim's hypothetical community of saints), but it is hard to imagine a society with no crime whatsoever.

Crime is useful

Saying that crime is normal may seem to imply that there's no point in having law enforcement. If crime can't be eliminated, if crime is inevitable, why bother hiring police officers?

Well, for one thing, enforcing laws does make it *less likely* that those particular laws will be broken. The police can't completely eliminate fraud, but enforcing fraud deters at least some potential con artists from practicing their devious craft. If there's a behavior that people in a society want there to be less of, putting cops on the case is a good idea even if they can't stop every single criminal.

For another thing, though, enforcing crime may actually have benefits for the rest of society. Besides the fact that everyone else sees the law upheld and is taught to think twice before breaking the law themselves, the enforcement of laws can be something that brings people together. Being united in disapproval, after all, is still being united. Whether it's petty crime in a neighborhood or sensational crime that makes national headlines, crime gives everyone something to talk about and to agree on. In effect, monitoring and supporting law enforcement is part of mainstream culture, and like all mainstream culture (see Chapter 5), it can create a common denominator that unites even people who are very different.

In ancient Rome, crowds would fill the Coliseum to watch criminals be thrown to the lions; in medieval society, public hangings were popular entertainment. Societies today are a little more delicate than that, but spectacular criminal trials can still draw attention across a country — even around the world.

The Social Construction of Crime

Although some crimes (for example, kidnapping) are very widely outlawed and others (for example, pumping your own gas) are outlawed only in a few places, all crime is socially constructed in that each society has to decide for itself what counts as a "crime." In this section, I explain how crime is constructed in two places: in the courts and on the streets.

In the courts

In 1692, over two dozen people in Salem, Massachusetts were executed, or died in prison, as part of a series of events that became known as the Salem Witch Trials. Men and women were convicted of witchcraft based on confessions forced through means like being pressed by rocks, and by the highly dubious testimony of neighbors — sometimes neighbors with a grudge to bear — who said that they had been haunted or cursed by the accused.

It's one of the most shocking episodes in American history, and it's been widely studied and discussed; Salem itself remains a popular destination, especially around Halloween, for tourists curious to see the town where the trials took place.

Many accounts portray the witch trials as a sort of inexplicable craze that overtook an otherwise normal town, but sociologist Kai Erikson wrote an entire book (*Wayward Puritans: A Study in the Sociology of Deviance*) explaining why the trials, though tragic, make sense in social context. Seventeenth-century New England Puritans were God-fearing people who sincerely believed that the Devil was at work on Earth in very concrete ways and that the courts were an appropriate place for his deeds to be exposed and punished. What's more, their legal system gave individual judges tremendous leeway in interpreting and enforcing the law.

By contrast, in U.S. law today, not only is it illegitimate to prosecute supernatural crimes, a much higher standard of evidence is required for criminal convictions — particularly where capital punishment is a possibility — and the jury system makes it harder for any one judge to go on a personal crusade. Today, an event like the Salem Witch Trials is almost unthinkable; although it was exceptional even in colonial America, the legal system at that time was constructed such that an event like it may have been a very real possibility in any number of communities.

Erikson's study provides a good, if extreme, example of how crimes are constructed in the courts and in the legislatures. An activity — witchcraft — that most Americans today don't even believe is possible was genuinely feared in colonial America, and it was considered the proper business of the courts to stamp it out. In every society, laws are made and ruled upon in organizations (for example, courts and legislatures) that have the often-difficult task of deciding where to draw the line between behavior that ought to be punishable and behavior that ought not.

What counts as a "crime" varies from year to year — even day to day — as societies officially change their minds and change their laws. Here are just a few examples of debates that are taking place in societies today:

- ✔ Should abortion be legal, or illegal?
- ✔ Should it be legal or illegal to drive a car, or run a factory, that pollutes the atmosphere?
- ✔ Should it be legal or illegal to use portions of copyrighted material in recordings you create and then sell? If legal, how large a portion should you be allowed to use?

Legislatures in countries around the world might decide either way on any of these questions. If they decide one way, the activity in question becomes a crime, and those who engage in it are subject to punishment. If they decide the other way, the activity becomes as unpunishable as witchcraft.

Complicating matters even further is the fact that no law is completely unambiguous; it's up to courts to decide whether the law applies in any given situation. Often this is simply a matter of establishing whether or not a violation of the law occurred (did the suspect, in fact, steal that car?), but in other cases courts need to take highly ambiguous laws and decide how to fairly enforce them according to appropriate social standards.

In Minneapolis, for example, the city where I live, there is a law against keeping as pets animals that are "wild by nature." Clearly this means that keeping a hippo in the house is a no-no, but I could walk into any pet store and buy a parrot. Are parrots somehow, by nature, domestic? What about a turtle, or a fish?

As it happens, the law was intentionally written to be ambiguous, so that courts could have leeway to decide on a case-by-case basis whether the keeping of a particular animal is inappropriate. The neighboring city of St. Paul, meanwhile, decided to take action to prevent what its city council saw as a potentially dangerous fad, and explicitly outlawed the keeping of sugar gliders.

If you had confessed to witchcraft in Massachusetts four hundred years ago, you might have been put to death. Today, proudly self-described witches run souvenir shops there. If I had a sugar glider in my pocket right now, sitting in Minneapolis, I'd be a law-abiding citizen ... but if I were to take my pet across the Mississippi River to St. Paul, I'd be a criminal. "Crime" is what people say it is — nothing more and nothing less.

On the streets

Police officers are on the front lines of the fight against crime, and their heroic efforts — often in the line of serious danger — keep citizens safe every day. But how do they decide how best to keep people safe: which laws to enforce, and when, and how? It's not always obvious.

Sometimes it's clear what cops have to do. They may come across a theft in progress, or witness an egregious violation of someone's rights, or be called to an urgent situation that demands immediate action. Often, though, police officers have a great deal of leeway in deciding when, where, and how to enforce the law.

Even in well-policed societies, it's impossible to enforce *every* law. For example:

- ✔ On the freeway, people routinely exceed posted speed limits by modest margins, gambling that as long as they don't push the envelope too far, the police won't ticket them.

- ✔ Most jaywalkers would be shocked to be stopped by a cop.

- ✔ Large numbers of people break copyright laws every day by burning CDs or sharing music online.

✔ Marijuana is widely — often openly — used in countries where it's officially illegal.

✔ Few people reach legal drinking age without ever having known the taste of alcohol, and at college campuses across the United States drinking is a primary social activity despite being nominally illegal for the large majority of undergraduate students.

As with the "exotic animal" law I mention earlier, some of the laws prohibiting these activities were written with the full understanding that they would be unenforceable in most cases; they're there to be selectively enforced, at the discretion of the law enforcement officers and the courts.

Other laws, though — for example, laws against murder, rape, violent assault, and large-scale theft — are written to be enforced as universally as possible, and possible violations can merit exhaustive investigations. On the streets, police officers need to decide how to divide their time and attention so as to prevent the worst crimes and prevent as many lesser crimes as possible.

This adds another level to the social construction of crime. The first level takes place in legislatures and courtrooms, and the second level takes place on the streets. If I know I'm not going to be caught at a crime, it *de facto* becomes not a crime at all.

In legal and academic use, the term *de jure* means "officially," and the contrasting term *de facto* means "in reality." In many cities, riding a bicycle on the sidewalk is *de jure* a crime (insofar as there are laws against it) but *de facto* legal (insofar as you're unlikely to pay any penalty for it).

It's clearly necessary for police officers to have this flexibility, but it creates the possibility for unfairness. For example, many women believe that male police officers will be less likely to give them speeding tickets if the women cry when they're pulled over. Even if this isn't true, it's reasonable to think that it might be!

More troublingly, some police officers discriminate by race when deciding which possible crimes (or crimes in the making) to pursue. A song by the group Spearhead says that "it's a crime to be black in America"; the truth behind the lyric is that in many neighborhoods, racial minorities are viewed with suspicion and are apt to get away with a lot less than whites. Despite concerted efforts by political and law enforcement leaders, discrimination in law enforcement is not apt to go away any time soon — no sooner than racism generally is apt to disappear. People dressing a certain way, or having a certain color of skin at the wrong place in the wrong time, unfairly risk mistreatment or undue suspicion.

The bottom line: "crime" is defined in legislatures, in courts, *and* on the streets.

Don't touch that file

Minnesota mom Jammie Thomas, like millions of Americans, used file-sharing software to exchange music over the Internet — an activity that's illegal in the United States when it involves copyrighted files, as almost all popular music files are. The Recording Industry Association of America (RIAA) detected Thomas's activity and asked her for a cash settlement in exchange for an agreement not to prosecute. Thomas refused, and the RIAA took her to court. When she was found guilty and fined $220,000, Thomas appealed the decision on the basis that the penalty was excessive. Instead of being overturned, the judgment was increased — to almost two million dollars.

Thomas's lawyers called the penalty "grossly excessive," and many Americans were inclined to agree. Even people who acknowledge the necessity of copyright law question whether individuals who share music with no intention to profit by it deserve to be held liable for monetary damages — much less multi-million-dollar damages. The RIAA stood by its decision to prosecute Thomas, saying that the recording industry was losing much more than two million dollars each year because people would illegally download songs rather than paying for them, and that just because the law couldn't be enforced in every instance didn't mean it was wrong to enforce it in any particular instance.

The Thomas case and the international discussion about it show that people know the law is a blunt instrument and that "crime" is what you get caught for doing. Essentially, some people claimed, fining Thomas two million dollars for sharing a couple dozen songs was like fining someone two million dollars for driving five miles per hour over the speed limit. It was unfair, they said, to so strictly enforce a law that millions of people reasonably assume every day that they can get away with breaking. Is it? The courts said no, but you may have another opinion.

Becoming Deviant

Like all sociologists, those who study crime and deviance have come to appreciate the wisdom of W.I. Thomas's dictum that a situation defined as real is real in its consequences. In this case, that means that someone defined as "deviant" is especially likely to become even *more* deviant.

In the 1970s, sociologist Robert W. Balch asked junior high students to imagine a boy being caught outside of class without a hall pass — a violation of school rules, but a fairly minor one that could easily be overlooked. Balch asked the students to guess how a teacher would treat the boy if he were considered any of several things including a "troublemaker," a "good quiet student," or a "hippie."

Unsurprisingly, the students overwhelmingly guessed that teachers would be especially hard on a "troublemaker" or a "hippie," and especially easy on a "good quiet student." In fact, they guessed that teachers would be harder on a reputed troublemaker who'd never actually broken the law than on a student who had been in trouble with the police outside of school but managed to "keep his nose clean" at school. In effect, they told Balch that the way a situation was defined — whether or not a boy was a troublemaker — was more important than the actual truth of the situation, whether or not the boy had committed a serious offense.

What's especially sobering about Balch's study is that it's easy to imagine a boy being labeled a "troublemaker" for actually causing trouble, but it's also easy to imagine someone being considered "trouble" simply because of his race (for example, being black in a majority-white school), his economic situation (for example, being a working-class student in an upper-class school), or his sex (just being a boy rather than a girl). In any of those situations, you might come to feel like you can't win.

Being labeled deviant, then, can actually *cause* deviance in two ways:

✔ It can cause you to be apprehended and punished for behavior that someone without that label would have gotten away with — for example, being outside of class without a hall pass, or driving at night with a broken headlight. That adds to your disciplinary record and essentially *makes* you "more deviant" than the people who did the exact same thing but got away with it.

✔ It can make you more likely than someone without that label to actually decide to be deviant because you're in a different set of circumstances. If you figure you're going to get in trouble whether or not you obey the rules, why bother obeying them?

The irony is that slapping someone with a "deviant" label is often intended to shame them into reforming whatever behavior caused a social group or authority figure to define them as deviant in the first place. In the circumstances mentioned earlier, being called "deviant" is unfair in the sense that it doesn't necessarily correspond to any actual deviant behavior — but of course, often it does.

A kid in school may actually have caused some trouble, and a man or woman on the streets may in fact have committed a serious crime. In those cases, calling them "deviant" — an "ex-con" or a "repeat offender" — is perfectly fair in the sense that it actually does describe their behavior. For that reason, it's not illogical or unreasonable for teachers, police, and other authorities to pay attention to that label. If a boy caused trouble once, it only makes sense to think he may be tempted to cause trouble again.

Still, the fact that "deviant" labels can have such serious consequences means that anyone concerned with fairness ought to be concerned with applying them, and with jumping to conclusions about someone's behavior based on any label they may have. This has implications for fighting crime and deviance — as I explain next.

Fighting Crime

Just because the idea of "crime" is socially constructed doesn't mean that crime is okay, or that crime is nothing to be worried about. What counts as "clean" is socially constructed too, but that doesn't mean you never need to shower! One of the reasons sociologists have spent so much time studying crime is to help understand why crime occurs and to give law enforcement officers tools to fight it. In this section, I explain how sociology can be used to help prevent crime — as well as to figure out what to do when people *do* commit crimes.

What works, and what doesn't

In 1997, a teenager named Michael Carneal opened fire at his school in Paducah, Kentucky, killing three students and injuring five others. People in the community said they had absolutely no warning — but was that true? All these things were known about Carneal before the shooting occurred:

His school work was sloppy, and his grades had recently dipped. He had stolen from and vandalized his school.

He was routinely subject to public humiliation, he had poor social skills, and he was a prankster who had thrown a stink bomb at school.

He had been caught looking at pornography on a school computer; in fact, he sold pornography to other students.

He had abnormal fears, and he had written disturbing essays.

He was brutal to animals, he had plastic weapons confiscated from him, and had brought two actual guns to school. He stole guns and money and kept rifles at a friend's house, he threatened his peers and physically hurt at least one classmate, and he openly fantasized about taking over the mall and the school. He threw a bike in a bonfire, owned a copy of the *Anarchist's Cookbook*, shot a cow, and spoke about solving problems with extreme violence.

Anyone in the community would have done anything to prevent the tragic shooting, and yet no one had been able to put together the pieces and prevent the crime. Why not? In the early 2000s, the U.S. Congress asked sociologist Katherine Newman to investigate why school shootings occurred and how they might be prevented.

With psychologists already investigating the problem of school shootings, Congress approached a sociologist because they understood that preventing crime is about more than just understanding "the criminal mind." There's no doubt that it's important to understand the psychological state of those who commit crimes — especially violent crimes — but law enforcement officials can't get inside the heads of all possible criminals, and they can't solve everyone's problems. What government agencies, schools, companies, and even families can do is to build *social structures* that help detect and deter crimes before they happen, as well as help to apprehend suspects after crimes have been committed.

A sociologically informed approach to fighting crime will focus not on the individual criminals but on the circumstances in which crimes are committed. A couple of important sociological insights into crime appear elsewhere in this book: Robert J. Sampson and Stephen Raudenbush's finding that fixing broken windows isn't the best use of police officers' time because people's perceptions of disorder have more to do with the people around them than with their physical surroundings (Chapter 2), and Christopher Winship's study of how a partnership between the Boston Police and black religious leaders helped to dramatically lower the rate of violent crime in Boston (Chapter 10).

Those sociological studies and others (also see Chapter 14) have shown that crime fighting shouldn't just be treated like a game of whack-a-mole, with police officers running to take care of whatever problems happen to arise. Of course they have to do a lot of that, but to *only* do that is to buy into the theory that criminals are "bad people" who just happen to be that way. If that were the only explanation for crime, then crime would be very difficult to predict — bad people can be anywhere.

It's also not enough to just keep tabs on the people who seem to have the strongest motives to commit crimes. That approach can lead to heavy-handed policing of low-income communities, possibly fraying relationships between citizens and cops, and ironically leading to even more crime. If understanding and fighting crime was as simple as figuring out which people might have motives to commit crimes, cops' jobs would be much easier and detective novels would be much more boring.

Sociologists emphasize that crimes take place in a social context, and a good way to prevent and detect those crimes is to help build a social context that makes crime difficult to get away with. When the Boston Police partnered with ministers in the community, they built a trusting relationship with allies who shared their interest in preventing violent crime and could help share influence and information.

So how can all this help prevent school violence? Newman's study produced a book-length report, *Rampage*, that she wrote with several colleagues; it contains detailed analyses of multiple school shootings and makes concrete recommendations that every school can learn from, drawing insights from microsociology (see Chapter 6), network analysis (Chapter 7), and the sociology of organizations (Chapter 12).

The way I opened this section was, intentionally, a little misleading — I mentioned a number of things that were known about Michael Carneal. But by whom were they known? No one person, it turns out, knew all of those things, or even most of them. All of those facts emerged after the shooting, when authorities, journalists, and scholars investigating the case talked to everyone who had any contact with Carneal. All those warning signs were known, but no one individual saw the whole picture. Think about how insights from these sociological perspectives might help administrators understand and prevent school violence:

- **Microsociology.** Many people who knew Carneal were surprised to hear of the shooting because they couldn't believe the Michael Carneal they knew would be the type of person to commit such a horrible act of violence. Erving Goffman, though, clearly points out that people can wear very different masks to different people. The "real Michael" wasn't the Michael his teachers saw, or the Michael his classmates saw, or even the Michael his best friends saw. The "real Michael" was *all* of those people, and it's important to remember that you can't count on any one individual to really know what a potential criminal is capable of. You have to combine multiple reports.

- **Network analysis.** It may seem surprising that so many school shootings occur in close-knit rural or suburban communities, rather than in the supposedly impersonal big cities — but being a part of a tight social network with many overlapping ties also means that there's no escape from uncomfortable social situations. If you're teased at school in the big city, you might go home to a completely different neighborhood with people who think of you differently, but in a small town, you're trapped.

- **Organizational analysis.** Sociologists who have studied organizations also understand that a dense network of social ties doesn't necessarily translate into a free flow of information. People may keep information to themselves because of personal animosities, a fear of being embarrassed, or a fear of being seen as a gossip. Sometimes there are important things that, whether for good reasons or not, you don't tell even your closest friends and coworkers.

One of Newman's recommendations was that schools open channels of communication, especially for potential warning signs, so that someone like a school counselor might have the information they need to appreciate which students are at risk of committing violent acts. Violent acts like homicide and suicide rarely take place without warning; the trick is seeing, and responding to, the signs.

As ads on the New York subway put it, "If you see something, say something." If you have any indication that a person you know is at risk of harming themselves or others, talk about your concerns with a trusted authority figure or a mutual friend. There may be other warning signs that you're not aware of, and sharing information may lead to someone intervening before it's too late.

Cars, crime, and kickbacks

In the 1970s, sociologist Harvey A. Farberman set out to study the market for used cars. He didn't expect it to be a study of crime — he wanted to conduct a microsociological study of how potential buyers interacted with car salesmen. He soon realized, though, that he'd stumbled upon a fascinating case study in the sociology of crime: a social situation where criminal behavior was all but guaranteed by the rules of the game.

In the car business — at least, at that time — the rules of the game were set by the car manufacturers. They had the power to license dealers and to determine how much inventory those dealers were forced to keep on hand. If a manufacturer decided that a given dealer would take on a certain number of cars to sell, that was that; if the dealer didn't have the money to pay upfront for the inventory, the dealer would have to borrow it with interest. Further, the profit to be made on each new car sale was very thin.

So how did dealers stay in business? They exploited their customers through fraudulent service and repair practices — overcharging customers for repairs and doing unnecessary repairs for large sums — and they exploited used-car wholesalers by demanding cash bribes on top of used car trade-ins they sold to the wholesalers for resale. That meant the wholesalers needed cash to pay the bribes, and they earned it by conspiring with *their* customers to defraud the government by receiving a portion of their payments in (untaxed) cash.

By the letter of the law, then, the car retail industry was absolutely packed with criminals. But, Farberman's observations showed, if any individual dealership obeyed the law, it would go out of business; and if *every* dealership obeyed the law, the entire industry would collapse. In setting their prices and policies, argued Farberman, car manufacturers maximized their profits but essentially forced dealerships into criminal practices. Farberman's study provides an example of a social situation where fighting crime could not be a matter of simply arresting all the criminals; to end crime in the retail car market, the way that market operated would have to be fundamentally changed.

America's high incarceration rate

What to do when crimes *are* committed? There's no easy answer to that question either, but again, sociology can lend helpful insight to decision-making authorities. The remarkably high incarceration rate in the United States today is a subject of much discussion by sociologists and criminologists, and by the end of this section it should be clear why.

In general, when a society catches someone having committed a crime, it doles out consequences. There are at least three reasons for this. (See the end of this section for a mention of incarceration as "eye for an eye" retribution.)

✔ **Deterrence.** It's believed that if potential criminals know that it's likely they'll face punishment for committing a crime, they'll be less likely to do so. The harsher the punishment, the greater the disincentive to commit the crime. In this way, people punished for committing crimes are serving as examples to others who might be tempted to follow the same path.

✔ **Prevention.** It's impossible to predict with certainty who might commit a crime, but if someone is proven to have committed a previous crime, it's thought to be a good bet that they'll be tempted to commit the same crime again. Imprisoning criminals helps keep them from committing more crimes.

✔ **Reformation.** If a person commits a crime, there may be something that can be done — psychological therapy, for example, or job training — that can help change the circumstances that led the person to commit that crime. Convicted criminals can be forced, in prison or on probation, to undergo treatment that might make it less likely they will offend again.

Does punishment work? Does it help prevent crime? To some extent, absolutely. The experience of societies in periods of lawlessness — say, due to natural disasters or civil war — shows that although most people can be counted on to behave responsibly, many will take advantage of the situation (and, therefore, take advantage of others). Obviously there are some people who are prone to commit terrible acts of violence, but many others will also commit petty thefts or otherwise behave selfishly in the absence of a rule of law. It's clear that there needs to be *some* form of meaningful punishment to deter and prevent crime.

But how much, and what kind? That's the hard question. Increasing penalties deters crime to some extent, but not always predictably. A potential fine of two million dollars would seem to be enough to keep people from sharing a few songs, but millions of people are apparently unconcerned and do it anyway. (See sidebar, "Don't touch that file.") For four decades the American government has waged a "war on drugs," dramatically increasing fines and prison sentences for drug-related crimes; it's had so little success at actually reducing recreational drug use that President Barack Obama's administration has decided to stop using the term "war on drugs" to describe America's anti-drug efforts.

Besides the fact that punishment doesn't always work at preventing crime, there are two additional points to consider when thinking about how much punishment to dole out, and for what crimes.

First, there's the fact that punishment is not free. Maintaining jails, prisons, and probation officers is a huge expense that normally must be borne by the innocent taxpayers who populate a society. They gain, of course, in being protected from the imprisoned offenders as well as by the fact that the possibility of being imprisoned helps to deter other potential offenders, but it's reasonable to ask whether at some point there are declining returns to that investment. How many people must be imprisoned, and for how long, to keep a society reasonably safe? Money spent on prisons might also be spent on police officers, hospitals, or scientific research. What's the best use of that money?

Also, incarceration can directly or indirectly *cause* crime. The theory is that prisons are places where offenders learn life skills and repent of their crimes, but often the reality is that prisons are places where convicts are under the negative influence (sometimes, the abuse) of other offenders, coming out more crime-prone than they were when they went in — plus, having a grudge to bear against the society that put them behind bars.

Sociologists have also paid close attention to the effect of *stigma*: a social label that causes others to think less of a person. Most employers, for most jobs, in most places, are allowed to investigate the criminal records of potential employees — not just determining whether a potential daycare employee is a convicted sex offender, but asking whether a potential grocery clerk or auto mechanic has ever been convicted of any crime whatsoever. A convict released from prison bears a very heavy stigma that may make it unusually difficult for them to find work or have healthy social relationships. Having been in prison gives a person a label of "deviant" (as explained earlier) that blazes like a neon sign, giving that person an uphill battle to earn trust and opportunities both in and out of the workplace.

The stigma of being an ex-prisoner can cause what sociologists call *secondary deviance*: crime or deviance that is a direct result of the *primary deviance* that first led the person afoul of the law. To some extent this is reasonable and unavoidable — who wouldn't want to know if a potential employee had been in prison? — but it's important to bear in mind when considering how many people to imprison, and for what crimes.

These debates are particularly relevant to the United States today because the "war on drugs" and other changes in U.S. law have led to an incarceration rate that's significantly higher than that of other developed countries. To some extent that observation is neither here nor there because the United States may be unique — maybe Americans are especially crime-prone, or maybe there would be much more crime if there weren't so many potential offenders in prison — but many sociologists and criminologists are concerned, and they believe that changes in U.S. policy are overdue.

Especially troubling to many is the fact that certain groups — especially African-American men — are vastly overrepresented in the U.S. prison population. To the extent that imprisonment does have a negative effect on the imprisoned, minority communities are bearing the brunt of that negative effect. Whether that is appropriate and humane is a question people disagree on — after all, people usually aren't imprisoned for nothing, and with a few exceptions, each individual in prison has in fact committed a serious crime — but sociologists insist it's a question that needs to be looked at very closely.

Many people believe that crimes should be punished, if for no other reason, for the reason that it's "only fair" — that is, that if someone hurts another person, the offender should have harm done to them in return. I don't include this in the list of reasons for incarceration because it's not an empirical argument: If you believe that people should be incarcerated in retribution for crimes, that is a moral belief, not an argument about how to reduce crime. (If you think that incarcerating criminals will make others hesitant to commit crimes, that would be considered a *deterrence* argument, as mentioned elsewhere in this section.) Whether or not you believe criminals should be punished in retribution for their crimes is something you have to decide for yourself, not something a sociologist can decide for you.

Part IV

All Together Now:
The Ins and Outs
of Social
Organization

In this part . . .

Social organization: It's a noble goal, and sometimes it actually works. If you've ever worked for a company, attended a school, joined a social movement, voted, paid taxes, or lived in a city or a suburb (have I caught you yet?), you've been a part of a social organization. In this part, I explain what sociologists have learned about the workings of social organizations.

Chapter 12

Corporate Culture: The Study of Organizations (and Disorganizations)

In This Chapter

▶ Connecting sociology and the world of work

▶ Understanding why bureaucracy works — and doesn't

▶ Being human in an inhuman organization

▶ Opening and closing organizational boundaries

▶ Searching for a purpose

*I*f I asked you to name a society, you'd probably name a country — the society of Kenya, or the society of Vietnam, or the society of the United States. It's true, those are all good examples of societies, but societies can also be smaller: a state or province, a family, and, of course, a corporation. (See Chapter 2 for more on what a "society" is.)

On a day-to-day basis, you may be more deeply involved in the society of your workplace or school than in any other society — including your own family! Corporations, schools, and other social organizations also occupy a lot of people's attention because they're consciously designed . . . and redesigned, and re-redesigned. Everyone wants to know what the best way is to organize a for-profit company or a nonprofit organization or a school or a religious organization so as to help that organization work as effectively and efficiently as possible, which also means keeping all of its members happy!

In this chapter, I explain how sociologists study and think about organizations such as these. I first introduce the general sociological approach to organizations, then explain how sociologists have come to appreciate that organizations are rational systems with purposes . . . but they aren't always rational systems, and they don't always stick to the same purpose. Of course, that might be something you don't need a sociologist to tell you.

The Corporate Conundrum: Making a Profit Isn't as Easy — or as Simple — as it Sounds

Sociologists — working in collaboration with economists and other organizational analysts, for example those at business schools — want to understand how organizations work, and that means acknowledging the reality that people in organizations are facing complicated choices and great uncertainty, and that they're working with limited time and information. Sometimes that means that they hit on brilliant insights, but sometimes it means that they crash and burn. Most organizations do some of each. For-profit corporations want to make profits, which seems like a pretty simple and straightforward task, but companies tie themselves in knots trying to accomplish it. New products, new advertising campaigns, mergers, acquisitions, executive retreats and skit nights…sometimes it seems like companies are running to stand still, or running and still managing to move backwards. "Making a profit" turns out to be a lot less simple than it sounds.

Take Starbucks, for example. The company's official mission statement is "to inspire and nurture the human spirit — one person, one cup, and one neighborhood at a time." Could they *be* any more ambitious? What's wrong with just selling coffee?

There's nothing wrong with just selling coffee — but corporate life is rarely that simple. Imagine that you founded a competing company; one that did not aspire to "nurture the human spirit," but just to sell coffee at a reasonable profit. Seems straightforward . . . until you try to do it.

Where are you going to sell your coffee? Are you going to operate stores, or are you going to have a mail-order operation, or both? Are you going to sell brewed coffee, or just the beans? If you're selling brewed coffee, are you also going to sell espresso drinks? Will you stock flavored syrups and three kinds of milk? What about hot chocolate? Tea? Snacks? You could reasonably extend your product line into all of these areas:

- Frozen drinks
- To-go drinks
- Drinks sold through grocery stores
- Coffee-flavored ice cream
- Coffee mugs
- Coffeemakers

> ✔ Stuffed animals wearing your corporate logo
>
> ✔ Music to listen to while drinking coffee
>
> ✔ Board games to play while drinking coffee

In fact, Starbucks sells all those things — and if you don't, your customers may wonder why not.

Then, after you've decided on a product line and an expansion strategy, you need to put into place a team to manage your employees. At a basic level, you need to manage payroll and benefits; beyond that, you need to worry about hiring, firing, and promotion. And what about training? Then there's the question of your corporate culture; you want to make your employees happy. Should you hold holiday parties or summer picnics? Maybe organize volunteer outings to help build playgrounds and clean up parks?

When you get that far, you're going to be looking at questions of optimal organization and product flow. Are you going to own your stores, or franchise them out? From whom are you going to buy your coffee, and how are you going to make sure they keep up with your demand at a price you can afford? Are you going to manufacture your own paper coffee cups, or are you going to hire another company to do that? If you're facing competition from a smaller coffee company, should you try to buy that company?

At every level of organization, there are many, many difficult choices — and the bigger your organization gets, the more choices and possibilities you have. Starbucks's mission statement does mention a "cup," but fundamentally it allows the company to do anything that might be considered "nurturing the human spirit," so long as that spirit nurturing turns a profit. That gives the company a lot of options, and potentially a lot of frustrations.

To begin understanding the sociological approach to organizations, in the next section I describe Max Weber's classic theory of bureaucracy.

Weber's Big Idea About Organizations

The great sociologist Max Weber, as I explain in Chapter 3, believed that over time, society has become more and more rational — that is, that society has become increasingly based on formal rules that are carefully planned and documented, are rigorously followed, and that apply to everyone regardless of who they are, where they come from, or what they believe.

Sound familiar? It might sound to you like the way things work at your school or workplace, where there are a million confusing rules and forms upon forms to fill out, and where it may seem like things would be so much easier if people would just focus on solving problems instead of nit-picking about every little thing. In one form or another, your school or workplace is a *bureaucracy* — and Weber believed that bureaucratic organization is one of the hallmarks of contemporary society.

Weber's definition of a bureaucracy is in many ways the starting point for today's sociology of organizations. According to Weber, bureaucracies have several key characteristics:

- ✔ A bureaucracy is an organization defined by written rules. A bureaucratic organization may have many different parts, but the relationships among those parts are defined in the rules — which also define the limits of the organization.

- ✔ Each person who works in a bureaucracy has a given set of responsibilities, which they are expected to fulfill within prescribed limits.

- ✔ Positions in a bureaucracy are organized in a hierarchy, where it's clear who has authority over whom.

- ✔ Bureaucracies hire and promote on the basis of formal credentials (like school degrees or professional certificates), training, and job performance — not on the basis of personal preference or affinity.

- ✔ Everything a person in a bureaucracy needs to perform their job is supplied to them by the organization — which, then, owns those supplies.

What this adds up to is that in a bureaucracy, a position is separated from the person *in* that position. The people in bureaucracies are essentially parts in a machine — and if a part in a machine breaks, it gets replaced by another part that's going to do the exact same thing.

By contrast, think about a group of friends. A group of friends is a social organization, with members working together to achieve goals (throw a party, go out on the town, share information about other groups) — but it's an informal organization, where who you are is intimately tied to what you do in that organization. Maybe you have an awesome home entertainment system for your friends to enjoy, but if for some reason you leave your group of friends, they don't get to keep the entertainment system. You don't leave an empty "position" in your group of friends; they may or may not bring in someone new, and if they do, that new person will have different possessions and qualities to bring to the group.

At a corporation, on the other hand, if you quit you don't get to take your computer and your desk — those belong to the company, and they'll be used by the person they hire to replace you, who will do more or less exactly the same thing you did. A company is a bureaucracy: a permanent, formal organization that follows a set of rules.

Getting a leg up on bureaucracy

For my niece Madeline's second birthday, my mom gave her a small table and chairs that came in a box sealed from the factory. When they opened the box to assemble the table, though, my mom and my sister discovered that the table had only three legs — clearly, there had been an error on the packing line and not all the parts had been included. Mom called the company and asked if they would please send a replacement leg so that the table would stand properly. No, she was told, she would need to pack the table back up and return the whole thing to the store, where it would be replaced with a complete table.

But, my mom said, it would be incredibly inconvenient to do that — and anyway, she'd already thrown all the packing material away. Didn't the company have a factory with *thousands* of little table legs? Couldn't they just grab one and send it to her? No, she was told; that would be a "special order" that would take several weeks to fulfill and would cost almost as much as buying an entirely new table-and-chairs set.

Mom tried again: What if the company opened a box with a complete table and chairs, took a leg out of the box, and sent it to Mom? The result would be the exact same as if Mom returned her set: The factory would have a table without a leg, and Madeline would have a table with four legs. Nope, Mom was told. They couldn't do that.

In the end, the company recognized how frustrated Mom was getting — and sent her *an entirely new table and chairs*, without making her return the one she had. Because of the company's bureaucratic organization, it was easier for them to do that than to break the rules and open a sealed box or take a table leg off the assembly line. Sometimes, when sticking to their own rules, bureaucracies end up acting in a paradoxical, wasteful manner. Many companies consider it better to be a little wasteful than to allow employees to break any rules and risk the resulting disorganization and confusion.

Because they're so impersonal, bureaucracies can seem unfair, unkind, and bizarrely ineffective. (See sidebar, "Getting a leg up on bureaucracy.") You may need something from a bureaucracy that seems simple and straightforward, but if the bureaucracy isn't set up to do that, it's not going to happen. Banks may refuse loans to good, reliable people because they don't have any credit history; bars may refuse to admit a grey-haired senior citizen who doesn't have a driver's license to prove he's over 21; and an ATM machine may eat your card because you accidentally mistype your security code.

There is, though, a reason that companies continue to organize themselves bureaucratically. Even if bureaucracies seem to be acting in an absurd manner, it may *collectively* benefit the entire company to set up firm rules and expectations from which employees are not allowed to deviate.

A friend of mine was given a troubleshooting job at a top software company precisely *because* she didn't have much experience with programming — the company had learned that when it hired technical whizzes for that troubleshooting position, the whizzes would come up with inventive solutions that no one else could understand, which made the software impossible for anyone else to fix when something else went wrong. The company just wanted someone who would follow the rules and do exactly as they were told in each given situation.

Furthermore, the fact that bureaucracies (officially, at least) don't discriminate can be for the better. The fact that loans are now based on credit scores means that someone can't be given a loan for being a "good guy," but it also means that someone can't be denied a loan because of their race or sex.

Still, being caught in a bureaucracy can seem uncomfortably impersonal — because, after all, it is. That's why Weber called rationality an "iron cage." (See Chapter 3 for more on Weber and his "iron cage.")

Rational Systems: Bureaucracy at its Purest

One of the best sociological books on the subject of social organization is Richard W. Scott's *Organizations: Rational, Natural, and Open Systems*. In the next three sections of this chapter, I borrow Scott's insightful typology to discuss these three different ways that sociologists have come to understand organizations. Every organization is rational, natural, *and* open; I'll explain what each of those terms mean, one by one. First, I describe "rational systems."

In Scott's typology, "rational," "natural," and "open" are three different ways to understand organizations, not three different kinds of organizations. Be careful not to be confused and think that some organizations are "rational," others are "natural," and still others are "open" — *every* organization has *all* of those qualities.

Measuring the shovels: Efficiency! Efficiency!

The term *rational system* refers to the fact that any organization is typically designed to work as efficiently as possible at accomplishing some set task. A bureaucracy as described by Weber (see previous section) is a classic rational system: an organization that works like a machine. In this sense, almost all formal organizations — that is, organizations with rules and defined membership — are rational systems. Just because they're not *always* rational doesn't mean they aren't designed with a goal in mind, or that they don't generally accomplish that goal in some form or to some extent.

An engineer-turned-management consultant named Frederick Taylor was the all-time greatest proponent of rational systems. He recognized that organizations weren't always rational, but he thought that was a problem that ought to be fixed. In Chapter 3, I explain that the first sociologists believed that sociological research could help to design the ideal society; if we were to understand exactly how societies work, we could fix social problems like we repair cars and TVs. Taylor had exactly this view of organizations, and in the early 20th century he actually undertook to study particular organizations and help their owners or administrators make them work better.

Taylor's approach became known as "scientific management" or "Taylorism." He would visit organizations and study every detail of how they worked, then recommend how their operations could be revised to make them work better. He had four main principles:

✔ Instead of guessing at how to do a task most efficiently, study the task scientifically and choose the method proven to be most effective.

✔ Select employees based on precise qualifications, and train them in the most efficient work practices rather than leaving them to figure things out for themselves.

✔ Supervise workers closely, and retrain them when necessary.

✔ Give managers the job of designing efficient work methods and supervising the workers who actually accomplish the tasks.

Most famously, Taylor observed steel mills and offered recommendations as to how to improve every aspect of the steel production process — from the specific tasks each worker was given to the communication systems used in mills to the way the mill floor was laid out and the way material moved from one part of the mill to another. He even went so far as to study the size of shovels used by workers and determine what size shovel allowed a worker to scoop the most coal over the course of a workday.

Tensions between labor and management were high in Taylor's time, and just as Comte believed that sociology could bring peace to society, Taylor believed that his version of scientific management could resolve labor disputes: If the ideal work conditions were determined by objective scientific observation rather than by the whims of managers, how could workers possibly argue with that?

Quite easily, as it turned out. Taylor appreciated the role of financial incentives and argued that his system fairly compensated dedicated workers — he held up one particular steel worker, Schmidt, as an example, and pointed out that Schmidt was working more efficiently under Taylor's system and making more money to boot. The steel company profited, and so did Schmidt . . . thus, scientific management was a win-win proposition.

Many workers and labor advocates, though, saw Taylor's methods as dehumanizing and brutal. In breaking down jobs into their individual components and telling each worker precisely how to do his job, his critics said, Taylor was taking away workers' autonomy and making their work miserable. Plus, it seemed to assume they were too stupid to know how to do their own jobs. The famous muckraker Upton Sinclair pointed out that yes, Schmidt was making 61 percent more pay under Taylor's system . . . but for doing 362 percent more work. When workers at one Massachusetts plant were subjected to Taylor's methods, they went on strike and inspired Congressional hearings where Taylor spent four days defending his methods.

Sociologists today agree that Taylor wasn't fundamentally mistaken in his belief that evaluating work processes objectively, especially in situations where tasks are rote, is a better strategy for efficient production than allowing each worker to independently create a work plan. Still, they also agree that Taylor made a basic error in thinking that it was a good idea to treat human workers like machines.

Even when there's fair pay for efficient work, people are not machines and they're apt to balk when it seems like there's no room for individuality, variety, or personal initiative in their work. Taylorism may not be wrong . . . but it's not exactly right, either.

The bounds of reason

Taylor's approach makes most sense when work is predictable and easily routinized — but of course, for many jobs that's not the case. In many cases, organizations and the people who work for them have to deal with ambiguous situations that change from week to week, day to day, or even moment to moment. In those situations, it's just not reasonable to expect a worker to follow a strict set of rules. Workers have to be flexible and make decisions based on changing circumstances.

So what can you do if you want to make someone in a job like that as efficient as possible? Well, you can take a few actions:

- You can equip them with general principles about what decisions to make in which circumstances. For example, you might tell a manager not to give any customers special accommodations unless it seems like they're about to switch their business to another company.

- You can try to localize the decision-making, so that the same people make the same kinds of decisions. For example, many stores have designated returns departments with people who are specially trained to accept returns — so busy cashiers don't have to make decisions about whether or not to accept returns.

- You can have people work in teams to make complex decisions, so no one worker is given all the decision-making power.

Even so, dealing with uncertainty is a major problem for most organizations; they spend a lot of effort trying to design and maintain systems that will stand up to different circumstances. (I explain more about the general problem of dealing with the environment in the section on open systems.)

Especially for the very complex decisions that are made by the highest-ranking members of an organization, a particular challenge is to decide how much information to gather before making a decision. Imagine you're running the coffee business I describe in the first section of this chapter, and you're trying to decide where to open your next location. You have to consider rents, local laws, the location of competitors, the potential supply of workers and customers, and many other factors. How do you know when you've gathered enough information to make the best decision about where to open your next store?

Herbert Simon, one of the all-time great scholars of organizations, coined the term "bounded rationality" to refer to the fact that the rationality of human decision-makers is "bounded" by the amount of time they have to gather information and make decisions — as well as, needless to say, by the limited computing power of their human brains. (For more on decision-making by individuals, see Chapter 6.)

Simon's work has been a major influence on management consultants, who are today's Frederick Taylors. Management consultants are specialists in organizational behavior — many consultants, in fact, have been trained as sociologists — who are hired by companies, as Taylor was, to serve as outside evaluators who can help a company design its operations as effectively and efficiently as possible.

Not only do management consultants have to consider the bounds on the rationality of the people at the companies they're studying, they need to consider the bounds on their *own* rationality. My friend became a management consultant after graduating from college, and I was surprised when he told me that his company might spend as little as two weeks studying a company before making a series of recommendations. When I asked why they didn't spend more time, he explained that they *could* spend a lot more time — but that probably wouldn't result in recommendations that were dramatically more useful. Two weeks, his firm had learned, is enough time to gather most of the important information about a company's operations.

The success of management consultants would seem to vindicate Taylor and his overall approach: Objective, scientific study can help improve business operations by a great deal. But why do businesses need to hire *outside* evaluators? Why hire a 21-year-old who knows nothing about your company to make management recommendations, rather than turning to a company veteran who knows all the organization's ins and outs?

There are a few good reasons for this, but one of them is that sometimes people are more willing to listen to an outsider than to someone who they know well. Someone you know well may have biases or conflicts of interest that might get in the way of his making decisions that are best for the organization. How can you objectively decide which of your employees' jobs to eliminate when you've become friends with all of them? People's rationality is limited not only by their time and brainpower, but by the fact that they *are* human, with human relationships and human needs. They're not robots, and that's the insight at the heart of the next perspective: the natural system perspective.

Natural Systems: We're Only Human

As the limits of Taylor's "scientific management" became clear, sociologists started to realize that understanding organizations means understanding the people who make up the organizations. People are *not* interchangeable cogs who behave like robots; they're human beings who behave like . . . well, like human beings. In this section, I first describe a famous set of studies that demonstrated the limitations of Taylorism; then I explain how this insight led to the "corporate culture" movement that has brought us innovations like Casual Fridays and logo-printed baseball caps. (Richard W. Scott, the sociologist who devised the rational/natural/open system typology, also considers the drift of organizational purpose to be an insight of the natural-system perspective; I discuss that idea at the end of this chapter.)

Making people feel special: The Hawthorne Studies and the Human Relations Movement

In the 1920s and 30s, a team supervised by Elton Mayo, a professor at Harvard Business School, undertook a Taylor-like study of productivity at the Hawthorne works, a manufacturing plant near Chicago. Like good social scientists, they took a measure of productivity under the initial conditions as a baseline, then subjected certain groups of workers to changes in their working conditions to see whether they could increase the workers' productivity.

In their experiments, the investigators tried changing many aspects of the working environment:

- They changed the levels of lighting, from especially bright to especially dim.

- They tried shortening the work day, to see whether that would increase workers' hourly productivity.

- They varied the length of breaks the workers were given.

✔ They tried giving the workers food on breaks.

✔ They varied the way workers were paid, experimenting with rewarding workers for individual productivity and rewarding them for overall group productivity.

This went on for years, and the researchers were confounded to see that no matter what they did, just about *every* variation they introduced improved productivity! At least in the short term, almost every change made to the work environment caused the workers' productivity to increase. In the end, Mayo concluded that the workers were becoming more productive not because of the nature of the specific changes, but because *they knew they were being observed.*

Even though in most circumstances the workers weren't being rewarded for the additional productivity, their behavior changed simply because of the way they felt about the situation. In later interviews, they explained to Mayo's team that they enjoyed being a part of the investigation and that they appreciated feeling like they were being paid attention to, that their opinions and experiences were noted and valued.

This discovery — which later became known as "the Hawthorne Effect" — provided Mayo and other sociologists with direct evidence that Taylor had been mistaken in thinking that the best strategy for increasing productivity was to take away employees' individual initiative, to tell them how to do their own jobs.

The workers who protested Taylor's policies, it turned out, had been right: people do their best work when they feel valued and respected, not when they're treated like robots. (If you've ever been treated that way at a job, you understand why it doesn't help workers' motivation!)

This insight provided the genesis of what was called "the Human Relations Movement." Based on the Hawthorne Studies and other research, Mayo argued that effective organizations need to pay attention to the relationships among their workers. Many people believe that the most important factor in job happiness is not the nature of your work but rather the nature of your coworkers: If you like the people you work with and feel respected by them, you'll give the job your all. People want to feel like they're part of a team, not like they're part of a machine.

This meant, said Mayo, that both sociologists and CEOs needed to pay attention to these aspects of corporate life:

✔ The relationships among workers, the social groups they form that overlap with their working groups. For people working in a company, their social relationships are just as important as — if not more important than — their working relationships.

✔ Communication among workers and management. Workers need to feel like they have a personal stake in the company, like their experiences and opinions are heeded and respected. Communication can't just flow from managers to workers; it has to flow from workers to managers as well.

✔ Managers' skill as leaders. A good manager isn't just a paragon of efficiency; they have social skills as well and can inspire workers to do their best. A manager who doesn't win their employees' respect and admiration isn't a good manager, no matter what their level of technical skill and professional judgment.

To be precise, the Hawthorne Studies didn't prove that workers' productivity improved if they actually had influence over their work situation; it improved if they *felt like* they had influence. Today's corporate culture movement is as much about cultivating workers' feelings toward their employers as it is about actually giving them a voice in their work situations.

Corporate culture: Trust falls and free coffee

Have you ever worked for, or heard about, a company that takes any of these actions?

✔ Holds corporate retreats so employees can get to know one another?

✔ Gives employees free coffee, soda, or even beer?

✔ Creates mousepads, posters, t-shirts, pens, and other items with the company logo?

✔ Allows employees to take break from works to play Foosball or ping-pong?

✔ Allows employees to bring pets to work?

All of these things would absolutely appall Frederick Taylor, a man for whom efficiency was the bottom line. None of these things have anything to do with getting a job done — in fact, they all seem like perks and activities that are liable to be distractions. So why are they such common practices in the corporate world?

These practices are the legacy of Mayo's Human Relations Movement. Today, owners of corporations appreciate that if workers aren't happy, they won't be productive. This is true of any workplace, but it's especially true of modern workplaces, where much of the routine work that formerly was done by people has been automated, and more people are called upon to be creative at work. The dot-com boom of the 1990s saw astonishingly open workplaces sprout up in Silicon Valley and other technology hotbeds, with workers being encouraged to come and go as they pleased, treating their workplaces as extensions of their homes. The Google corporate campus is famous for its open plan, its comfortable feel, and its amenities like food, drink, and exercise equipment.

Today, a great number of businesspeople and social scientists study the work environment in what is known as the study of "corporate culture." Some of these studies are very practical — how many parties should a company hold each year? — and some of them are abstract and academic, looking for parallels between the way corporate culture works and the way culture works generally (see Chapter 5). What they all share is a fundamental acknowledgement that life at work is about much more than just "getting the job done."

One danger with attending to "corporate culture" is thinking that a surface layer of attention to employees as individuals is good enough — that it can remove the need for an organizational structure that actually gives those employees a voice in how things are done.

Larry Summers's hard lesson in soft skills

"Soft skills" is a management term used to describe what you might call "people skills": the ability to get along with others and win their trust. In his five years as president of Harvard University — ironically, the same institution where Elton Mayo founded the Human Relations Movement — Lawrence Summers learned the hard way just how important "soft skills" are.

Summers became president of Harvard in 2001, amidst great fanfare and excitement. He was a brilliant economist who had been one of the youngest people ever tenured at Harvard and then had served as Secretary of the Treasury under President Bill Clinton. He had lots of ideas about how to increase Harvard's efficiency, and he wasn't afraid to ask hard questions about the status quo. Harvard's governing body hired Summers because they knew he would have the tenacity to push for a major campus expansion they viewed as important.

After Summers was in office, though, he made one human-relations misstep after another.

Faculty and administrators felt that he ran the university like a rigorous graduate seminar, asking his tough questions in a way that made them feel threatened, uncomfortable, and disrespected. Cornel West, a professor of African-American studies who was one of the university's most popular faculty members, abruptly left for Princeton University when Summers offended him by suggesting that West was neglecting his academic research. Most damningly, Summers tactlessly suggested to a conference on women in science that they should consider whether the traditional dominance of men in math and science was partially due to men's greater inborn ability in those areas. Eventually, the arts and science faculty voted that they had no confidence in Summers, and he resigned in disgrace.

As sound as Summers's organizational ideas may have been, his experience at Harvard demonstrated the danger of being insensitive to your employees' feelings. As Elton Mayo knew, a leader who fails to inspire is a leader who fails.

Getting down to business: Dolly knows best

In the 1980 movie *9 to 5*, Dabney Coleman plays a sexist, know-it-all boss who thinks he knows how to run an office. He doesn't allow his workers to display any personal belongings; their bare desks are arranged in perfect rows. "An office that looks efficient," goes his motto, "is efficient!" He's inattentive to his employees' personal needs, and in fact sexually harasses his secretary, played by Dolly Parton.

When an unusual chain of circumstances leads to Coleman being absent from the office for several weeks, Parton and two other employees — played by Lily Tomlin and Jane Fonda — sign his name to memos changing office policies. Personal photos and decorations are encouraged, new flexible time-share arrangements are instituted, and the company even opens a daycare for the convenience of working parents. Coleman is flabbergasted when he returns, but before he has time to change anything back, the chairman of the board arrives and personally praises Coleman for the dramatic rise in productivity Coleman's brought about with "his" new policies.

The movie plays this all for laughs, but it reflects a very real change in corporate culture that was taking place at that time, as women — often working mothers — poured into offices and companies that once ran Tayloresque operations with rows of men sitting in desks and working from nine to five came to terms with the reality that the members of their new workforce had different needs. The movie reflects companies' growing understanding that workers are not interchangeable, and that running a workplace based on standards of pure "efficiency" is actually not all that efficient.

In a study of corporate whistleblowers, sociologist Jim Detert found that almost all companies encourage their employees to communicate openly with management — but that when employees actually do express grievances or make suggestions, they're very often dismissed offhand. (Executives are then mystified when it's revealed that there are major problems with their operation — "Why didn't anyone *tell* us?") Mousepads, polo shirts, and flashy performance awards are no substitute for corporate policies that genuinely respect all members of an organization.

Open Systems: The Whole Wide World of Work

Both the rational-system and the natural-system perspectives attend to life *inside* of organizations; but over time, sociologists came to realize that it's impossible to really understand any organization without understanding its environment: all the social conditions surrounding the organization. In this section, I discuss the topics of setting organizational boundaries, seeing organizations as networks, institutional isomorphism (a.k.a. the "me-toos"), and organizational mission drift.

Keeping the riff-raff out: Setting organizational boundaries

The fundamental insight of the open-system perspective is that no organization is an island.

Think of a very simple organization: two kids running a lemonade stand. The life of the organization is in its relationships with the outside world. These kids need a steady supply of lemonade mix from the kitchen cupboard or the grocery store; and they need an equally steady supply of customers who will buy the lemonade. With a more complex organization, such as the coffee chain I describe at the start of this chapter, the organization's relationships with the outside world can be fearfully complex.

First, they have their suppliers. Just to name a few:

- Coffee growers
- Paper cup manufacturers
- Providers of heat, water, and other utilities

Then, they have their customers, including:

- Individuals who buy coffee
- Franchisees who buy the rights to sell coffee
- Supermarkets who buy coffee in bulk

Finally, there are all the other individuals and organizations they must deal with:

- Governments and regulatory agencies
- Landlords
- Transportation companies
- Competitors

If any of these people make any significant change, the organization is going to have to change, too. Frederick Taylor might be able to walk into a Starbucks today and come up with an ideal workflow and organization, but that might all change tomorrow if circumstances change. Changing operational procedures is costly and troublesome for any organization, especially if an organization needs to exert effort just to find out what conditions *are*; so organizations seek to minimize uncertainty.

One relatively straightforward way to minimize uncertainty is to absorb uncertain elements of the environment right into your organization.

Coffee suppliers giving you a hard time and changing their prices often? Buy a farm and grow your own coffee! Franchisees getting hard to negotiate with? Then operate your own stores! Landlords giving you headaches? Buy your own building!

The logic is appealing, and in fact many large companies do expand to own almost the entire chain of production. A retail store might operate its own factory in China, ship its own products to the United States, distribute them itself, and own and operate its own stores; just about the only things those companies don't own are their customers!

Companies can further insulate themselves against instability by expanding into other lines. The company that owns the Gap mid-price clothing retailer, for example, also owns the high-end Banana Republic chain and the low-priced Old Navy chain; whether sales sag at the high end or the low end of the market, Gap, Inc. has its other stores to help pick up the slack. Some companies, known as "conglomerates," even go so far as to buy completely unrelated businesses — like diversifying a stock portfolio.

At some point, though, it becomes unwieldy to manage. Companies often find it more efficient to outsource operations like cleaning, transportation, and security, rather than try to run those things themselves. In other words, organizations need to set their boundaries — they need to decide which operations will be part of the organization and which will be part of the environment. The best answer is rarely obvious, but it's a question that all organizations need to consider.

Organizations as networks, networks in organizations

In Chapter 7, I describe the network perspective in sociology and explain what network analysts have contributed to the understanding of society. Understanding the complex nature social networks is key to understanding organizations.

Most of my focus in Chapter 7 is on networks of individuals: Your personal network is the network of individuals you're acquainted with or otherwise connected to. If you read that chapter and the earlier sections of this chapter, you can see how network analysis fits well with the natural-system view of organizations. You have a professional network that might be drawn on a map of your company's bureaucracy: There are people you're officially expected to know and interact with in certain ways as part of your job.

On top of that, however, you also have a *personal* network at your company: You have friends at work, and your personal relationships certainly don't overlap perfectly with your professional relationships. This distinction becomes important when you consider that professional information can flow through personal networks just as quickly, if not even *more* quickly, than through professional networks.

To add another layer of complexity, consider the fact that your personal and professional networks both spread well beyond your company. Many of these connections have little or nothing to do with your professional work, but many of them do — companies are connected by complicated webs of personal ties in addition to all the professional ties they need to maintain. This can be extremely tricky for companies to negotiate, and sociologists appreciate that a company's environment impacts that company through both personal and professional networks.

Institutional isomorphism: If that company jumped off a cliff, would your company jump off a cliff, too?

If you've been reading this chapter from the beginning, you've seen how the tidy world of Frederick Taylor has come unglued as social scientists have revealed one reason after another why understanding organizational life isn't like understanding a machine. To some extent it's accurate to say that an effective organization is designed like an efficient machine, but the more closely you look at the realities of organizational life, the more clear it becomes that "efficiency" and "effectiveness" are very often not things that can be objectively measured.

When organizations face so many choices about what to do and how to do it, it can be hard to see what they're "supposed" to be doing. You may recognize this feeling from your own life: Think of your first day at a new school or in a new job. You walk into the place with a general idea of what you're supposed to be doing, but there's still a lot you don't know and you're not going to be explicitly told. What are you supposed to wear? What are you supposed to talk about? How often are you supposed to take breaks? If the coffee is gone, whose problem is that? What you'll probably end up doing is just looking around and doing whatever everybody else is doing.

Organizations — from governments to retailers to nonprofits — have the same problem, and often they solve it in the same way: by doing what everyone else is doing. This is called *isomorphism*.

Sociologists Paul DiMaggio and Walter W. Powell note that there are three different reasons why companies behave in an isomorphic manner — in other words, why they copycat one another.

- ✔ **Coercive isomorphism** happens when an organization feels like it needs to act in a certain way or it will be punished (formally or informally). For example, a country that doesn't respect certain human rights will find itself facing economic sanctions from the rest of the world — if it drafts children into its army or denies women the right to vote, it will be ostracized from the global community.

- ✔ **Mimetic isomorphism** is instinctive behavior in response to uncertainty, like when you're unsure what to wear so you decide to wear what everyone else is wearing. Say that hypothetical coffee company doesn't know whether or not to sell tea; it might be profitable, or it might not. What to do? Why not see what the *other* coffee companies are doing, and follow suit?

- ✔ **Normative isomorphism** is, according to DiMaggio and Powell, the result of professionalization. Though individual health clinics, in a private healthcare system like in the United States, compete with one another for patients, it's in the interest of the entire medical field for doctors and nurses to be trained only at certain accredited institutions. This means that healthcare professionals across the United States are similarly trained and are bound to follow similar procedures no matter where they work.

Sociologist John Meyer has spent his career studying institutional isomorphism, and he believes that the pressures for organizations to conform are so great that they'll often converge on the same way of doing things even when it seems completely illogical. He points out, for example, that tiny, desperately poor countries will found their own national airlines even when their people are starving; they feel they need to win the respect of the international community, and they don't think they can do that without having things like a national airline. Again, this may remind you of your own behavior — have you ever spent money on a status symbol when you really ought to have used it for something else?

In Chapter 5 I explain the sociological difference between "culture" and "structure," and the debate over the role culture plays in society. The work of John Meyer and like-minded sociologists is a demonstration of the importance of culture: If structure were all that mattered, each organization would do exactly what its unique circumstances dictated, regardless of what other organizations are up to — unless those organizations are directly forcing compliance with a certain behavior. In many cases, though, cultural ideas about what they're "supposed" to be doing actually define how organizations see themselves and set their priorities.

The world's smartest sheep

A colleague and I spent several years studying universities around the world; specifically, we looked at changes in the academic subjects that were taught and studied there. We found that to an amazing extent, universities from Malawi to Jamaica to England to Japan maintained similar curricula, and that their curricula changed in the same ways over the course of the 20th century. The social sciences (especially sociology!) became studied much more frequently around the world, and the humanities much less frequently. This was true even among countries that were very different in many ways — faculty at their universities seemed to imitate one another like sheep in a field.

Why did all these universities change in the same ways? All three of the mechanisms identified by Paul DiMaggio and Walter Powell (see "Institutional isomorphism" section of this chapter) were at play. To some extent universities needed to pursue certain subjects to please funders and attract students (coercive isomorphism), to some extent they converged on the same way of doing things because all their faculty were trained at the same institutions (normative isomorphism), and to some extent they just pursued certain subjects because that's what everyone else was doing (mimetic isomorphism).

It's an especially interesting example of isomorphism, we think, because universities claim to present *the truth*. The subjects taught at colleges are supposedly the most important subjects for people in the world to know about. The fact that university curricula are becoming more and more similar around the world is evidence, we believe, that people in different countries are becoming more and more similar in the way they see the world, in what they think is important to know and do. (See Chapter 16 for more on globalization.)

Mission drift: Searching for a purpose

If you need any further evidence that social organizations are more than just machines doing set jobs, consider how often their missions drift from what they were originally "designed" to do.

- Political parties may change their positions over the decades, as other parties rise and fall and different coalitions come together to support the parties. The current Republican Party in the United States is the same party that President Lincoln was part of in the 1860s, but it's not certain that Lincoln would consider himself a Republican today.

- Businesses may switch their products as the market changes. For example, when the success of Starbucks demonstrated how much customers were willing to pay for a cup of coffee, Dunkin' Donuts switched its business model and now makes most of its profits not from doughnuts but from coffee.

✔ Charismatic leaders may sway the focus of an organization. For example, as leader of the Guggenheim Foundation, Thomas Krens controversially turned the organization's focus from maintaining its landmark museum in New York City to expanding is presence with new museums in cities around the world.

As several sociologists have noted, when established, organizations tend to focus on preserving themselves rather than on fulfilling their mission; if self-preservation leads down a different road than the organization initially followed, it will tend to go down that road.

Occasionally this means a dramatic about-face in an organization's purpose, but more often changes in organizational purpose occur in a gentle drift. One function that used to be performed is no longer performed, and one new function is added. A former goal is dropped, and a new one acquired. Before you know it, the organization is doing something very different than it was doing in the first place.

Given that complex organizations may have a large number of potential goals to achieve, this "mission drift" can happen very easily. In fact, some sociologists wonder whether it even makes sense to think of complex organizations as having any real "purpose" in any meaningful sense of that word.

In 1972, social scientists Michael D. Cohen, James G. March, and Johan P. Olsen invented what they called the "Garbage Can Model" of organizations. When very complex organizations are put in highly uncertain situations, Cohen, March, and Olsen argued, the result can be that the organization's behaviors seem to have little to do with either problems to be solved or with reasonable solutions to those problems. There are any number of actions the organization can take at any time, and they're taken almost randomly, as though they were being pulled out of an overflowing garbage can. Each action has some costs but reaps some rewards, and the organization lumbers along aimlessly.

Cohen, March, and Olsen's classic example was a university: There are so many different things a university can do — regarding teaching, research, administration, public outreach, student life — that might qualify as part of its mission, and a university's decision-making structure is often so sprawling and decentralized, that a university can seem to be doing a little bit of everything at once, without a clear purpose to any of its actions. No wonder Larry Summers was frustrated! (See sidebar, "Larry Summers's hard lesson in soft skills.")

All this may make it sound like organizations are completely ineffective — and indeed, it often seems that way! But in fact they are not; they're powerful means to accomplish collective goals. If the nature of those goals drifts around from time to time . . . well, that's how people act individually. Why shouldn't they act that way collectively?

Chapter 13

The Rules of the Game: Social Movements and Political Sociology

In This Chapter

▶ Understanding the role of government in society

▶ Thinking about power: how it's shared, and not shared

▶ Getting social movements off the ground

*W*hen you're paying your taxes or applying for a passport, it may seem like government is all-powerful. Government decides what you can and can't do, where you can and can't go, what money it takes and what money it lets you keep. With all these rules, regs, and restrictions, it seems like "government" and "society" are the same thing.

It's true that government has a unique role in society; it's the manager of society, determining the rules of the game and the allocation of resources. But government is only a *part* of society: Government is affected by social forces outside itself, and it often changes. Sometimes those changes are sudden and violent — as in political revolutions — and sometimes those changes are gradual, with laws and policies shifting slowly over many years or decades.

Political sociologists study not only the way government works, but the way it interacts with other social institutions. In this chapter, I first explain, from a sociological perspective, what government *is*. Then I explain how sociologists think about power in society, and finally I summarize what sociologists have discovered about social movements formed to effect change in government and society.

Government: Governing and Being Governed

So what *is* government, and how does it work? Those are big-picture questions, and sociologists who study them have to step way back and consider many different societies at many points in time. In this section, I first explain what "the state" is, and then tell you what we know about the causes of political revolutions — the points at which everything can change, and at which all bets are off.

Social structure and the state

The United States uses the term "state" to refer to one of the 50 little governments that make up the nation, but sociologists and political scientists use the term "the state" to refer to the overall government. Like many social institutions, "the state" (a.k.a. "the government") is something people know when they see it, but it can be slippery to define. Think of all these different examples of governments:

- Traditional rule by wise elders (A tribal chieftain and a tribal council)
- Imperial republic (The Roman Empire)
- Monarchy (King Arthur and the Knights of the Round Table)
- Democratic republic (The Canadian Prime Minister and Parliament)
- Theocracy (The Supreme Leader of Iran, with a Council of Guardians and Assembly of Experts)
- Communist republic (The Chinese President, National People's Congress, and State Council)

They're all very different, but what they have in common is that they're the *legitimate users of force.* In other words, a government is, fundamentally, that organization in society that reserves for itself — or has delegated to it — the ultimate right to use force to compel people to behave in a certain way. If you are going to use any kind of force to bend people to your will, you had best have the support of your society's government or you could find yourself in trouble.

Beyond this basic, defining characteristic, governments take many different forms. They arise, persist, and end for different reasons. Some governments are pure dictatorships, where a leader enforces their will over a group of people simply because they have influence over the army and the police and can punish anyone who does not do as they say. Most, though, at least nominally govern with the consent of the governed — in other words, they have the support of the majority of the people in their power. In most countries today, the majority of citizens support the *system* of government, even if not the specific people who are in power at any given time.

Political scientists and legal scholars are specifically interested in the workings of government, sometimes very particular governments. They share many interests with sociologists, but fundamentally, the reason you'd call yourself a "political sociologist" instead of a "political scientist" is that you're interested in the workings of society *generally*, not just in the specific workings of government. The core questions political sociologists ask about government are:

> How does government work, *and* . . .

> How does it *interact* with the rest of society?

Look back at the list of government examples. It includes several different types of government, such as theocracy, monarchy, and communist republic. Sociologists would like to know how each of those types of government work, but they'd also like to know *why* different societies have different types of government. Is it just a coincidence that China is a communist country, Canada is a democratic republic, and Iran is a theocracy? (A "theocracy" is a country where religious leaders also control the government.) Maybe . . . or maybe there's something about each of those societies that caused those different types of government to arise. That's what sociologists would like to know.

They'd also like to know how each of those different types of government interacts with other social institutions, such as the economic system and the educational system. Governments are officially "in charge" of the people they rule, but there are many powers that governments don't have:

- ✔ They can't change culture and customs, though they can influence both (see Chapter 5).

- ✔ They can't control the economy, though they can influence it (also see Chapter 5).

- ✔ They can't enforce *all* their laws *all* the time (see Chapter 11).

- ✔ They can't control the outside world (governments, like other organizations, are open systems — see Chapter 12).

All of these other institutions — culture, the economy, other governments, and outside powers — influence governments in complicated ways, and political sociologists are curious about all those interactions. That's what the rest of this chapter is about.

The big takeover: Causes of political revolution

When it comes to government, political revolution is about the biggest change there is. In a revolution, an existing government is forcefully overthrown and replaced by another.

Political revolution has been a hot topic among sociologists from the very beginning, in part because sociology was born in a world wracked by revolution (see Chapter 3). The European revolutions of the 18th and 19th centuries were horrifically violent and disruptive, and one of the reasons a scientific approach to society seemed so appealing was that if sociologists could determine the *causes* of political revolutions, they could possibly help to prevent them — or at least to help people carry them off in a more peaceful, less disruptive manner.

After 200 years of investigations, sociologists still haven't come up with a "recipe for revolution," but their investigations have made clear just how precarious governments really are. If you live in a country with a functioning government that is reasonably stable, does a good job of meeting people's basic requirements, and is at least somewhat responsive to its citizens' changing needs and demands, consider yourself lucky — that government is one of the greatest achievements of the human race.

Think about all the actions that can destabilize or topple a government:

- ✔ An environmental catastrophe, like a drought or natural disaster (for example, the Rapanui of Easter Island who ran short of resources and fell into disastrous conflict with each other)

- ✔ An outside attack by an aggressive neighbor (for example, European nations in the Second World War)

- ✔ Internal fighting or disorganization among the people in the government (for example, the American Civil War)

- ✔ Too much economic inequality, which can cause the have-nots to rise up and take over (for example, the French Revolution)

- ✔ A cultural challenge to the justification for the system of government (for example, the Russian Revolution)

In large, complex societies with relatively elaborate governments, there is rarely any one single cause that can be isolated as *the* reason for a revolution. Usually economic, social, and political factors interact to weaken a government's grip; then a charismatic opposition leader or external challenge becomes the straw that breaks the camel's back.

The challenges of understanding political stability and instability are well understood not only by sociologists but by leaders who have tried to stabilize their own governments or — in some cases — the governments of other countries. Various world powers that have tried intervening to topple other governments have further learned that there's no magic trick that can induce a revolution, either.

Still, "nation building" has become its own discipline, studied by military and political leaders the world over who want to help build stable, peaceful governments both inside and outside their own countries. It's not easy, but there are some common principles sociologists and other social scientists have established as being important for a government to gain and keep the support of its citizens.

- A functioning infrastructure, with people's basic needs (food, health, shelter, transportation) being met

- A stable economy, with people able to find legitimate work to feed themselves and their families

- A transparent system of government, where people feel that officials are honest and accountable for their actions

- Official respect for cultural and religious traditions

- A sense of independence from foreign influence, especially the influence of foreign powers not seen as friendly or supportive

It sounds simple, but it's extremely tricky. A functioning government that successfully balances the needs of a large, diverse group of citizens requires the trust and support of those citizens — and in the wake of war or turmoil, or if a previous government was corrupt or irresponsible, people may be very wary and reluctant to trust the official powers.

When you read the news, you may sometimes find it difficult to trust your own government. Does it deserve your support? Your government needs to earn your trust and support, and the trust and support of your neighbors, every day — when governments are unable or unwilling to make their citizens happy, things start to get ugly.

Though sociologists have learned a lot about the causes of political stability and instability, there's no perfect formula for determining whether a government will stand or fall. You may be able to think of contemporary examples of governments that fail to meet their citizens' basic needs and yet still stand strong — why? It may be that there is no sufficiently organized opposition, or it may be that they've manipulated their citizens into believing that there is no superior alternative.

But how do they *know?*

To ask what factors cause political revolutions is to ask a *big* question. As I explain in Chapter 4, sociologists who ask big questions have to make do with fewer comparative cases than sociologists who ask little questions. If I want to know what factors cause a person to vote one way or another, I can survey millions of people (providing I have the time). If I want to know what factors cause a political revolution, I don't have that many examples to look at. What's more, if I'm surveying individual people, I can survey a bunch of people who are all living at the same time, in very similar conditions. If I'm looking at political revolutions, I'm going to have to go back in history for examples, which means that I'll be looking at revolutions that happened at different times and in different places. That can make them hard to compare for similarities and differences.

One of the best-regarded sociological studies of political revolutions is Theda Skocpol's *States and Social Revolutions*, published in 1979. It's a careful analysis of revolutions in France (1789), China (1911), and Russia (1917). Skocpol's study has been influential, but it's also been criticized — as have been many similar studies — for having too few examples. Sociologists point out that you would never try to build a theory of job change based on studying only three people, so how can you build a theory of revolutions based on only three countries? Don't you have to look at many more examples to see what the patterns are?

There's no easy answer to that question: Ultimately, every sociologist has to decide for themselves what counts as valid evidence. If you don't have hundreds of revolutions to go on, does that mean you should give up even trying to understand them — or should you do the best you can with the evidence available to you? Sociologists may disagree about the answer to that question, but what they do agree on is that *all* evidence should be carefully, systematically examined and that, even though evidence is always limited, more is always better than less.

Sharing (or Not Sharing) Power in Society

Questions about the state and social movements tend to boil down to questions about *power* in society. What *is* power? Who has it, and when do they (or don't they) share it? If one person has more power, does that necessarily mean others have less? In this section, I summarize the two main ideas sociologists have about power in society — the idea that power is a limited quantity that cannot be shared, and the idea that power is a collective good that everyone can work together for.

Conflict models: Every man, woman, and child for themselves

One way to think about power is as *influence over other people*. This is probably the most "common sense" way to think about power: If I have a lot of power, I have the ability to compel a lot of other people to do as I want them to. If I have only a little power, there are few people I'm in a position to coerce, and I'm going to spend a lot of time doing what other people want me to do.

This is what's known as a *zero-sum* view of power. It means that there is a limited amount of power to go around, and if I get more power, you must have less. Either you have power over me, or I have power over you. It's as simple as that.

Naturally, in this view, power is something that everybody wants. If I don't have power, that must mean that someone else has power over me; while that person might choose to be nice to me, they might just as easily make a decision that I'm unhappy with. The best-case scenario for me would be to have all the power for myself, and that way I can call the shots.

This way of thinking about power doesn't necessarily mean that one person in a given society needs to have all the power — different people may have power in different situations, or for different reasons. I might have power because of my money, for example, while you might have power because you're ridiculously good looking. A third person — let's call him Don — might have power because of his extensive social connections. We each have some power, and each of us can be especially influential in different situations.

Still, when the rubber hits the road, only one of us can come out on top. If all three of us run for elected office, we can each try to use our power to win:

> I can buy lots of ads for my campaign.

> You can make lots of personal appearances and wow voters with your good looks.

> Don can work his connections and try to get influential people to persuade voters on his behalf.

We can probably each earn lots of votes, but only one of us is going to get the most votes. In a zero-sum model of power, power may have different sources, but it all ultimately comes down to the basic question of *who gets their way*.

Sociologists who think this way about power are often called *conflict theorists* because they theorize that everyone is in conflict with everyone else, pretty much all the time. Sometimes they might work together to achieve certain shared goals, but when their common purpose is achieved (or frustrated), they'll part ways. If this is how you think about power, you likely think of a political party as an uneasy coalition of people who make a truce to put a candidate in power, but might otherwise have nothing in common.

The granddaddy of conflict theorists was Karl Marx. In fact, this kind of theory about the social or political world is often called a Marxist theory. As noted in Chapter 3, Marx believed that power and influence in society were largely about material goods: food, clothing, land, and other resources, represented in a modern capitalist economy by money.

Marx distrusted money because it's like liquid power: It flows easily from one person to another, and it can be easily used by one person or group of people to gain advantage over others. If your assets are in the form of land, a house, cattle, skills, or even social connections, I might be able to swindle you out of those things — but it's going to be a lot easier for me to swindle you out of your money.

Precisely as Marx would have feared, when the Soviet Union ended and Russian citizens were given large sums of money representing their share of formerly state-owned enterprises, many were quickly cheated out of it and were left with nothing.)

You can see why Marxist political thinkers are often concerned with the influence of money on the government. In fact, Marxists tend to see the government as essentially a tool of the wealthy, something that exists at the pleasure of — and for the convenience of — people with money. A Marxist, zero-sum view of political power is to some degree behind each of these concerns about politics:

- ✔ **Campaign finance.** Should wealthy candidates (and candidates with wealthy supporters) be allowed to spend as much money as they want on their political campaigns, or should there be laws to equalize funding among all candidates?

- ✔ **Lobbying and gifts.** Should corporations and other organizations be able to employ lobbyists whose job is to get the attention of officeholders? Should the access and privileges of lobbyists be limited? Should officeholders be limited in the type and amount of gifts they're able to receive — to prevent "gifts" from being used as bribes?

- ✔ **Term limits.** Should officeholders be able to stay in office for as long as they can gain the majority of the vote, potentially accruing more and more power and influence with each term and becoming harder and harder to beat — or should officeholders be subject to term limits, preventing them from serving beyond a certain amount of time?

These and other issues reflect people's underlying concern that one person or group of people might have too much influence, for too long, over what the government does. They reflect a concern that the government will use its power for the good of one or a few rather than being fair to all.

A big debate among political sociologists concerns "the autonomy of the state." The question, in other words, is whether the government actually has any independent influence and power in society, or whether it's strictly a tool of other interests. Marx believed that the state, at least in modern capitalist society, had little autonomy — that it was essentially a tool of the bourgeois. This was a view shared by 20th century Marxist C. Wright Mills (see Chapter 3), whose book *The Power Elite* suggested that if the wealthy told the government to jump, the government's answer would be, "How high?"

Others point out that the government does have a lot of independent power, by virtue of its unique role in society. The government, after all, has the guns; even the wealthiest members of society must obey the government's laws, or they'll find themselves on the wrong side of a set of jail bars. In revolutions like the Russian Revolution, the government can seize the assets of the wealthy and redistribute them (or keep the assets for itself); short of that, governments can raise taxes on whomever they please. In many countries, people with high incomes pay a greater share of their income in taxes than do people with low incomes.

What conflict theorists on both sides of this debate agree on is, though, that power is zero-sum: Whether the wealthy have it, or the beautiful people have it, or the government has it, *someone* has it — and that means that someone else doesn't, or a lot of other people don't.

Pluralist models: Fair is fair

The Marxist C. Wright Mills attacked the Durkheimian Talcott Parsons for having too rosy a view of society. Parsons thought that modern industrial society actually worked pretty well — in fact, better than any previous form of society — to meet people's needs. When Mills accused Parsons of forgetting that a privileged few "power elite" were in charge of everything, and were bending everyone else to their will, Parsons snapped right back with some valid observations criticizing the Marxist view of power.

Parsons believed that power was not zero-sum: that giving power to some didn't necessarily mean taking it away from others. How could that be? Parsons pointed out that there simply has to be *someone* in charge, or society would descend into chaos and nothing would get done. If no one has the power to make decisions, then no decisions get made. When society is effectively organized, choosing one person or group of people to give power to actually gives *everybody* more power over their collective situation.

To understand how this works, think about a coxswain on a rowing team. The "cox" doesn't row at all; they just sit at the end of the boat and coordinate the rowing by calling out to the rest of the team. In a sense, the cox has "power" over the rest of the team in that they can tell the rowers what to do and when to do it — but everyone on the team understands that without a cox, the team's rowing would be uncoordinated and they would be wasting a lot of effort. By giving power to the cox, all the team members gain power over their opponents; if each team member kept for themselves the "power" over when and how to row, the whole team would lose.

Of course, that's all well and good when it comes to a rowing team whose members agree on what needs to be done (fast and efficient rowing), but does that view of power make any sense for large, complicated industrial societies? In situations where it's far from clear what the best course of action is, won't any leader be tempted to take the course of action that's most rewarding for the people they like — or for the people who are paying them off?

That's certainly a possibility, but Parsons also believed Mills was empirically wrong in saying there was a "power elite" working behind the scenes. When things aren't going your way, it may seem like the world's conspiring against you...but is it actually? If your boss yells at you, your dog pees in the house, and your son gets in trouble at school, does that mean they all had a secret meeting somewhere and decided to do everything they could to make your day miserable?

Political sociologists with a *pluralist* view of power point out that when you closely observe actual working societies, it's rare to find power concentrated in the hands of a few, and — far from conspiring to work to their collective advantage — the people who are in positions of power often argue among themselves.

Consider all the different types of power people have in a contemporary society:

- **Political power:** Heads of state, members of a legislative body, mayors and aldermen — presidents, prime ministers, supreme leaders, queens and kings

- **Economic power:** Captains of industry, wealthy families — CEOs with princely salaries, people with vast property holdings, people with money stuffed in their mattresses

- **Cultural power:** Entertainers, artists, writers and thinkers — famous actors, bestselling authors, TV hosts

- **Network power:** Well-connected socialites and "power players" — agents, lobbyists, neighborhood gossips

- **Human capital:** People with special education, skills, or talents — engineers, professional athletes, good plumbers

Median voter theory and "common sense"

The median voter theory, first formulated by economist Duncan Black, holds that where voter's political preferences range along a continuum from very liberal to very conservative, in a two-party election candidates will end up gravitating towards the middle rather than taking extreme positions that risk alienating moderate voters. I was explaining this theory to a student once when a friend of mine, overhearing, said, "Jay's going to hate it that I'm saying this . . . but that sounds like a fancy name for simple common sense."

She was right — I *did* hate it that she said that! Why? Because dismissing any theory about the social world as "common sense" suggests that it can't be empirically tested. Sure, to an American used to a two-party system, the idea of a political spectrum running from right to left with two more or less centrist candidates sitting in the middle seems very familiar, but there are all sorts of ways the median voter theory could be wrong — or, at least, incomplete.

For one thing, who's to say the political spectrum runs from right to left? Where would a libertarian who's socially liberal but economically conservative fall? What if voters' views are more complicated than big government (liberal) versus little government (conservative)? That would be hard for the median voter theory to explain.

And what if voters' preferences don't fall in a bell curve — what if there's a big group of very conservative voters and a big group of very liberal voters, and few in the middle? What if voters abandon a candidate who strays too far from their ideals? What about third-party candidates — when do they make an impact? These are all questions that challenge or complicate median voter theory; theories that seem like "common sense" aren't always right.

It's sometimes the case that the people in these various domains agree with one another about which direction a society should go, but very often it's not — and furthermore, the people within each domain rarely agree with one another! Within each of these domains of power, there's a diverse spectrum of people with different interests and desires.

If this is starting to sound like everyone's in a rowboat without a cox, that's exactly — a pluralist might say — why society delegates authority to particular people to make particular kinds of decisions. In a well-functioning pluralist society, the decisions that end up being made at least roughly balance the needs of all the different people in that society. Some voices may be louder than others, but in the long run, most people get heard.

Is this actually how society works? Well, there are many different societies that work many different ways, and certainly in some cases the decisions that are made are hardly "plural" at all. There are dictatorships and other types of society where, in fact, the power *is* concentrated among a very few people. Many sociologists, though, believe that a pluralist model is a better model for the way the world actually works than a Marxist model is.

Robert Dahl, a political scientist whose work is widely respected by sociologists, responded directly to C. Wright Mills in the 1950s and 60s. In Dahl's most famous book, *Who Governs?*, he presented New Haven, Connecticut as a case study in pluralism. Dahl scoffed at the idea that any kind of secret cabal was running New Haven — instead, he argued, the city government did its best to balance the competing interests of all the different people it governed. Sometimes people felt slighted and got angry, sometimes people took advantage of others, but by and large, Dahl said, New Haven was a democratic city — "warts and all."

Dahl and other pluralists believe that's the way government works, at least in democratic societies: by helping large, diverse groups of people work in their own best interest.

Social Movements: Working for Change

In the perfect pluralist society, democratic voting and fair representation would be enough to bring about a system of laws and policies that appropriately balance the interests of everyone in a society. It never quite seems to work out that way, though — in part because there is no such thing as a perfectly democratic society, and in part because many of the most important institutions in society are not governmental at all. For that reason, people often find it necessary to organize social movements to work as a group for the kind of changes they want to see.

In this section, I explain how social movements get off the ground and mobilize supporters — and how and why they succeed.

Getting off the ground

A social movement, in the sociological sense, is more than just a bunch of people who say they want something: it's *an organized effort to achieve social change*. Social movements can be very small, or they can be very large; they can be very successful, and they can be complete failures. Nonetheless, what all social movements have in common is that they represent concerted efforts to bring about social change. They typically represent people who feel that their voices are not being heard through other channels; that they don't have the means to get through to the powers that be without an organized effort to make their demands known.

There are many different kinds of social movements, with many different kinds of goals. From community-organizing groups like ACORN to religious groups like the Christian Coalition to lawless groups like the Ku Klux Klan, a social movement is any group of people organizing to bring about social change.

Social movements often target governmental officials and agencies, but they sometimes also target corporations or influential individuals. Most social movements seek to raise public awareness of the issues with which they're concerned; in fact, some social movements seek to do nothing *but* raise public awareness.

Social movements' efforts may take many forms. Most social movements involve one or more of these efforts:

- ✔ **Rallys, marches, and parades:** Public gatherings to show the world how many people feel a certain way, and how strongly they feel it.
- ✔ **Coordinated demands:** Letters, e-mails, or other messages to the movement's target(s).
- ✔ **Publicity:** Advertisements, posters, graffiti, or other means of spreading a group's message.
- ✔ **Civil disobedience:** Members of a group defying the law to show how strongly they feel about their cause, especially when their cause involves a law they find unjust.

Social movements do not necessarily have to be coordinated from the top down; in fact, most large social movements are diverse, with different organized groups working towards some shared goals and some different goals. Groups within a social movement may also disagree on the *means* of achieving a goal: For example, some groups may believe that violent vigilante efforts are justified and necessary whereas other groups believe that efforts should be exclusively peaceful.

So why do social movements arise? It's a question sociologists have been studying for a long time, and the answer isn't obvious. After all, everybody wants *something* in society, but not everybody is going to go down to City Hall and picket over it, write letters about it, or even tell anyone else how they feel about it. There are any number of grievances that exist in any given society; which ones turn into full-fledged social movements? There are at least two good answers to this question; they come from relative deprivation theory and resource mobilization theory.

Relative deprivation theory

One answer that seems to make sense goes by the name of *relative deprivation theory*. According to relative deprivation theory, people are spurred into organized action when a gap opens up between what they *think they deserve* and what they are *actually getting*. In other words, if society is setting a group of people up to think that they ought to have something, but then doesn't give it to them, they feel "relatively deprived" and are inclined to take their grievances to the streets.

As an example, think about the women's suffrage movement of the late 19th century and early 20th century. In the United States (and in many other countries) at that time, there was a concerted movement by women — with the support of sympathetic men — to gain the right to vote. This effort definitively succeeded with the ratification of the 19th Amendment to the Constitution, guaranteeing all women the right to vote.

That amendment, though, was not ratified until 1920 — and women had been without the guaranteed right to vote for all of American history up until that time. Why was there no major suffrage movement in the 18th century, or in the early 19th century? Certainly there were plenty of women who were unhappy about their lot during those times, but they didn't form a major suffrage movement until later.

Relative deprivation theory would say that women didn't organize a mass suffrage movement until they felt *relatively deprived* of the right to vote. As the 19th century neared its end, the idea that any group could be legitimately deprived of the right to vote was under increasing attack from all sides. Slavery had ended, and in many places people of all races could vote. (Jim Crow laws, sadly, kept African-Americans in many places from actually voting until decades later.) Women in certain other countries were gaining the right to vote in the late 19th century, and some U.S. states and territories were granting suffrage (that is, the right for women to vote) for elections within their jurisdiction.

All this meant that a woman in 1900 who was living in a state where she was unable to vote could read about plenty of other examples of women who did have the right to vote. A hundred years previous, in 1800, a woman unable to vote would not have been able to point to many examples of women who could legally vote — so though both the woman in 1800 and the woman in 1900 were equally deprived of the right to vote, the woman in 1900 would *feel* more deprived.

A useful aspect of this theory is that it's helpful for explaining why there are just as many social movements in wealthy societies as there are in poor societies. Objectively, people in some societies are more deprived than people in others — but what inspires social movements, according to this theory, is a sense of *relative* deprivation.

If relative deprivation theory still seems confusing, think about a child whose father spontaneously decides to buy him a one-scoop ice cream cone; now, think about a child who is given the same one-scoop cone while his sibling is given a two-scoop cone. Which child is more likely to get upset?

Resource mobilization theory

Many sociologists, though, feel that relative deprivation theory is not enough to explain how and why social movements arise. Not only are there just as many social movements in wealthy societies, note those sociologists, when you start counting them you realize that there are even *more* social movements in wealthy societies than in poor societies. These sociologists — in fact, most sociologists studying social movements today — prefer a theory called *resource mobilization theory*, a term coined by sociologist Douglas McAdam.

Why? Because coordinating a social movement isn't just about sharing a grievance. Just because a significant number of people feel deprived of something doesn't mean that they'll be able to get together and coordinate a social movement. For that to happen, they need resources such as:

✔ Leaders with the time to coordinate the group's activities.

✔ Communication resources, like mailing lists, phone trees, computer networks.

✔ Money to buy advertisements and other attention-getting devices, as well as to buy other resources.

✔ Social resources, such as contacts in the government, the media, and other spheres of influence.

✔ Transportation resources, such as planes, trains, and automobiles.

Those resources are all more readily available in wealthy societies, so it's easier for people to mobilize social movements in wealthy societies than in resource-poor societies. Resource mobilization also explains why certain groups within a particular society are able to generate social movements, whereas others aren't. It's not necessarily the case that people involved in big, elaborate social movements feel more aggrieved than the people whose grievances don't lead to social movements — it's just that some people are better able to access the necessary resources for a social movement than others are.

This way of thinking about social movements is especially popular among Marxists, who — as I explain in the previous section "Sharing (or Not Sharing) Power in Society" — are concerned about the impact of money and power on political outcomes. Marxists point out that it's exactly the people who *already* have many advantages who are able to mobilize social movements to give themselves even *more* advantages, whereas the people with relatively few advantages — the people who have the most basis for demanding social change — are also the people with the fewest resources to mobilize social movements. That can lead to an unfair situation becoming even more unfair.

Think about how much easier it is to start a social movement now than it was before the development of the Internet. Before, you'd have to make phone calls or drop flyers to organize rallies; now, you can create a Facebook event and the word will spread like wildfire. This is an illustration of why sociologists emphasize the importance of resource availability in the generation of social movements.

Rounding up the posse

If one question is how social movements get started, another question is how people become involved in them. Even in the case of large, widespread social movements, most people in a society — even most people who care greatly about a given issue — do not become involved. Why?

One answer comes from microsociology, and points to the importance of frames. As I note in Chapter 6, a "frame" is a definition of a social situation. What I think my role is in a given social situation — including how, and whether, I need to act — depends on the frame around that situation. Whether or not a person chooses to join an active social movement depends, at least in part, on whether or not the situation is framed as one that person has an interest in.

This becomes especially important when you consider the fact that sometimes the grievances social movements fight for are quite removed from the lives of the people whose support the movement needs. In the women's suffrage example above, the aggrieved, deprived group is quite clear: it's women. In other cases, it's not so clear; to mobilize supporters, social movements need to convince as many groups of people as possible that the movement's cause is something the groups have a stake in.

As an example, think about the animal rights movement. There are many different organizations involved in that movement, with different goals and methods, but the general goal is to end practices that harm or cause suffering to animals. To mobilize as many supporters as possible, the various groups involved in the animal rights movement place a number of different frames around the issue.

- ✔ To attract supporters who are concerned about the environment, advocates portray animal rights as an environmental issue: raising animals for food, they point out, requires more resources and creates more pollution than raising grains and vegetables does.

- ✔ To attract supporters who are concerned about their health, advocates portray animal rights as a health issue: eating vegetarian, they say, means you'll be healthier.

- ✔ To attract supporters who are pet owners, advocates portray animal rights as a moral issue: they spread photos and videos of animals being mistreated to win the sympathy of people who would never want their pets to be treated that way.

- ✔ To attract people who are conscious of their social status, advocates portray animal rights as something it's cool to be worried about: they have attractive people pose for ads — sometimes unclothed ("I'd rather go naked than wear fur") — to suggest that caring about animal rights is something that hot, high-status people do.

Taking it to the extreme

The sociology department at Harvard is located in the same building as the psychology department, and when I was in grad school the building would be given enhanced security when there were animal-rights protests in the Boston area. Why? Because the building supervisor was concerned, justifiably based on his past experiences, that ardent activists might try to break into the building and free the caged monkeys used for psychological experiments.

The supervisor's fear demonstrates the fine line between agitating for social change and forcibly bringing that change about. All major social movements, from the Civil Rights movement to the environmental movement, have involved some significant elements of lawlessness. Sometimes it's fairly minor — say, occupying a college building to protest a tuition hike — and sometimes it escalates into outright armed rebellion.

Is violence in a social movement justified? That all depends on whether or not you agree with the movement's goals. Does it work? Often, yes . . . but then again, it sometimes backfires and embarrasses more moderate members of the movement, especially when people get hurt. The decision to obey or defy the law in the course of a social movement will always be a matter of judgment.

Social movements can sometimes seem ridiculous, and sometimes they invite ridicule by using humor or intentionally extreme methods to get their point across. Still, social change is a serious matter, and throughout history people have gone to extremes to bring about the changes they seek. Sometimes that may seem hard to justify, but at other times, doing too little seems even worse.

Sometimes being mobilized into a social movement is simply a matter of having the issue framed in a way that is compelling to you.

Interestingly, sociologists have also found that it's often the case that people active in social movements did not necessarily have strong pre-existing beliefs in line with the movement's principles — that is, that belief may follow action rather than vice-versa.

In the late 1990s, sociologist Ziad Munson set out to study the U.S. movement to make abortion illegal. He knew that many millions of Americans believed that abortion was wrong under most or all circumstances, but he also noted that only a small fraction of those people became active in what was known as the "pro-life movement," the organized movement to prevent abortion with the ultimate goal of making it illegal. Munson arranged a series of interviews with activists in the movement, seeking to understand what led them from being passive supporters of the movement to being active supporters of the movement.

He was surprised to discover that many of his supporters reported that before they became active in the pro-life movement, they had not had strong views on the issue at all — in fact, some even said that they would have considered themselves "pro-choice" (that is, in favor of keeping abortion legal), and had switched their views *after* becoming active in the pro-life movement. What happened in these cases was that people typically became involved in the movement through friends and family: licking envelopes or making signs to support someone they cared about. After they started participating in the movement, they found that their beliefs about the issue became much stronger — that they turned into dyed-in-the-wool advocates for the pro-life cause.

Even, it seems, when it comes to an issue as personal and where views are held, by many people, so strongly, people can more easily be induced to act than to believe; after they start acting, their beliefs may follow. For this reason, social movements may have as much luck going through personal networks and offering other incentives (even material rewards) for people to act as they'd have appealing to people's fundamental beliefs.

What it means for a social movement to be successful

Some social movements quickly meet with success, some find success only after many years, and some social movements meet with no success at all. Is there any way to understand why some movements succeed and others fail?

With an eye to exactly this question, sociologist William Gamson studied several dozen organizations involved in social movements. After careful study, he concluded that (you've heard this before!) it wasn't quite that simple. To "succeed" or to "fail" can mean different things in different contexts.

Gamson offered at least four different outcomes that social movements can meet, depending on whether or not they're accepted as legitimate organizations and whether or not their material goals are met. Here are the four outcomes Gamson saw:

- ✔ **Full response.** When a movement is recognized as legitimate *and* achieves its goals, it's unquestionably been a success. This is the kind of success that the Civil Rights movement has had after many years of struggle: Not only do African-Americans have the universal right to vote and to gain employment without discrimination, the movement's leaders have been given much recognition. In the United States, Martin Luther King, Jr. Day is a national holiday.

- ✔ **Preemption.** Social movements may experience bittersweet victories when they realize their goals but are not accepted as legitimate organizations or as welcome movements. Music fans who have organized digital file-sharing networks to pressure record companies to loosen copyright restrictions have met with some success — companies have lifted certain protective measures, and have pulled back from their initial strategy of prosecuting copyright violators — but nonetheless, those fans have never been recognized as acting legally or legitimately. In this way, the goal of their movement has been "preempted" by the record companies.

✔ **Co-optation.** This happens when a social movement wins recognition, but doesn't actually meet its goals. Gay pride festivals are now major civic events in many cities around the world, but some gay rights activists believe that their movement has been co-opted: that governments are visibly welcoming to gay rights organizations even as they fail to actually grant the rights (for example, marriage rights) that the organizations demand.

✔ **Collapse.** When a movement fails to achieve its goals *and* fails to win recognition, it simply collapses. For example, the movement to re-legalize polygamy in the state of Utah has failed to either change the law or to be recognized as legitimate. There are still a number of people who practice polygamy, but they often do so secretly and have been unable to muster anything resembling a genuine social movement.

The success of a social movement is sometimes a matter of having a charismatic leader, sometimes a matter of successful framing and mobilization, and sometimes a matter of raw resources — but often it's a matter of whether or not the society is disposed to accept the movement's demands, and whether or not there's a genuine opportunity for those demands to be met.

When it comes to understanding the success or failure of social movements, it's handy to remember the Latin phrase *carpe diem*: "seize the day." For a social movement to succeed, the time has to be ripe — that is, it has to be the right "day" — but the movement must also successfully mobilize supporters to fight for its cause. That is, the movement has to do its share of seizing.

Chapter 14

Urban Sociology and Demographics: (Ain't No) Love in the Heart of the City

1 don't know about you, but I've never seen a sociology textbook that has a photo of a small town on the cover. Cover images tend to portray bustling cities with towering skyscrapers, sometimes with people moving so quickly they blur. Why is that? After all, a village is a society, too.

Urban life is at the heart of sociology. As you can read in Chapter 3, sociology was founded at a time when cities were growing rapidly as people moved in search of jobs and new opportunities. When they did, they would encounter — many for the first time in their lives — people from different religions, different races, different places.

When you're among people who are similar to you, it's easy forget about the fact that you're all operating under a set of assumptions and expectations about the social world. In the city, there's no getting around the fact that there are many different traditions and languages and ways of life: many of them are right in front of you when you walk down the street. It can easily make you curious about society, and about how all those different people can possibly get along together.

In this chapter, I begin by talking about classic sociological studies of the city. I then talk about urban change and diverse neighborhoods, and finally look to the future of the city. Can cities remain peaceful, productive places for everyone to live? Sociologists believe they can, but they acknowledge that there's always going to be tension, always going to be diversity and change. That's what urban life is all about.

Sociology in the City

Sociologists have always looked to the heart of the city for people and situations to observe. Urban life is enormously complex, and it will always be a challenge to understand how it works. (It's often a challenge just to live it!) In this section, I explain how 19th century sociologists understood city life, and how 20th century sociologists threw themselves right into the thick of it.

The loneliness of a crowd

"The lonely crowd" is a cliché (and the title of a classic sociology book that actually has more to do with suburban life than with urban life), but it is one of the paradoxes of social life that being in a crowd of people can indeed be lonelier than being alone. Hundreds or thousands of people may be in the same *place* as you, but if don't or can't relate to them, it can feel very isolating — even frightening.

That's a new feeling for people who move to big cities from small communities: the feeling of almost always being surrounded, even crowded, by people, but by people who don't necessarily know or even care who you are or where you came from. On a bus or subway car, you may have your face jammed into the armpit of someone who's completely ignoring you. For a number of reasons, that's not pleasant.

The sociologist who's best known for writing about why it *feels* different to be in a city than in a small community was a German named Ferdinand Tönnies, whose most important work was published in the late 19th century.

In his book *Gemeinschaft und Gesellschaft*, Tönnies explained what he saw as a difference between *Gemeinschaft* — a world usually translated into English as "community" — and *Gesellschaft*, which is usually translated as "society."

For Tönnies, *Gemeinschaft* characterizes a community that feels like a community. It's characteristic of a group you're usually born into, and like other members of the community, you share many things in common. You naturally feel a kinship with other people in *Gemeinschaft* because you have a set of shared interests and, for that and other reasons, you do many of the same things. Examples of groups bound by *Gemeinschaft* include:

> ✔ Farming communities
>
> ✔ Families
>
> ✔ Religious communities

Gesellschaft, on the other hand, characterizes a group of people who come together by choice, usually for very specific practical reasons. When you opt to move to a place or join a group because there's something in particular that you want to accomplish — not necessarily because you feel any particular affinity for the other people in that group — the bond you share with the other people in that group is the impersonal bond of *Gesellschaft*. Examples of these groups include:

> ✔ Urban business centers
>
> ✔ Corporations and trade cooperatives
>
> ✔ Universities
>
> ✔ Political parties

In *Gemeinschaft*, when you encounter someone you can safely assume that he or she has a lot in common with you and is, or wants to, share a personal relationship — in other words, that he or she is your friend. In *Gesellschaft*, people are together for a very specific reason and may otherwise want nothing to do with one another. In fact, in some such groups (for example, in business ventures), close personal relationships may be discouraged or even outright forbidden!

In *Gemeinschaft*, bonds among people are intimate and personal. In *Gesellschaft*, bonds are practical and impersonal.

Groups characterized by *Gemeinschaft* are generally much more comfortable, and if you ever read Tönnies's writing, you may get the feeling that he prefers *Gemeinschaft* and wishes there could be more of it. From a sociological perspective, though, *Gemeinschaft* isn't something you can just put in a can like paint and spray wherever you think the world needs some peace, love, and understanding: it's the result of living among people who have a lot in common with you. In most social situations today, the fact is that you just *don't* have much in common with the people around you and it would be silly to pretend that you do.

When I was living in the Boston area, a neighbor from St. Paul — the quieter, less crowded city where I grew up — came to visit, and as we walked through downtown Boston he turned to me. "I keep saying hi to people," he said, "but they don't say hi back!" Were people in Boston less friendly than people in St. Paul? Yes, but for a reason. When you're walking down a crowded city street, you're continually passing people who you are not friends with and may never see again. If you stop to say hi to everyone, you'll essentially be wasting breath that could be saved for the people you *are* friends with.

Tönnies believed that society, over time, was increasingly characterized by *Gesellschaft*: it's becoming more urban, more diverse, and more bureaucratic. All those things can make society feel less friendly and warm, but they're happening for many reasons — including many good reasons — and short of some terrible disaster, the clock is unlikely to turn back (see Chapter 16 for more on social change).

Gesellschaft is something people are going to have to learn to live with . . . and, in fact, most people are doing so quite happily. Diverse urban life is full of surprises: new people, new experiences, new ideas. Sometimes the surprises are nasty, but most people today have decided that urban life is worth that risk.

Street corner society

Look on any city street at any given time, and you're apt to see people buzzing about, going to and fro, jumping in their cars and hopping out of cabs, selling things, buying things, arguing, making out . . . it can be dizzying to see how much activity is going on at any given time. It may seem like there's no pattern, no sense to be made of it at all.

Smile! You're on candid (sociological) camera

William Whyte is a big name in urban sociology: it was shared by two different men who both made major contributions to the discipline. William Foote Whyte was the sociologist whose participant observation was the basis for his classic book *Street Corner Society*; William H. Whyte was the author of *The Organization Man* (see the section "The rise and fall of the suburbs") and a pioneer in visual sociology, the use of cameras to document social life.

William H. Whyte and his team turned video cameras on a number of spaces in New York City, watching to see how people used the spaces. They made a number of fascinating findings, and they had the video evidence to back them up. (You can use a search engine to find their film *The Social Life of Small Urban Spaces* for viewing on the Internet.)

Even in the crowded city, Whyte and his team found many urban spaces were usually deserted; people flocked to a few busy plazas even when they were planning to sit alone. Why? Because the most common activity among people observed by Whyte's team turned out to be — that's right — *watching other people*. And, it turned out, people liked to be watched! Whyte expected smooching lovers to be found in private, secluded spaces, but most often they sat or stood right in the center of things for everyone to see. Further, people having private conversations would stand in the middle of the sidewalk, forcing people to step around them.

The next time you're out and about in a big city, watch to see how people gather and use spaces. Even people who are "alone" really aren't: They're relating to all the people around them in ways that fit the circumstances of the city.

Over time, though, if you watch carefully, patterns will emerge. You'll notice the shopkeeper who always comes out for a smoke break at three specific times each day, the bus driver who helps the little old lady up the steps with her shopping cart each Tuesday morning, the kids who come home from school every weekday and pass by the musician playing his guitar. You'll notice cops on a beat — and, maybe, criminals on their own beats. There are rules and regularities to even the most chaotic urban neighborhood.

Though many different research methods have been used to study urban life, the research method most closely associated with urban sociology has been ethnography: hitting the streets to talk to city residents and understand how their lives and relationships work. From the Chicago School on down (see Chapter 3), this has been an enormously productive pursuit that has yielded some of the most important studies in all of sociology.

One of the most famous studies is described in the book *Street Corner Society* by the great American sociologist William Foote Whyte. Over the course of several years in the 1930s, Whyte lived among the predominantly Italian-American residents of an inner-city neighborhood in Boston. His careful study shows many of the complex aspects of life in that place at that time:

- ✔ The tension between neighborhood-oriented "corner boys" and the upwardly mobile "college boys."
- ✔ Local politics, with officeholders and candidates for office working to win the allegiance of important individuals and families.
- ✔ The prevalence of organized (and disorganized) crime, with racketeers knit into the neighborhood's social fabric.

The most memorable, and poignant, aspect of *Street Corner Society* is Whyte's description of the complex relations among a gang of "corner boys"; he captured the way they had to balance their personal friendships and relationships with complex social forces. Over Whyte's years of observation, various boys' fortunes rose and fell, and those boys in leadership positions faced hard choices about how to use their influence with their peers.

Books like Whyte's — and, to be sure, there have been many more excellent studies along these lines — demonstrate the complex nature of urban life, even in communities that look desperate and disorganized. Many Bostonians dismissed the North End neighborhood where Whyte lived and worked as a "slum," but Whyte's book paints a complex picture: one that isn't always pretty, but does show the strong webs of social organization present in the neighborhood.

Street Corner Society was also pioneering in Whyte's use of the research method known as "participant observation," in which the researcher joins a social group and participates in activities along with its members. (See Chapter 4.) The method has its drawbacks — it can be hard to objectively analyze a group of which you're a part, which is something you know if you've ever tried to figure out your own family — but it's hard to imagine that Whyte would have been able to paint so rich a portrait if he had stayed at arm's length from the people he was hoping to understand.

Changing Neighborhoods

Cities aren't static — they're always changing. If you've lived in a neighborhood even for a year, you've seen it change; and if you've lived there for longer, you've seen it change even more. Sociologists have long been interested in how and why neighborhoods change their character (and their characters). In this section, I explain how sociologists think about urban transformation.

It's 10 PM. Do you know who your neighbors are?

Do you know who your neighbors are? Could you step out your front door, point at each house or apartment building, and say who lives there? When you walk down your street, do you know the names of the people you pass?

Based on sociological studies of neighborhoods, I'm going to guess that you probably don't — and that you feel at least a little bad about it. TV shows, political campaigns, and Currier & Ives prints of community ice rinks send the message that your neighborhood is very important, and that your neighbors ought to be your bosom buddies. Your parents may talk about how, when they were young, everybody knew and trusted everybody on the block, how if you misbehaved in front of the neighbor lady, she'd punish you just like your own mom would.

There are indeed many communities that are tightly knit, but there are many more that aren't. Most people today don't identify with their neighborhoods as being important to their identities; it's just where they happen to live. They each probably know a few people who they happen to come across or who they've borrowed sticks of butter from, but they don't really see their streets as being *their* streets.

The "good old days" shouldn't be romanticized: people have always been mobile, and there has always been variety in the types of neighborhoods they've shared. In certain pockets, multiple families may have lived on the same city block for decades or even generations, but that kind of stability has never been universal, or even the norm — especially in urban neighborhoods as opposed to rural communities.

Some aspects of urban life, though, have indeed changed over the past several decades:

- ✔ Transportation and communications technology allows people to have much more frequent and meaningful interaction than in the past with others who are far away, and though in general this supplements rather than replaces interaction with people who they see in person, it is certainly true that sitting on the porch and watching the world go by isn't quite as compelling as it was 50 or 100 years ago.

- ✔ Immediate families are smaller and more independent than they once were.

- ✔ Rising wealth and living standards around the world mean less sharing of community resources — including housing. It was once common for families to host unrelated, paying boarders in their private homes; that practice is much less often seen today.

- ✔ From grocery shopping to entertainment, more activities are done at large urban or suburban centers and fewer are done at small neighborhood establishments. This is more efficient, and saves money for everyone.

- ✔ For a number of reasons (both parents working, increased participation in educational programs, safety concerns), children are much less frequently encouraged to play in the areas directly outside their homes — especially unsupervised — than was formerly the case.

All these factors, and more, have contributed to the declining significance of neighborhoods as centers of activity. It's very easy to know almost nothing about your neighbors — to come and go in your car and possibly even to live in a home for years without having any significant interaction with those living near you.

That said, it would be a mistake to think that this overall trend means that your neighborhood simply doesn't matter any more!

There is tremendous variety among types of neighborhoods and types of communities. True, many neighborhoods are only loosely connected — but many neighborhoods are very tight-knit, with neighbors socializing and supporting each other. This is true for different reasons in different types of neighborhoods. In relatively wealthy neighborhoods, residents may have more resources to communicate among themselves, to host events, and to mobilize around causes like street repair and public safety . . . but in less wealthy neighborhoods, residents may have more incentive to band together and support each other.

The importance of your neighborhood goes beyond just the influence of the people you share it with. Your neighborhood impacts your access to transportation, utilities, and other resources; it impacts your safety as well as your educational and work options; it may even directly impact your health if pollution or housing quality are significant factors. Those things are, in turn, affected by the people who live around you.

Neighborhoods on the tipping point

You don't need a sociologist to tell you that neighborhoods change over time. What's a little trickier is knowing *how* and *why* they change. Urban sociologists have spent decades studying patterns of neighborhood change, and they've come up with some interesting theories about what's going on.

The invasion-succession model: Make room, make room!

Sociologists in — and influenced by — the Chicago School likened neighborhoods to biological ecosystems. Robert Park, a major figure in that crowd, espoused a model that became known as the *invasion-succession model.*

According to the invasion-succession model of neighborhood change, a neighborhood — like a forest or a prairie — hosts a number of "species" that exist together in harmony. In my neighborhood in Minneapolis, for example, you might say that there is one social "species" of older, wealthy people who own large homes. With more space than they can use, they rent their extra rooms and carriage houses to members of a second social "species": young, single adults who are upwardly mobile but don't yet have the means or desire to buy their own houses. These two "species" exist together in harmony.

But what if a new "species" moved in — say, entrepreneurs who wanted to run businesses out of their houses? That might spur conflicts over parking, traffic, and the neighborhood's historical character. Any of the following things might happen:

- ✔ The neighborhood might somehow find a way to accommodate this new "species" of resident.

- ✔ The current residents might band together to drive out the "invaders," and the neighborhood would remain as it is.

- ✔ The entrepreneurial "invaders" might cause the longtime residents to move out, making more room for new business-oriented "invaders," who would ultimately succeed the former residents and create a new local "ecosystem."

This way of thinking about neighborhood change has been of great interest to sociologists hoping to understand transitions in neighborhoods' racial composition. If a neighborhood has predominantly residents of one race, then if residents of another race move in, the existing residents may feel threatened and try to make the newcomers feel unwelcome; if more and more of the new-comers move in, though, the neighborhood may reach a tipping point where the previous residents simply decide to leave.

This model of neighborhood change seemed to make a lot of sense in the early 20th century, when open racism was still common; in some ways it's still useful today, whether it's used to describe changes in neighborhoods' racial composition (unfortunately, many neighborhoods are still racially seg-regated, and residents of a different race may feel unwelcome) or changes in the occupation or income level of residents. Sociologists today, though, realize that neighborhood change happens for more reasons than simply because of "invaders" changing a neighborhood's demographic composition.

For an interesting and controversial look at neighborhood change today, take a look at Bill Bishop's book *The Big Sort: Why the Clustering of Like-Minded America is Tearing Us Apart.* Bishop believes that people's tendency to move to neighborhoods where people share their political beliefs and cultural inter-ests is damaging to the larger community because it means there's less oppor-tunity for exchange and dialogue. Others would argue that it's for the better if people feel they have a lot in common with their closest neighbors. What do you think?

The life and death of neighborhoods

Another influential theory of neighborhood change was the "life cycle" theory, in which neighborhoods are thought of as being more like organisms themselves than like ecosystems.

The sociologists who invented the life cycle model believed that neighbor-hoods went through repetitive cycles of change. First, a neighborhood would be developed, and people would start to move in. As it attracted more resi-dents and more development, a neighborhood would enter its prime — but eventually, the neighborhood's infrastructure would start to decay, the quality of life there would start to decline, and residents would move out in pursuit of newer, nicer neighborhoods. Eventually, the neighborhood would be in bad shape, and would need to be redeveloped, starting the cycle all over again.

This model makes a lot of sense: If you think about your own city, you can probably identify neighborhoods that seem to be in each of the "stages" of neighborhood life. There's the shiny new suburban community or downtown development where everybody seems to want to move; there's the vital neigh-borhood with popular businesses and longtime residents; there's the declining neighborhood where another business seems to close every day; and there's the dangerous neighborhood where crime is frequent and where no one lives unless they can't afford to live anywhere else. In the case of the latter neighbor-hood, you have probably heard calls for "renewal" and "redevelopment."

This way of thinking about neighborhood change acknowledges that urban life is more than just a big game of Risk, with "invading armies" of different groups trying to "take over" different neighborhoods. In fact, many of the healthiest, most vibrant neighborhoods have incredibly diverse social "ecosystems" and can easily accommodate newcomers without making the longtime residents feel threatened. The life cycle model also takes into account the importance of neighborhood infrastructure: building quality, local services and amenities. It's true that when buildings, streets, and other human-made artifacts reach a certain age, they start to decay, and many people find it easier to just move away than to replace the old stuff.

Still, sociologists realize that this way of thinking about neighborhood change also has its limitations. Failed experiments in "urban renewal" (see sidebar "Out with the old and in with the new . . . for better or worse") have made clear that you can't just hit the restart button on a neighborhood — that neighborhood change is a complex process that involves location, infrastructure, demographic change, social networks, and many other factors.

The rise and fall of the suburbs

I teach at a college in Eagan, Minnesota, a suburb of St. Paul. Eagan is only a short drive from the central city; it's green and hilly, parking is copious, and a big shopping area near the freeway has one of just about every big chain store you can name. Life is relatively easy in Eagan, and that's why most Americans prefer to live in communities a lot like it.

Ever since there have been cities, there has been a market for housing at their outskirts, accessible to the commercial activity and entertainment in the cities' centers but with more affordable space. Many inner-city residential neighborhoods started out as suburban areas when the cities were smaller, and older cities like London and New York City have inner-ring suburbs that are themselves hundreds of years old, with beautiful (and hugely expensive) historic houses.

Most neighborhoods that are now called "suburbs," though, are products of the highway system, which allows people to drive great distances at high speeds. The highway system means that a person can reasonably commute to work in, say, St. Paul from not only Eagan, but from a city like Hugo — which is 20 miles away.

The suburbs built in the United States after World War II seemed to promise "the American dream": on a single income (usually the father's), a family could have a freestanding house with its own yard. For reasons of both efficiency and style, many suburbs built at that time — and since — have featured houses that are very similar in appearance.

Out with the old and in with the new . . . for better or worse

The life cycle model of neighborhood change (see section "The life and death of neighborhoods" earlier in this chapter) inspired a wave of calls for "urban renewal" in the middle of the 20th century. The idea behind urban renewal was that decaying or dangerous neighborhoods could be reinvigorated with massive investments in development. Sometimes this worked, but often it didn't. In downtown Boston, a successful example of urban renewal sits right next to an unsuccessful example.

Starting in the early 19th century, Boston's Scollay Square neighborhood was a buzzing hub of commerce and entertainment — including, especially after 1940, the kind of "entertainment" that involved women wearing lots of sequins and feathers with not much underneath. By the 1960s, the neighborhood was seen as seedy and was completely torn down; in its place went what is now called Government Center, a vast plaza that houses Boston's City Hall and other government buildings. The development has been widely criticized for replacing a vibrant neighborhood with a cold, windswept expanse where no one really wants to go.

Right across the street, though, an aging fish market next to the historic Faneuil Hall was turned into an outdoor shopping mall in 1976; the resulting Faneuil Hall Marketplace was instantly hailed as a triumph of urban renewal and has been packed with residents and tourists ever since. People come from all over to stroll among inviting gift shops, entertaining street performers, and vendors selling seafood and other local specialties.

Why did Faneuil Hall Marketplace work so well in rejuvenating a troubled neighborhood, and Government Center fail? There are many answers, but one answer is that no one was displaced in the building of the marketplace. A lesson from Boston's experiences is that just because a neighborhood strikes some people as unsavory doesn't mean it's "dying," and that when a neighborhood is destroyed, you can't grow a new one overnight no matter how much money you spend.

Sociologists have always been fascinated by suburbs: Although it's clear that many families find them highly desirable as places to live, sociologists have often been troubled by certain aspects of suburban life:

✔ In his bestseller *The Lonely Crowd*, sociologist David Riesman worried that suburban life was helping to turn Americans into "other-directed" people who did what everyone else was doing instead of what their "inner compasses" told them to do.

✔ Sociologist William H. Whyte made a similar argument in *The Organization Man*, which painted the suburbs as cookie-cutter neighborhoods where people lived bland, interchangeable lives.

✔ In *The Levittowners*, a study of the first new-model American suburb, sociologist Herbert J. Gans observed how racially and economically homogeneous the suburbs were, and wondered whether suburbs were contributing to social segregation.

Sociologists also, however, acknowledge that residents of some suburban communities have social bonds that are very tightly knit — perhaps even *too* tightly knit. Whyte's study of a growing suburban community in *The Organization Man* shows how many residents were kept almost dizzyingly busy with schedules of card games, church meetings, and other social functions. Residents were able to rely on one another for everything from child care to a stick of butter to emotional support. Far from being isolating, the suburbs were intensely social. The suburbs' relative homogeneity was both a cause and an effect of that aspect of suburban life.

At first, sociologists like Gans were concerned at the "white flight" represented by suburban growth, with relatively wealthy — often white — city dwellers abandoning urban neighborhoods for the shiny, safe suburbs. As those mid-century suburbs have aged, though, they've become less desirable and more diverse. Many well-to-do families have left older suburbs like Levittown; some heading for the newer, shiner "exurbs" that lie beyond the suburbs and others heading back into the city, where they contribute to the process of gentrification (see the section "Gentrification and the new creative class" later in this chapter).

Many post-war American suburbs are now populated by a diverse mix of long-time residents and new arrivals priced out of their inner-city neighborhoods. Some are home to thriving enclaves of immigrants from places like Africa and East Asia. Though the houses may still be "cookie-cutter," their residents are anything but.

Life in the City: Perils and Promise

As they have always been, cities are places of great hope, great promise, and — like any place — real dangers. Some people live in cities because they've always dreamed of being there, others find city life to be a nightmare from which they can't escape. In this section, I address the conflicts and tensions inherent in city life.

The upper class, the lower class, and the underclass

Diversity of all sorts is among the essential features of big-city life, but not all urban neighborhoods are particularly diverse. Some neighborhoods are primarily occupied by wealthy people who own lavish homes or high-rise condominiums, some are primarily occupied by working-class people who live in modest homes or rent decent but not luxurious apartments, and others are downright rough, occupied by people who wish they could afford to live elsewhere.

As I note earlier in the section "Changing Neighborhoods," an essential insight of urban sociology is that your neighborhood isn't just a place where you live, it's a place that *affects* your life. Residents of expensive neighborhoods don't just get the nice, expensive house or apartment they're paying for; they also get everything that goes with living in that neighborhood:

- ✔ Good schools
- ✔ Well-kept public spaces and parks
- ✔ Well-maintained roads and sidewalks
- ✔ Good police protection
- ✔ A thriving business community, with multiple shopping and dining options

Those things make easier the lives of people who already live in relative comfort. In theory, these things should all be available to *all* residents of a city — but in reality, poorer neighborhoods tend to lack those amenities. Residents of a poor neighborhood are likely relatively poor to begin with; in addition to having to get by with limited money, they suffer the disadvantages of living in a poor neighborhood:

- ✔ Overcrowded, understaffed schools
- ✔ Public spaces and parks that are not as accessible or well-maintained as those in wealthier areas of town, and that may sometimes play host to dangerous or criminal activities
- ✔ Roads and sidewalks that are poorly maintained
- ✔ A police presence that may be inadequate, hostile, or so overwhelmed with serious crimes that isn't very responsive to ordinary residents' concerns
- ✔ A depressed business community, with few job opportunities and limited shopping options

To find jobs, good schools, and reasonably priced consumer goods, residents of poor neighborhoods are often forced to travel long distances by car — or, if they can't afford a car, by public transportation. At home, they may face physical danger and other challenges. Plus, they likely find it relatively difficult to make the social connections that will help them get up and out of poverty.

To describe these exceptionally challenging circumstances, sociologists sometimes use the term *underclass*. Sociologist William Julius Wilson, in his 1987 book *The Truly Disadvantaged*, argued that members of the urban underclass are those left behind when people who could afford to fled the city for the suburbs. As manufacturing jobs dried up in the 1960s, 70s, and 80s, members of the urban underclass were especially vulnerable and had a hard time maintaining steady employment, sometimes turning to crime, drug use, and other destructive activities.

Though a disproportionate share of the underclass are minorities, Wilson believes that the challenges of the underclass have less to do with racism than with simple economic realities. "White flight," says Wilson, wasn't just white flight — it was the flight of people of all races who could afford to leave the troubled inner cities. The disappearance of middle-class blacks might, in some ways, have created much more of a challenge for inner-city African-American communities than did the disappearance of middle-class whites.

Gentrification and the new creative class

Elijah Anderson's 1990 book *Streetwise* tells the stories of two neighboring inner-city communities: "Northton," a predominantly black neighborhood plagued with low employment, high crime rates, poor health, and other problems; and "the Village," a diverse neighborhood that's on the upswing.

Many Northton residents could be described as members of the underclass, and Anderson notes that the community is home to fewer and fewer role models as the guru-like "old heads" of the neighborhood die, move out, or are simply marginalized as young people in the community fall under the sway of less constructive influences. By contrast, Anderson's Village neighborhood is steadily becoming wealthier — and whiter. The challenge faced by the Village is the challenge of *gentrification*.

The word "gentrification" is derived from the word "gentry," which describes wealthy landowners in traditional European society. Gentrification is the process by which neighborhoods become steadily wealthier, especially inner-city neighborhoods that have long been relatively affordable.

If you live in a city, you've seen gentrification happening, even in you haven't heard the process called by that name. Think about a neighborhood in your city where the "creative types" have been moving — the artists, the single professionals, the people who enjoy living where "the action" is. It may be a working-class neighborhood, it may be a "tough" neighborhood downtown. The new residents move there because it's affordable and conveniently located, but as more and more well-educated people with relatively high incomes move into the neighborhood, you start to see the signs of gentrification:

- ✔ "Hip" bars and coffee shops
- ✔ Art galleries and theaters
- ✔ New construction, including housing renovations and expansions

These things all serve to, over time, increase the desirability of the neighborhood — which makes houses and apartments there more valuable, which makes them more expensive to buy or rent. This can create tension between the new residents and the longtime residents, who not only see the character of their neighborhood changed, but also find themselves increasingly priced out of their own communities.

Neighborhoods have always gone up and down in value over time, but gentrification has particularly been a concern among sociologists and urban planners over the past few decades, as inner-city neighborhoods have become more desirable to what Richard Florida, a scholar of urban life, calls "the creative class."

According to Florida, members of the "creative class" are becoming increasingly central to economic life in developed countries. As manufacturing jobs move overseas, life in countries like Germany, the United States, and Australia is increasingly dominated by people who essentially *think* for a living. They may be software engineers, businesspeople, artists, or filmmakers. What they have in common is that they thrive in diverse, dense communities that give them many opportunities for intellectual and social stimulation. Where do they find these communities? Often, in inner cities.

Are those inner cities ready for the creative class? Ready or not, here they come.

Order and disorder on the streets

Chances are that today, your city looks a lot like mine, Minneapolis.

- ✔ There's a central city that's home to important economic, political, and cultural institutions; within that city there are pricey residential neighborhoods, hip "up and coming" neighborhoods, sturdy working-class and middle-class neighborhoods, neighborhoods home to large (and growing) immigrant populations, and "tough" neighborhoods where you don't want to spend too much time after dark.

✔ There are affordable inner-ring suburbs where life is often still regarded as "nice," but not as nice as it was in the 1950s, when they were the place to be. They're still *a* place to be, but not *the* place to be.

✔ There are exurbs, where young families and older retirees move when they want the space and comfortable safety that the inner-ring suburbs once offered. Much of the city's new-home construction is happening here.

People often move to the exurbs and suburbs because they seem safe, and in some ways they are: Though suburbanites have their share of problems, crime rates are generally lower in the suburbs. Most importantly, though, the suburbs *feel* safer.

What is it that makes a neighborhood feel safe? What is it that makes a community feel like a place you want to live, or don't want to live? Why are crimes so much more frequent in some neighborhoods than in others?

In Chapter 2, as an example of a sociological study that's helped policy-makers find out what "really matters," I cite a study by Robert J. Sampson and Stephen Raudenbush that surprisingly challenged the idea that small signs of seeming disorder in a neighborhood — for example, broken windows in houses — cause people to think those are lawless places where anything goes. It is true, found Sampson and Raudenbush, that people are more likely to commit crimes in places they perceive to be "disordered," but they judge urban disorder not by the condition of windows and walls but by the people they see there. Specifically — and unfortunately — they tend to associate a significant minority presence in a neighborhood with "disorder." (In fact, this holds true even for observers who are themselves members of minority groups.)

Of course, all cities are disordered to some extent; that's part of their appeal. In his book *The Geography of Nowhere*, social critic James Howard Kunstler observes that what makes cities exciting for some — and scary for others — is that, unlike in a suburban community, when you walk down a city street you have no idea who you're going to run into. If you live in the city, you're going to have at least glancing interactions every day with a lot of people who are quite different from you and whom you may see only once in your life.

What should a city look like? Kunstler is a proponent of a philosophy called "New Urbanism." He and other New Urbanists believe that cities worked best before they were so sharply divided into commercial and residential zones, when urban areas had a mix of uses. They tend to favor:

✔ Affordable housing integrated with more expensive, luxurious housing.

✔ Housing integrated with commercial establishments — for example, apartments above stores.

✔ Pedestrian-friendly public plazas.

✔ Accessible, affordable public transportation.

Can New Urbanism bring diverse, lively environments to the inner city? In some cases it's worked, but in other cases — for example, a Disney-sponsored New Urbanist city called Celebration — it's fallen flat.

New Urbanism may be a useful way of thinking about successful city spaces, but whether or not the Chicago School sociologists were 100 percent right in thinking of cities as "ecosystems," it's clear that successful neighborhoods are like successful natural ecosystems: They're hard to build from scratch, they're tremendously valuable, and they're surprisingly fragile.

Part V
Sociology and Your Life

"I'm tired of letting everyone pull my strings."

In this part . . .

*E*nough about the whole wide world — what about *you?* What does sociology have to do with *your* life? As it turns out, quite a lot. In this part, I explain how your life is influenced by your society — from birth to death, and at all points along the way.

Chapter 15

Get Born, Get a Job, Get a Kid, Get Out of Here: The Family and the Life Course

*I*n a recent production of J. B. Priestley's play *When We Are Married* at the Guthrie Theater in Minneapolis, audience members enjoyed the story of three couples who were married on the same date in 1883 meeting to celebrate their shared 25th anniversary. The actors were, or were made to appear to be, in their 60s. No one except me seemed to find that peculiar — but they should have! Why? Because in 1883, the average age of marriage for women was under 21. The actors should have been in their 40s!

As with all other social norms, it's easy to assume that the way things are in your society is the way they've always been, or the way they are everywhere else. That's rarely true, though; and it's especially not true with respect to the timing and progression of steps through the life course. Different people, at different times and in different places, have had widely varying ideas about what makes "a good life."

In this chapter, I explain how the life course itself is socially constructed. First, I discuss the social construction of age (at both ends of the spectrum, childhood and old age); then, I explain how demographers study the life course. Finally, I explain how sociologists study the always-timely issue of health care, and how family life has changed over time.

The Social Construction of Age

Age itself isn't socially constructed — the body's basic life cycle is the same for all people, everywhere. To say that "age" is socially constructed is to say that people's ideas about what is necessary and appropriate for people at each stage of life varies from place to place and from time to time. In this section, I explain how ideas of childhood and old age have varied, and continue to change.

The "invention" of childhood

A historian named Phillippe Ariés made headlines (well, academic headlines) in the 1960s with his bold assertion that the idea of childhood was "invented" in the Middle Ages. According to Ariés, before that point in history, people didn't think of kids as being all that different from adults: They were just a little smaller. As soon as possible, kids became involved in the economic and productive life of society; they weren't regarded as needing any kind of special treatment just because they were below a certain age.

Historians today agree that Ariés overstated his case by a long shot, that the essential dynamic of family life — with parents loving their children tenderly, sometimes coddling them while also often encouraging them to do chores and achieve tasks — has been just about the same since the beginning of history. Still, Ariés was on to something: For most of human history, childhood wasn't nearly as distinct from adulthood as it is now. Think about the ways that children today are regarded as being different than adults:

- Children cannot legally vote, sign contracts, or take independent responsibility for themselves — rights that are guaranteed to all adults.

- Children are not allowed to work for pay (except for teenagers, within strict limits), and they are forced to attend school.

- Children are seen as being especially vulnerable and innocent, and are in need of shelter from the dangers of the world.

For much of human history, none of those things were seen as being true. Until very recently — a couple hundred years ago — most children did not attend grade school, let alone high school. They were needed to help support their family by working on the family farm (or, later, in factories), and the skills they'd be learning in school (even reading and writing) were seen as luxuries, not necessities. As for their innocence . . . many people, including the Puritans who settled America, believed that children were fundamentally sinful, and were in need of strict discipline to mold them into responsible adults.

Interestingly, along the way children acquired some specific rights that they did not previously have. Today, children in most countries have the right to seek legal protection (or to have protection sought for them) if their parents or guardians abuse or overwork them. Plus, it's increasingly the norm in educational and family settings to allow children a lot of say in what they do and when. ("Would you like to play in the block area or in the art area? What book do you want to read? Where do you want to go today?") That's much different than when children were meant to be seen and not heard.

Why the change? Has society simply become more . . . enlightened? Well, yes, but it's also true that the seismic social changes that gave birth to modern society (and to sociology — see Chapter 3) changed the place of children in society.

As a society develops, industrializes, and urbanizes, it eventually undergoes what demographers (people who study trends in population) call a "demographic transition." At that time, both mortality (death rates) and fertility (birth rates) fall steeply: Fewer people are born, and they live longer. This happened in the United States and in Europe between 100 to 200 years ago.

After a demographic transition, there are fewer children around, and because they live in a (relatively) high-tech, industrializing society, they need to go to school for many years before they can be productive members of society. This means that they need to be supported by their parents for many years — instead of supporting their parents through their work, as was formerly the case. Is it any surprise, then, that most parents have fewer children than they used to?

So the children who do come along are bigger deals than they used to be. They're not *loved* any more than they used to be — parents throughout history have always loved their children — but they are the focus of more schooling, more money, and much more attention. That is new, and that is the main reason why childhood today is so much different than childhood was just a few hundred years ago.

Are kids today spoiled? If being "spoiled" means being doted upon by overly accommodating adults, then that's a matter of judgment. If being "spoiled," though, means being guaranteed an education and protected from forced labor . . . then yes, they're spoiled rotten.

To understand the profound difference between childhood today and childhood just over a century ago, consider that in the late 19th century — as sociologist Viviana Zelizer has pointed out — parents were invited to insure their children's lives to compensate the family for income deceased children would have made had they survived. Today, by contrast, the cost of raising and educating a middle-class child in the United States can exceed $250,000. Children may represent a "net gain" emotionally, but certainly not financially!

Dad, can I take the car?

Anyone who's read Jane Austen's *Pride and Prejudice*, or seen a film adaptation of the story, has an idea of how courtship worked before the 20th century. Couples got married without ever exactly "dating": They would make each other's acquaintance in public settings, and if the match was deemed suitable (at least by their families, and ideally by the members of the couple as well), they'd become engaged and that was that.

What you did as a teenager may have surprised your parents, but it would have really *mortified* your great-great-great-grandparents. There's still some controversy around whether or not teenagers should have sex, but just about everyone agrees that it's proper for there to be a stage of life during which young people go about independently with members of the opposite gender (or, now, whichever gender they're attracted to), hang out with friends, be alone together, and at least do a little smooching.

Modern adolescence was born in the early 20th century, as attending high school became widespread and technology (notably, the automobile) gave young people a measure of independent mobility. The whole commercial culture of adolescence — from soda fountains to school dances to youth fashions — sprang up around that time.

Ever since then, "adolescence" has been expanding to fill more and more of the life span. Today, 12-year-olds often act like 16-year-olds — running around at all hours and having a series of boyfriends or girlfriends — but so do 30-year-olds! A major reason for this is the increase in college and grad school attendance, with many people taking until their mid-20s or even their 30s to finish schooling and settle down to begin a career. It's hard to do homework when you have a toddler walking around . . . just ask anyone who's tried!

18 again: The new senior citizens

Just as the earliest stages of life have been changing rapidly in recent years, so have the later stages.

People in the final decades of life have always been an important part of society, serving as leaders and mentors and supporting younger people as they raise children and take up leadership positions. A number of changes over the past century, though, have completely transformed seniors' experiences and essentially created an entire new stage of life.

For one thing, there's simply much *more* of life than there used to be. My grandma will occasionally include in her e-mails and letters statements like, "I'm 89!" She seems almost surprised to still be alive — and no wonder. She's already lived over 30 years longer than most other American girls born in 1919. Grandma's great-granddaughter, though — my niece Madeline, born in 2007 — can reasonably expect that she and most of her peers will easily reach the age of 80. Further, medical advances have dramatically improved the quality of life for older people.

Additional social changes that have changed the experience of being past "middle age" (whatever that is) include:

- ✔ **Economic changes** that have made things both easier and harder for senior citizens. On the one hand, jobs relying on experience and knowledge rather than physical endurance have become more plentiful and lucrative; but on the other hand, economic tumult means that more and more seniors find themselves unexpectedly out of work — and possibly facing age discrimination (see Chapter 8) when they apply for new jobs. Further, Baby Boomers have now reached what used to be considered "retirement age," but many are finding themselves without the pension plans their parents had and thus forced to continue working, at least part-time.

- ✔ **Childbearing changes** have meant that people are having children later and later — in some cases, even after age 40. This means that not infrequently, people reach their 60s still supporting their children in college or grad school. With a predominance of two-earner families, grandparents also find themselves more essential to the day-to-day care of their grandchildren than they would have been 50 years ago.

- ✔ **Changes in relationships** — including a divorce rate around 40 percent — and reproductive technology (yes, Viagra) have meant that more and more seniors are dating and leading active sex lives.

All this adds up to a very different experience for today's seniors than their parents and grandparents had. The title of this section — "18 again" — is tongue-in-cheek, but it's not a joke. Seniors today often lead lives with a mix of work, family responsibilities, romance, and recreation that's not dissimilar to the kind of life a teenager or college student leads. (In fact, increasing numbers of seniors are going back to school and *becoming* college students.) The only differences? Seniors go to bed earlier . . . and do more drugs.

This sounds like fun, and that's absolutely true: Whether living independently, with friends or relatives, in retirement or assisted-living communities, or in nursing homes, seniors today are leading notably exciting, fulfilling lives. Though people over 50 didn't grow up with the Internet, they've learned quickly and are fueling much of the growth of social networking sites and other online communities.

It's also true, however, that seniors today face a historically unique set of stressors. With families being small and economic times being tight, seniors can't count on their children to support them — in fact, they're having to support their children for unprecedentedly long periods of time. Most of them have not had life-long jobs, and robust pension plans or retirement savings accounts are fewer and fewer. Government subsidies help, but are hard to live on. What this means is that not only are seniors *able* to live active lives, many of them *have* to live active lives — they need the income. Being able to be up and at 'em and on the job every morning when you're 70 is great, but being forced to is not.

Social scientists project that over the next few decades, the number of people age 65 and over will grow at three times the rate of the population generally — so seniors are going to become a bigger and even more important part of society.

Running the Course of Life

From a sociological perspective, understanding the life course doesn't just mean understanding *what* happens over the course of a life; it means understanding *when* it happens. In this section, I explain how sociologists, demographers, and other social scientists study the incidence and timing of life-course transitions.

Demographics and life transitions

Demographics is the study of population patterns — in other words, the study of how populations of different groups of people grow, shrink, and move over time.

If you're interested in TV, you may have heard the term used in connection with ratings. TV producers pay close attention to the demographics of their audience because they need to report that information to their advertisers. Here are the kind of information advertisers want to know:

- How many people watch a program?
- Where do they live?
- How old are they?
- Are they men or women?
- Are they married or unmarried?
- How much money do they make?

This is important information for advertisers because they want to target their products: If you manufacture pantyhose, you probably don't want to advertise on a program watched mostly by men — unless they're drag queens or bank robbers.

Demographic information is also essential, however, for many other organizations. Governments need to know how many representatives to assign to a state (the primary purpose for the U.S. census), as well as where to put libraries and mailboxes and swing sets. Corporations need to know where to open new electronics stores, bakeries, and day care centers; and nonprofit organizations need to know where to focus their efforts to support single mothers, or elderly Lutherans, or people with HIV. Demographic data are also, of course, very important to sociologists as well as other social scientists.

Demographers, and sociologists interested in demography, tend to be particularly interested in *life-course transitions*. Those are the points at which people transition from one stage of life to the next. Some transitions (aging, for example) are gradual, but most are quite abrupt: Even if they're a long time coming, they happen more or less instantly. Important life-course transitions include:

✔ Birth

✔ Completing stages of education (grade school, high school, college, grad school)

✔ The beginning of labor-force participation (in other words, getting a job)

✔ The start of dating and sexual activity

✔ Moving out of one's parents' household

✔ Childbearing

✔ Cohabitation (moving in with a romantic partner)

✔ Marriage

✔ Divorce

✔ Death

Gathering data on these can be tricky; some are matters of public record, but others need to be gathered with surveys or other techniques (see sidebar, "Counting and recounting"). These are the essential signposts of life, though, and with these transitions come enormous changes in people's activities and goals. Having accurate demographic data is invaluable for understanding how communities work — and how they change over time.

Counting and recounting

When you hear someone tell you that "the population of Boise is 205,314," or "the average Canadian male has first sexual intercourse at age 16," or "700 million people watched the Oscars," do you ever wonder how the heck they *know* that? You should. Demographic data are gathered by a variety of means, none of them perfect.

It may seem easy to call someone up and ask how old he or she is, but in actuality surveys are hugely expensive — and the better they are, the more expensive they get. The U.S. census aspires to survey every single American resident, but it's impossible to reach that goal. The Census Bureau itself estimates that it missed over six *million* people in the 2000 census . . . and that's just for the bare headcount. More detailed demographic information comes from the census's long form, which was intentionally only sent to about 16 percent of households. That doesn't mean the long form data are inaccurate, but it does mean that there's greater room for error there — and there's even more room for error in smaller, privately administered surveys.

Among surveys commonly used by sociologists, the number of respondents range from tens of thousands at the high end — larger sample sizes are highly unusual, especially when data are detailed — to mere hundreds at the low end. Many sociological studies derive from just a few big surveys where data are publicly available; few sociologists have the resources to survey thousands of respondents.

As I explain in Chapter 4, having a relatively small sample size doesn't mean that data are inaccurate, just so long as the group you managed to survey is actually representative of the population you want to study. That's easier said than done (and as you can see by the last sentence, it's not even that easily said). Statisticians have developed some extremely impressive tools for analyzing data, but when someone throws a bunch of demographic data at you to prove his or her point, it's not a bad idea to read the fine print.

Different shapes of the circle of life

The average American man graduates from high school at 18, moves out of his parents' house at age 22, gets married at age 27, and has his first child at age 32. Does that describe any actual American man you know? It might, but it probably doesn't. Those are averages calculated from data on many thousands of men, but each individual American man follows his own course.

So do those averages mean anything at all? Absolutely. They describe the normative life course in American society. They describe the typical path of life for American men, and they're roughly equal to the averages seen in similar countries. Americans know about what those averages are, and men know that if they go through those transitions earlier or later than average — or not at all — they're unusual.

Of course, "American men" is a vast group, comprising well over 100 million people. It includes white working-class men in Philadelphia, Latino architects in Miami, black dentists in Oregon, and Asian farmers in California. Each of those groups has its own averages, and for various reasons they're all different. Demographers, and sociologists interested in demography, spend a lot of time trying to figure out *how* life course transitions are different among different groups of people, as well as *why* they're different and *when* they happen for each group. This may include asking questions like:

- Why do people whose parents are college graduates become financially independent at a later age than people whose parents are not?
- Why do women typically marry at a younger age than men?
- Why do divorce rates vary among races and ethnicities?
- Why do people in some states retire at earlier ages than people in other states?
- Why are small towns typically populated by older people than are big cities?

Just starting to think about what the answers to these questions might be, you can see how life course transitions are deeply tied to all other aspects of society. The average age of, say, marriage is tied to a range of things including education, dating and courtship practices, the economy, and the law. If it varies — as it does — from group to group, that's typically for a range of good reasons, and it falls to sociologists and other social scientists to sort those reasons out.

Because the sequence and timing of life transitions varies among social groups, that means it varies from place to place, from society to society, and from time to time. Another task that keeps sociologists and demographers busy is figuring out why those transitions vary over time. As I note in the introduction to this chapter, people today marry several years later than they did in the fairly recent past . . . why? Since 1883, the shape of life has changed . . . and it will continue to change.

The very nature of life course transitions changes over time. Transitions that may seem momentous and universal at one time and in one place may disappear as important life markers, and others may arise.

Retirement, for example, was not too long ago regarded as a hugely significant life transition. When a man or woman had finished a successful career, they stopped working and commenced to spend the rest of their life on pursuits they chose, living off retirement savings or a pension. Today, that life transition is disappearing. More and more people are working throughout their lives, and changing companies or even changing careers as they do so.

The number of people who officially "retire" after multiple decades at one company (or in one career) is declining, so young people today don't expect to "retire" as their grandparents did. One result of this is that they're less likely, among other things, to save money for retirement.

A life course transition that's becoming increasingly common, on the other hand, is cohabitation. Just a few decades ago, a couple who lived together before marriage was seen as exceptional, and "shacking up" was something you might not even talk openly about. In some circles, that's still the case; but increasingly, cohabitation is a normal step in relationships that may or may not lead to marriage. In acknowledgement of this as well as of the increasing prevalence of couples who openly live together in same-sex relationships, invitations to events are now more likely to say "partners invited" than "spouses invited." Cohabitation is becoming a newly common transition in the ever-changing life course.

Taking Care: Health Care and Society

No matter what bad things happen to members of our family, my grandma has a single response: "At least you have your health!" Not just for her, but for many people, health is *the* fundamental concern in life: Without your health, it's hard to enjoy anything else. Further, it's a family concern: Your health can affect your employment, your mobility, your life expectancy, and many other aspects of your life that have a profound bearing on your family.

Sociologists have found, however, that "health" can mean different things to different people — and that providing health care is a matter of making hard decisions, both for individuals and society. In this section, I explain why.

Deciding what counts as "healthy"

It may seem absurd to think of health as something that's socially constructed. After all, a broken arm is a broken arm, no matter what society you're in. That's of course true, but if you're asked whether or not you're "healthy," you could answer that question in many ways, and in doing so you'll consider what is normally considered healthy in your society.

Even if I make the question more specific and ask whether you need treatment for a health concern, your answer will vary depending on what treatment options are available to you and your family. Think about all these different examples of people seeking medical treatment:

✔ A 69-year-old woman has ovarian cancer and goes with her husband to a clinic to receive chemotherapy.

✔ A 41-year-old man has an appointment with a counselor to talk about emotional problems he's been having since the end of a relationship.

✔ After starting a new relationship, a 26-year-old woman visits her gynecologist to request a prescription for birth control pills.

✔ A 12-year-old boy has broken his collarbone skateboarding, and his mother takes him to the emergency room to have the bone set and a cast put on.

✔ A 52-year-old man goes to his dentist to have a root canal performed.

✔ A 37-year-old woman is having back pain after childbirth and receives acupuncture to relieve the pain.

Those are all legitimate health issues, but they would have been treated very differently — or possibly not at all — in different places and times. Why does the definition of what counts as "healthy" change over time and from place to place?

One obvious factor that changes is technology. As the ability to treat health issues grows, the bar for what counts as "healthy" goes up. Today, medical professionals have the ability to replace missing teeth, excise unwanted fat deposits, do full-body cancer scans, and perform thousands of other treatments that would have been impossible just a few decades ago. This means that the number of different health issues any given person can be treated for at any given time has grown significantly. That's not to say any given family can necessarily *afford* to have those things treated or would *choose* to have them treated, but the possibilities are there.

Another aspect of health that varies, though, is a society's — and a family's — notion of what lifestyle and bodily state corresponds to the picture of "health." Having conspicuously visible fat in the belly and elsewhere has been regarded in many societies as being especially healthy; in most societies today, it's considered healthier to be on the thin side rather than the heavy side. This is a result of changes in:

✔ **Knowledge:** Medical professionals today understand that being obese increases one's risk of heart failure and other health problems.

✔ **Material circumstances:** Because of changes in agriculture, transportation, and food-processing technology, it's now more expensive to eat a healthy diet of vegetables than to eat a poor diet of junk food. Thus, being thinner is an indicator of greater wealth.

✔ **Culture:** Prominent opinion-makers in the media and in social networks have promulgated the idea that thinness is attractive.

Is ADHD socially constructed?

After decades of debate, psychologists have arrived at a definition of a disorder now called attention deficit hyperactivity disorder (ADHD), a condition in which individuals experience inattentiveness and/or impulsive behavior to an extent that interferes with their daily lives. Common treatments for ADHD include medications like Ritalin that often help increase attention span, concentration, and self-control.

ADHD has been diagnosed with increasing frequency in recent years, especially among children, and has become a matter of much debate among parents and educators. Some believe that many children diagnosed with ADHD are simply unusually active, and that medicating children for the condition is tantamount to drugging them into submission. Others — both children and adults — have found that taking medication has completely transformed their ability to get work done and has significantly enhanced their lives. When my friend's doctor prescribed Ritalin for her, he explained that some of his patients liken it to putting on a pair of glasses: It brings clarity.

It's hard to blame people for being suspicious of the medical establishment, which has not always worked well in the past (as recently as the 1950s, doctors were appearing in cigarette advertisements to tout their favorite brands). Still, most people find that professional associations like the American Psychological Association are generally trustworthy, and when they decide — as in this case — that a disorder is "real," then it's best to assume they're right.

Definitions of health and sickness have always changed, and will always do so. Sociologists (and physicians) agree that the current medical consensus is by no means the final word on what diseases "actually" exist. Still, unless you're ready to write off the medical establishment entirely — and some are! — the best you can do, in medicine as in sociology, is to find the most reliable data and interpret them as well as you are able. You can refine your views as more data become available. Right now, the best evidence suggests that, though it's not for everyone, medication can be enormously helpful for many people who have ADHD.

Mental health is an area where attitudes particularly vary among societies. At the extreme, mental states like schizophrenia that may be regarded as dangerous or unhealthy in some societies may be regarded as special or blessed in others; short of that, though, opinions may vary widely from one society to the next about whether it's desirable to seek treatment for depression, attention deficit disorder, learning disabilities, or anxiety. Even within a given society, different individuals may have strikingly different views on those matters. (See sidebar, "Is ADHD socially constructed?")

When families are making decisions about health care, they are influenced by the attitudes in their society — and, if they have immigrated, in the society from which they came — as they decide whether to pursue preventative medicine, emergency medicine, traditional or holistic medicine, or nothing at all.

The complex challenges faced by families in making health-care decisions are also challenges faced by governments, as they decide where, how, and when to devote resources to their citizens' health care.

Organizing and distributing health care

Because health is so fundamentally important, there will always be debates over how health care is organized and distributed within societies. Everyone wants the best possible care for themselves and their loved ones, but the best possible care is extremely expensive.

Many governments and health care organizations aspire to guarantee adequate — ideally, far better than merely adequate — health care for all their citizens, but if every single person had unlimited access to all existing medical treatments and technology, the cost could be so high that a society would hardly be able to afford much else. If your family finances have ever been strained by the cost of health care, you understand the challenges that leaders in your government are facing.

What this means is that, one way or another, every society must somehow determine how and when various treatments will be provided — and how they'll be paid for. Sociologists often study health care both to help improve it and because the medical establishment is a fascinating social institution.

A sociologist's overall perspective on the health care establishment will depend on whether he or she leans more in the direction of Durkheimian functionalism or Marxism. (See Chapter 3 for more on those perspectives.)

  ✔ A **functionalist** will likely pay attention to the overall norms — formal and informal — defining who is "sick" and how they'll be treated. Talcott Parsons believed that "sick" is a particular role in society, a role that varies among societies of different sizes and at different stages of development. Just as there is always crime in society, there will always be the sick; but if a society defines too many people as sick, not enough work will get done and too much money will be spent on health care. If a society defines too *few* people as sick and fails to attend to basic health needs, it will suffer in the long run.

  ✔ A **Marxist** will emphasize that different parties have different material stakes in health care. Providers and insurance companies want to provide as much care as possible providing they're generously paid for it, but the patients want that care provided at low or no cost. The government could conceivably adjudicate between them, but is likely to be in control of the wealthy and thus to favor their interests.

Of course, this isn't just a black-or-white proposition: Most sociologists today don't fall strongly in either of those camps but instead have a view akin to Weber's: that different groups and individuals have real material interests, but that the conflicts among them play out on a field where the ground rules are set by cultural norms. For example, hospitals or insurance companies find themselves under siege when they deny lifesaving care to children; that care might be vastly expensive, and the children's families may be unable to pay the cost of that care, but there's a strong social norm discouraging anyone from allowing a child to die if there's anything that can be done to prevent it.

What all sociologists agree on is that health care organizations are exactly that — *organizations* — and they are apt to behave like all other complex organizations. I explain in Chapter 12 that organizational life is about much more than just "getting the job done," it's about managing the people in the organization as well as managing the organization's relationship with its surroundings. This is just as true for hospitals and clinics as it is for coffee shops, despite the fact that the stakes are much higher.

Medical professions — especially the profession of physician — are deeply institutionalized: To become a doctor or a nurse, you have to go through long training that provides not just an education in how the human body works, but an education in how to *be* a doctor or a nurse. Members of those professions tend to go about various practices and procedures in certain ways; as with any profession, some of those traditional practices are wise and provide continuity and reliability whereas others may be bad habits that ought to be broken. Consider that when training to be a doctor, residents (young doctors learning the ropes) often work for shifts of over 24 hours. By the end of those shifts, they're exhausted and, evidence suggests, more prone to make mistakes — but the current system is a longstanding tradition and has been resistant to change.

Doctors have more extensive training than do nurses, and have traditionally been the authorities in medical settings. Nurses, however, argue that their close day-to-day experience with patients (a doctor may see a given patient much less frequently than that patient's nurses do) give them a valuable perspective that doctors too often neglect to consider, just because the doctors are "the experts."

Medical professionals can be just as hesitant to believe evidence that contradicts their beliefs as everyone else is. A doctor may diagnose a patient based on a quick assessment or a hunch, and then may be slow to notice or accept subsequent evidence that they may have erred in their initial judgment.

Medical professionals are human beings, and medical organizations are human institutions. As such, they're subject to the same forces that make it alternately inspiring and frustrating to be a part of a complex organization. It may seem scary to think that your and your family's health is in the hands of an organization that makes the same kind of mistakes your company or school makes, but it's the truth — and only by accepting that can sociologists and others work to make medical organizations safer, more effective, and more efficient.

Families Past and Present

Have you ever noticed how many books, movies, and TV shows are about family life? Families are at the heart of most people's lives, and they're endlessly fascinating to people trying to understand the human condition. No sociologist (or author or filmmaker or anyone else, for that matter) can tell you how your family works, but sociology can help you understand the social patterns that influence your family. In this section, I first describe the history of the family and then explain what social scientists know about families today.

The way we never were

The family in the 1950s *Dick and Jane* series of reading primers for children featured a father in a business suit (the implication being that he's the breadwinner), a mother in an apron (the implication being that she's the homemaker), a son, a daughter, and a dog. That's become the default image of "the family" that pops into many people's minds, but it's certainly not representative of most families today — and there were many, many families it wasn't representative of even then.

The 1950s, which still loom so large in people's imaginations as an era of idealized family life, were a unique time in recent history. Many men were returning home after fighting in World War II, and they were settling down with their partners to start families in the so-called "Baby Boom." It was a time of relative prosperity, and both social norms and government policies encouraged the building of new homes in suburban settings.

Since then, there have been many conspicuous changes in family life. More families have two earners (rather than a single earner supporting the entire family), more children are born out of wedlock, and more marriages end in divorce. These changes are sometimes portrayed as a decline in "family values."

You're entitled to your opinion about what the best family structure is, and to argue for government policies that promote that structure, but be careful when using phrases like "family values." There are many different kinds of family, and your family values may not be the same as your neighbor's.

As I explain in Chapter 5, cultural change and structural change almost always go hand-in-hand, and it can be very difficult to sort out what caused what. There have certainly been some significant changes in cultural ideals regarding family life: Divorce, single parenting, and unmarried partnership are all more commonly accepted than they were five or six decades ago. Whether or not you regard this change as something bad, it's important to be aware that there have been some real structural changes — that is, changes in basic social conditions — since the post-war era:

- ✔ The economy is more turbulent, and it's much more challenging for a single individual to secure and hold a job that will support a family over several decades. Many more families *have to be* dual-income families than was the case in the 50s.

- ✔ Developments in law and corporate policies, some spurred by the efforts of same-sex couples unable to marry, have made it easier for unmarried couples to enjoy some of the practical benefits — insurance coverage, shared child custody — of marriage. (Still, however, it's much more difficult for unmarried than married couples to access these benefits.)

- ✔ Though sociologists of gender still see a "glass ceiling" (see Chapter 9), implicit and explicit discrimination against women in educational and professional settings have sharply declined, making it easier for women to pursue careers on the same terms as men. When women today choose to leave jobs to raise children, because women are making relatively more money today, that choice is likely to have economic consequences that are more significant for the average family than they would have been in the 1950s.

- ✔ Advancements in contraceptive technology — most notably, the refinement and legalization of the birth control pill — have given men and women the option to be sexually active without conceiving children. Exercising this option is a personal choice, but previously, it was far more likely that sexual activity would result in pregnancy (with abortion being illegal and unsafe), so people were making choices about marriage and family life in a very different universe of possibilities.

So change in family life has definitely happened, for a number of reasons — but that said, the 1950s were not the idyllic time they may seem to have been. In her bestselling book *The Way We Never Were*, historian Stephanie Coontz deflates what she calls "the nostalgia trap": a trap in which people assume that because family life was more homogeneous in the 1950s, things were better then.

Among other things, Coontz points out that authorities often looked the other way in cases of spousal and child abuse, that it was not unusual for working fathers to spend a disproportionate amount of their income on luxuries for themselves, and same-sex relationships were almost entirely taboo. The divorce rate, though it's risen since the 1950s in most countries, plateaued at about 40 percent and has now remained stable for many years. And marriages continue to happen at a high rate; in fact, it's now *more* common for unmarried women in middle age and older to eventually marry (or, if they're divorced, remarry) than it was in the past.

Coontz and other historians of the family also point out that in the big picture, the 1950s were a very unusual decade — probably for reasons having to do more with the economy and post-war social policy than with people's values. The relatively low divorce rate in the 50s was just a temporary dip; in the United States, the divorce rate has been rising since the 1860s. Many changes in family life — from women's increasing economic and social freedom to the removal of children from the workforce — that are often seen as originating in the 1960s actually began a century earlier, in the Industrial Revolution.

Going it alone: The challenges of single parenting

People become single parents for many reasons. Often, there's a divorce or death that leaves one partner with custody of children; sometimes grandparents or other relatives take custody of children whose parents can't care for them; in other cases, people choose to have children while single; and then, of course, there are accidental pregnancies.

These all result in very different family situations, but what they all have in common is that the single parents face enormous challenges. That's not to say that life is always a bowl of cherries for partnered parents, but single parents generally have fewer financial and personal resources to draw upon as they raise their children. This will certainly mean that they have less personal and professional flexibility than partnered parents; and the financial challenges they face mean that children of single parents, who are disproportionately poor in the first place, are more likely than the children of partnered parents to grow up in poverty and to suffer the consequences of that difficult situation.

Single parents need a lot of support from their families and their communities. Some find it unfortunate that single parenting is more socially acceptable today than it was in the past, but the past shouldn't be romanticized.

My grandmother became a single parent when my grandfather died of cancer while my grandmother was pregnant with their sixth child. In their small farming town, Grandma sensed a lot of uneasiness about her unusual situation — in fact, she felt somewhat stigmatized — and she ultimately sought out other single parents; they bonded together for mutual support. Single parents today may (or may not) feel less of a stigma than my grandmother did, but they need just as much help and support to give their children the safe, happy lives they deserve.

Family life, like every aspect of social life, has always changed and will continue to change. Just as there's no such thing as a "perfect family," there's no such thing as a perfect norm of family life. Each family is different, for better and for worse.

The family today

What *is* "the family today"? Sociologically speaking, a family is any group of people who live together in mutual economic and social support. Usually families are connected by blood ties as well as emotional and financial ties, but as the saying goes, family is as family does. In this section, I consider a few of the most important issues facing families today.

Work — at home and outside the home

The division of labor in families has been a topic of contention for as long as there have been families; in recent decades in particular, the growing number of two-career families have been struggling to figure out an efficient and equitable way of dividing the tasks that have to be done in the home and out of the home.

In her 1989 book *The Second Shift*, sociologist Arlie Hochschild put her finger on the challenge facing many two-career families: Both mother and father work full-time jobs outside the home, but after work it's the mother who takes on the "second shift" of caring for the couple's children and managing other household tasks. What especially frustrated many of the women Hochschild talked with was that their husbands nominally accepted the idea that household labor should be equitably divided . . . they just didn't *do* their share.

Happily, evidence suggests that in the years since 1989, men have done a lot of catching up: Their household contributions now come closer to matching the work they admit they should do. Today, an unprecedented number of fathers are involved in tasks — from bathing children to sweeping floors to baking meatloaf — that most of their fathers and grandfathers could hardly have imagined taking routine responsibility for. Women still do the majority of household labor, but the gap is closing.

Men getting up off the couch has picked up some of the slack in the constant amount of household labor that needs to be accomplished in a shrinking amount of time . . . but getting things taken care of around the home is tough for any working family. Families that can afford to do so outsource housework and childcare, hiring nannies or housecleaners, many of whom travel from poorer neighborhoods (and even countries) in search of higher wages. Hochschild has written of the challenges faced by nannies who are mothers themselves, struggling to care for both their own children and their employers' children. Wealthy countries are "exporting emotional labor," says Hochschild. This will continue to be a challenge in the years and decades to come.

Kids today! They grow up so . . . slow?

Childbearing rates are falling in developed countries around the world, and no wonder! Kids are expensive, and they're getting more expensive all the time. Just 200 years ago, most children contributed significantly to their family's livelihood, often by helping out on the family farm or by taking paying work. Today, children are required to attend school well into their teenage years; most finish high school and many go on to attend college or even graduate school before beginning their careers in earnest.

Children in low-income families often still contribute significantly to their households by caring for younger siblings or by contributing income to the family, but most children in developed countries work only to earn experience and discretionary spending money. Parents who can afford to do so (including many who must stretch to do so) often find themselves entirely or partially supporting their children well into the children's 20s.

As I note in the sidebar "Dad, can I take the car?", the semi-autonomous state associated with adolescence is becoming increasingly the norm for children both young and old. Both because of technologies like the Internet and changing social norms, young children have more social autonomy than they've ever had; at the other end of the teenage years, young adults are remaining dependent on their parents for longer and longer. This is a big change in family structure, and families are still trying to figure out how to handle it.

Though child labor laws now limit the nature and extent of work that can be done by young people, teenagers normally seek some kind of employment — and in tough economic times, they may feel the pain even more acutely than mature workers. Having not completed their education, teenagers need to seek jobs that don't require complex skills or training, and those jobs are often the first to dry up when the economy goes south.

Marriage: What's in a ring?

The institution of marriage is not going away. A large majority of people, in societies around the world, still aspire to make a public lifelong commitment to a partner; most do marry, many more than once.

That said, the meaning of marriage is changing. Marriage was once primarily a legal arrangement; now, the legal aspect of marriage is generally seen as secondary to its emotional aspect. A spouse is still, in a sense, a business partner; but he or she is also now expected to be a lifelong love and a best friend. That's a tremendous amount of weight to put on a relationship. It works well for many couples, but the increased emotional expectation put upon marriage has surely been one of the factors leading to the increasing divorce rate over the past century.

Because the legal aspect of marriage is now seen as secondary, marriage is less universally seen as a necessary bond for loving couples. Out-of-wedlock births have been rising sharply in the past few years, and a big part of that growth has been accounted for by committed couples who begin families together without bothering to get married. That can create legal challenges for unmarried couples, but for various reasons people are increasingly using their growing freedom to live together and even raise children together without being married. Among them are millions of gay and lesbian couples who are not legally able to marry.

Again, though, marriage is not going away. Notably, older adults are increasingly marrying, whether for the first time or in the wake of divorce or widowhood. Life is getting longer, and many middle-aged and senior adults are finding new love in their later years — love that they're celebrating by getting married. (Or remarried. Or re-remarried.)

A return to the extended family

Among the many unrealistic aspects of the Dick-and-Jane image of the family, perhaps the most unrealistic is the suggestion that the nuclear family is an island unto itself. It may or may not take a village to raise a child, but it's absolutely true that every family draws on the support of extended family members including blood relatives, relatives by marriage, friends, coworkers, neighbors, and other community members. Dick and Jane's parents couldn't have done it by themselves, and neither could yours or mine.

That said, the mid-century nuclear family, in its own single-family home, was more independent than families before or since. Throughout history, families have lived together in compounds, houses, or apartment buildings. It's long been routine for aged parents to live with their children, for married sisters to move in with their brothers, and for hired help and other people to be brought in to boot. The idea that a couple should live alone with their young children, support themselves financially, and do everything else themselves is relatively new, and it's already crumbling.

All the developments outlined in this chapter — extending adolescence, more school, later marriage, fewer children, longer lives, economic pinches — add up to an increasing reliance on extended family members for emotional and logistic support. Grandparents are increasingly involved in their grandchildren's day-to-day lives, parents are increasingly involved in their grown children's lives, middle-aged children are increasingly involved in their grown parents' lives, and everyone is texting and e-mailing and calling and Facebooking everyone else 24/7.

It all gets a little crazy sometimes . . . but, well, that's family.

Chapter 16

Future Passed: Understanding Social Change

From the very beginning (see Chapter 3), sociologists have wanted to understand, predict, and influence social change. Historians may be content with understanding social change in *retrospect*, but sociologists want to understand the fundamental, universal processes by which societies change . . . and if you understand those processes, you should be able to predict what's going to happen in the future!

Wouldn't that be nice? In practice, of course, it's very difficult to predict how societies will change, no matter how much you understand about society. Think about meteorologists: Despite centuries of scientific observation and with all the most sophisticated technological tools at their command, they can't predict the weather with any more than approximate certainty. The forces determining the weather are simply too complex and subject to unpredictable variation for meteorologists to do much better.

And yet, they *can* predict the weather with reasonable accuracy. If the 6 o'clock news on Wednesday says it's going to rain on Friday, it probably will. Similarly, sociologists and other social scientists can't tell you with perfect accuracy who's going to win the next election or which neighborhoods will rise in value, but they can make an educated guess that will more than likely be accurate.

In this chapter, I first explain the Big Three sociologists' (Marx, Durkheim, and Weber, for those who haven't been paying attention) views on social change because they set the terms for all future sociological debate on the subject. Then, I explore some likely scenarios for existing societies; finally, I consider the future of sociology itself.

Why Societies Change

As in most other aspects of sociology, debate over social change often returns to the ideas of Marx, Durkheim, and Weber — not just because they're Marx, Durkheim, and Weber, but because together they laid out three views of social change that represent three convincing but distinctly different arguments for why and how societies evolve. Understanding their views on social change is a good starting point for understanding how sociologists today think about the subject.

See Chapter 3 for more on Marx, Durkheim and Weber, the "big three" sociologists.

Marx: If it's not one revolution, it's another

In all things, Karl Marx emphasized the importance of the material world and the distribution of resources. Marx thought that societies changed as different social groups fought over things like food, land, and power.

Marx was what's known as a "stage theorist": He thought that social change happened not gradually, but relatively suddenly. A society might be in one stage for centuries, then over the course of just a short period it might totally reorganize itself and move to the next stage. Further, he believed that the basic progression of stages was essentially universal and inevitable — just as all human beings go from being infants to toddlers to young children to adolescents to adults, Marx believed that all societies have to work through certain conflicts on their way to a final utopian stage — which, he believed, all societies would eventually achieve.

In Marx's ideal society, everyone would have access to their share (or, if they had special needs, more than their share) of social resources, and everyone would contribute their share (or, if they had special abilities, more than their share) of resources to the common good.

Similar to Durkheim and Weber, Marx did a tremendous amount of historical research. When he looked at human history, Marx saw a series of historical stages, in each of which there were divisions among social classes. The nature of those classes changed, thought Marx, from time to time — slaves and slave owners, feudal lords and serfs, merchants and farmers. Each period of time, thought Marx, had its own "mode of production" in which the various classes were organized in a particular way to do the work required to provide for everyone's needs.

None of the modes of production, though, have been perfect. In a perfect society, everyone would work together happily and harmoniously to grow food, build houses, and do everything else that needs to get done. That would only happen, though, said Marx, if the division of the fruits of the labor were equal — if everyone got a fair share of the goods created by the classes' collective labor. That's never happened.

To understand Marx's theory of historical change, think about trying to get somewhere on a bike when your friends keep jumping on. One of your friends might hop on the pegs on the rear wheel, another might jump on the handlebars, and maybe someone even tries to sit on the bike's crossbar. You can keep going for a little while — and, for your friends, that's nice while it lasts — but before too long you'll get tired and have to stop, or maybe even wipe out, in which case everyone is likely to get hurt.

For Marx, every mode of production has in one way or another been like that. Society can exist for a while with one class doing more than its share of the work and reaping less than its share of the rewards, but over time, that class builds resentments and anger — even as it becomes more and more crucial to everyone else's well-being. Eventually, the exploited people can't take it any more and rise up in opposition or otherwise sabotage the system. At that point, the system is essentially broken and needs to be rebuilt. The rebuilt system — the next mode of production — will be superior to the previous mode of production in some ways, but it will have its own problems that will eventually lead to its downfall.

Most attention (in this book and elsewhere) has been given to Marx's theory about what's specifically going to happen next: that the current mode of production — capitalism — will give way to communism. Marx believed that the proletariat, who are being exploited by the bourgeois, would one day revolt and overthrow the inequitable system to replace it with a perfectly fair communist system, in which each person contributes what they can and takes what they need.

So why hasn't this happened? That's not an easy question for Marxists to answer. For all its imperfections and injustices, capitalism has actually been spreading around the world since Marx's time. Some societies that have experimented with communism (notably the defunct U.S.S.R.) have relapsed to capitalism, and the world's biggest nominally communist society — China — is becoming *de facto* more capitalist every day. Where's the revolution?

There are at least a couple of different answers. Some Marxists believe the revolution is still coming: that inequality is continuing to grow, and that revolution has only been thwarted by cunning maneuvers on the part of the bourgeois. (For example, exporting inequality — see Chapter 8.) Thinkers like

Noam Chomsky and Ralph Nader believe that people in power are oppressing the disadvantaged just as much as they ever were, that the system is just as corrupt as it ever was, and that revolution is necessary, perhaps inevitable.

Other Marxists observe that significant changes in technology and economic organization have made the division between the haves and have-nots less stark than it was in Marx's time. Technological progress has lifted the standard of living around the world, so *everyone* is objectively living better than they were in the 19th century. Both technological and social changes have created a large middle class that didn't exist in Marx's time (see section "The growth of the middle class," later in this chapter). If this situation persists, the revolution Marx anticipated may not come about because the circumstances Marx saw have changed dramatically.

The bottom line is that for Marx, social change is about conflict: about groups fighting for resources and power. Marx believed that when a communist utopia is finally achieved, social history will essentially come to an end because there will be no more conflict to drive social change. We'll see!

Durkheim: Increasing diversity

Emile Durkheim agreed with Marx that social change followed a certain predictable progression, but he strongly disagreed with Marx about the nature of that change and the reasons for it. (See Chapter 3 for more on Durkheim's life and work.)

The fundamental point to understand about historical change, said Durkheim, is that society is getting bigger and more complex. That's happening for a number of interrelated reasons. As technology develops, societies are able to sustain greater and greater populations of people who travel and communicate in wider and wider circles.

For tens of thousands of years of human history, people had to work very hard all the time at procuring the basic necessities such as food (first by hunting and gathering, later by farming) and shelter (from the elements and from each other). Everyone had to help with these basic tasks, leaving little room for real diversity. In a hunting-and-gathering band, it isn't really constructive to have a wide-ranging and vigorous debate about where the band will roam next — much less about what language should be spoken or about the meaning of life. Everyone had to pitch in with the basic tasks, and that was that. If you didn't like it, you could leave and try to go join another band where you'd inevitably be doing just about exactly the same thing.

As technology developed, there was more need for a division of labor. A small farming community might have specialists in raising crops, specialists in raising animals, and specialists in facilitating trade. There became the need for specially trained blacksmiths, builders, and shopkeepers. Eventually, societies supported standing armies of professional soldiers whose job was to keep the wolves (actual and figurative) at bay. There started to be genuine diversity: The life of a farmhand was wildly different from the life of a shop-keeper or a knight-errant.

Today, people work at an astounding variety of extremely specialized occupations. My cousin's husband works at an auto plant, where some days he does nothing but screw dome lights into trucks' ceilings. My sister works at a firm where she sells software services that facilitate communication between retailers and suppliers. I'm writing a book that might be of interest to some people studying a particular academic discipline, very few of whom will take their studies in that discipline far enough to earn a living from it. Globalization has connected people around the world, but that means the people connected include a rickshaw driver in Vietnam, a stockbroker in Manhattan, and an artist in Uganda. All three of those people exist in the same global society, but they couldn't even speak with one another if you put them in the same room together.

Durkheim believed that all aspects of social change are tied to this sweeping historical change. This diversity makes society stronger — not just in the sense that you get to meet interesting new people, but in the sense that when people organize themselves into a division of labor, they're able to accomplish more. If each of the workers at an auto plant were given responsibility for building a car from start to finish, their jobs might be more interesting, but they'd get far fewer cars built. If everyone in society did the same job, that job would be farming or hunting, and everyone would be right back to the prehistoric days — complete with comfy rock floors to sleep on and handy flint knives to prepare food with. Only because of the division of labor can we have waterbeds and Ginsu knives.

As the division of labor increases, profound social change comes with it. People need to accept — in fact, *embrace* — diversity because their livelihoods depend on it. All aspects of society change to accommodate the increasing division of labor.

- Laws become less about forcing citizens to do certain things and more about keeping them from infringing on other people's prerogative to do different things.

- Governments — and all other social organizations — become more open and democratic rather than closed and hierarchical.

- Formal education increases across society, to prepare citizens to enter an increasingly specialized workforce.

- Religions become more tolerant, more ecumenical, and less dogmatic. (The relatively few exceptions are especially visible, but the fact that they stand out proves the overall rule.)

- Social statues and roles become much more flexible.

Durkheim identified this change as the transition from "mechanical solidarity" to "organic solidarity." More on this transition — specifically as it applies to religion — is in Chapter 10, but in terms of social change, the important point to understand is that Durkheim believed that social change is driven by increasing diversity and *functional differentiation*. Unlike Marx, Durkheim believed that what fundamentally drives social change is people cooperating to bring about a better world rather than groups competing for a share of the world that exists.

Sound a little pie-in-the-sky? Maybe . . . Marx would certainly say so! Still, consider the fact that an international group of researchers recently showed that global conflicts have been declining over the past half-century, both in overall number and in the number of fatalities. Does this mean that there's another great conflict simmering and waiting to erupt (as Marx would say), or does it mean that peace is on the march (as Durkheim would say)? Only time will tell.

Weber: Into the iron cage

Max Weber came after Marx and Durkheim and was familiar with their work. He also conducted a great deal of historical research, and he had his own ideas about what forces bring about social change. (See Chapter 3 for more on Weber, who many sociologists today consider the most insightful sociologist of all time.)

Weber agreed with Marx that history was often marked by conflict, and that the results of conflicts could have profound consequences for the direction society would take thereafter. He agreed with Durkheim, though, that conflict over material things wasn't the bottom line; that ideas and values could be even more powerful than hunger. When he put those two ideas together, what Weber ended up with was a theory of history that didn't have the inevitability of Marx's or Durkheim's.

For Weber, history was a little bit like a mystery novel that you open on the last page. You know how the story ends, but you don't know how it got to that point. The butler's dead, but was he killed by the rich heiress because he knew too much? Or was he killed by the maid after he was unfaithful to her? Or perhaps was he killed accidentally by a person who mistook him for someone else? The ending may not seem to make any sense, but of course if you went back and read the story from the beginning, it would all become clear.

The trick is that when it comes to understanding social change, "the book" is thousands of years long and includes every word ever written. That's a lot of information to sift through, but *somewhere* in there is the explanation for why society is the way it is. What this means is that Weber didn't have a tidy overall theory of history the way that Marx and Durkheim did.

The historical theories of Marx and Durkheim are sometimes described as *teleological* — meaning that they saw history as inevitably progressing toward a particular end. Weber thought that historical change happened for a reason, but that its end was not predetermined and that future events could not be foretold, they could only be guessed at.

Things happened to turn out this way, said Weber, but they *could* have turned out differently if the complex play of ideas and interests had taken a different turn. If Marx or Durkheim read the last page of that novel, they would say the butler obviously *had* to die. In fact, they would predict, if you opened every mystery novel in the library, the butler would be dead at the end of every one of them. Marx might guess that it was because the heiress killed him in every one, and Durkheim might say that no, it was the maid in every case — but the point is that they would both say the outcome was really never in question. Weber would say that things could have been different, and he wouldn't be too surprised to find that a different character ended up dead in every different novel, maybe even the ones that started the same way.

To illustrate his point, Weber cited the examples of different countries. Chinese society is just as old as German society, and look how differently things turned out in those two countries! If those countries are looking more and more the same, that has to do with the current pressures of globalization, a Weberian might say, than with the fact that the two countries' histories had to converge. If they were on two different planets, they might look even more different than they do today.

Weber had specific ideas about how the Western world ended up in the "iron cage" of capitalism. Broadly, Weber believed that the world is caught up in a cycle of "rationalization," where tradition, custom, and local identity are giving way to systematization, standardization, and planning. This has many advantages — it makes the world more fair and lets things be accomplished more efficiently — but it can also make the world seem colder and more impersonal. Anyone whose neighborhood coffee shop has been replaced by a Starbucks, or whose independent bookstore has been put out of business by Amazon, probably understands a little bit about what Weber meant.

If you're interested in reading more about Weber's ideas, see Chapter 10 for his views on the role of religion in history and Chapter 12 for his ideas about bureaucratization.

What Comes Next?

At the beginning of this chapter I liken sociological forecasting to meteorological forecasting — it's impossible to predict exactly what's going to happen. Just as meteorologists can tell when there's a storm front coming, though, so do sociologists have a fair sense of what the most important changes affecting societies are, and they can make an educated guess about how things will shake down. In this section, I describe four major developments that are already taking place and will continue to be hugely important in shaping the future of societies around the world. Finally, I mention what we can learn from the past about looking to the future.

Globalization

You've probably heard it said that "the world is getting smaller." Obviously that's not literally true: What it means is that advances in transportation and communication effectively bring people and places around the world closer to us. In this sense, the world has been "shrinking" since the beginning of human history. In the following sections, I discuss advances in transportation; advances in communication; and the social effects of globalization.

Transportation

In 1873, when Jules Verne published his novel *Around the World in 80 Days*, it seemed almost impossibly daring to travel completely around the globe in under three months' time. Today, you can fly around the world in a tiny fraction of that time: just a couple of days. It's not cheap to do so, but you certainly don't need to be fabulously wealthy to pull it off: You could do it for about the price of a 15-year-old car.

The prevalence and relative affordability of passenger air travel means that a middle-class citizen of a developed country can comfortably manage to visit other continents at least a few times in their life, and can fairly routinely fly around their own continent.

In 1873, the fastest way to get from place to place was by train, or perhaps by water if the winds and currents were favorable. Today, if you're not flying you can drive from city to city at speeds ranging from 55 to 90 miles an hour. This means that not only can you road-trip across a continent in a few days, you can comfortably commute each day from one side of a sprawling metro area to the other. For example, here in Minnesota, towns that are today considered suburbs of the Twin Cities were considered way out in the country when my dad was young.

Still, you don't cross the ocean every day, but you *do* constantly use products manufactured on the other side of the world. Just as profoundly important as increased human mobility is the increased mobility of things. Last summer I went to an "ice bar" in Minnesota, where I drank from glasses made of ice. I was surprised — but not shocked — to learn later that the glasses had been made in *New Zealand* and shipped to Minnesota in frozen form. Transportation technology is now such that it's more cost-effective for that company to manufacture all its ice glasses at a central facility in New Zealand and ship them to ice bars all around the world than to freeze the glasses at each individual ice bar.

Communication

I'm almost finished writing this book, and I've never even met my editors. They're in Indiana, I'm in Minnesota. We've been sending chapters back and forth by e-mail. That's something, of course, you could do by standard mail, but we'd never be getting this entire book written and edited in six months if we were doing it that way! And if we were using standard mail, it would certainly matter how far away I was; with e-mail, I could be sitting in Hong Kong and things would get done just as quickly. E-mail is so efficient, in fact, that postal services around the world are struggling with the rapid decline in mail volume — especially the volume of business mail. The daily delivery of standard mail to average households may soon be a thing of the past.

The development of reliable Internet service in major cities — and, increasingly, small towns and rural areas — around the world is an unprecedented advance in communication technology. Massive volumes of information ricochet around the world in virtually no time, at relatively tiny cost.

There have been game-changers before, though: the printing press, the telephone, radio broadcasting, television broadcasting. Each has created such a seismic change in the way people live that they've taken decades to adjust to. The volume of information available to the average middle-class person now is so great that there's an increasing demand for "aggregators," or people whose job it is to take information freely available to anyone and to sift through it to tell you what the bits *you* need to pay attention to are.

There's no substitute for personal contact — and, as I note in Chapter 7, most of your communication via phone and Internet is probably with the people you see often in person anyway — but the world is now available to you with an immediacy that would have made Jules Verne's head spin.

What globalization means

In the words of Marshall McLuhan, you and I truly do now live in a "global village." The impact of globalization is already apparent — after all, it's been happening for thousands of years. Still, the process of globalization is speeding up, and by the time you're the age your parents are (or would be), you'll have seen much more change in your lifetime than they have in theirs.

One absolute certainty is that places around the world will become more similar to each other. Travel now, if you can, because whatever places you travel to, they'll never again look as different from your home town as they do now. Language, culture, customs, food — all those things are becoming more and more similar around the world.

This may seem depressing, but it's happening for a reason, and not necessarily a bad reason. The newspapers in Minneapolis and St. Paul are both hurting financially and have been laying workers off left and right, in part because more and more people read news online, often reading out-of-town papers like the *New York Times* or the *Guardian* of London. And why wouldn't they? The *New York Times* has a news staff without parallel, and there's no way the Minneapolis *Star Tribune* or the St. Paul *Pioneer Press* could compete with the *New York Times* for quality and quantity of coverage of national and international issues.

That does mean some local voices are lost — just as the prevalence of Hollywood movies means that people attend local entertainments less, and just as the growth of McDonald's fast food restaurants means that some neighborhood diners go out of business? A local theater company could never produce a blockbuster movie, and a local diner could never produce food as cheaply and quickly as a McDonald's restaurant can, so people choose to go to the megaplex and eat fast food.

Of course, that's the Durkheimian perspective — that globalization is fulfilling a function. A Marxist would say that huge, growing conglomerates are stifling small enterprises, and that we're all poorer (culturally and otherwise) as a result. There's truth to that as well, but it's worth observing that technology is multiplying *everyone's* choices. When my dad was growing up, you could get your news from the *Pioneer Press*, and that was it. Today, you can read virtually any newspaper in the world for free online. Just because we all have the same choices available doesn't mean we have to *make* the same choices. (Often, of course, we do . . . and if you've been reading since the beginning of this book, you should have a lot of good ideas as to why.)

Globalization isn't just about cultural choices, though: It's about structure as well, about jobs and governments and the economy. Transportation technology has allowed people in developed nations to own big televisions and fast computers for relatively small sums, but it's also meant the loss of millions and millions of manufacturing jobs in those countries as that work goes overseas.

As I write, the United States is just emerging from an economic recession that affected the rest of the world; there's no way it could not have! Today, all countries around the world are tied in a global economy. There isn't a world government, but communication and cooperation with *all* countries are increasingly essential for every national government. Globalization is tying every single person on Earth more and more tightly to every single other person, and that process is only going to accelerate in coming years. Like it or not, we're all in this together.

Increasing — and decreasing — diversity

Has the place where you live been growing more diverse every year? It would be very surprising if it hasn't. Even as globalization is making places more similar to each other, it's also making them more diverse. Maybe 30 or 40 years ago you had a one-of-a-kind local diner instead of a McDonald's, but the crowd of people who ate there was probably a lot more homogeneous than the crowd you'll find there now.

One of the results of globalization has been an acceleration of the pace of immigration. There's always been immigration, of course, but 200 or even 100 years ago it would have been hard to imagine large populations of immigrants from Somalia and Laos streaming into Minneapolis and St. Paul over just a few years' time, as has happened in recent years, markedly changing the Twin Cities' social landscape. Whether for jobs, political asylum, or simply wanderlust, people are moving all over the world at an unprecedented rate.

It's worth repeating: The world has *always* been diverse. Immigrants to the United States and Europe today are moving for many of the same reasons — and having many of the same experiences as — immigrants to those places 100 years ago. Tension, sometimes productive and sometimes destructive, among different groups living in the same place has always marked human society.

That said, social diversity, by many measures, has increased over the past several hundred years and will continue to increase for the foreseeable future. Whereas some societies remain stubbornly intolerant, overall, societies around the world embrace diversity much more fully than they did in the past. The idea that not everyone in their neighborhood will dress the same way, or speak the same language, or worship the same god, or celebrate the same holidays, is something that people today are much more likely to take for granted than their parents or grandparents were.

Further, communication and transportation technology has allowed for the formation and maintenance of what sociologists call *transnational communities*: groups of people who identify and communicate with one another despite the fact that they are geographically spread around the globe.

From her St. Paul home, my friend Julia maintains a Web site for news and discussion about issues related to the Kenyan community, a community that is far larger than the people actually living in Kenya. On Julia's Web site, people who are living in Kenya, who have emigrated from Kenya, who have family in Kenya, or who are simply interested in issues regarding Kenya can all connect and share their views. It would have been impossible for that global Kenyan community to connect so meaningfully before the advent of the Internet. Further, like many emigrants, Julia returns to Kenya every couple of years. It's expensive to do so, but it would have been far more expensive 50 or 100 years ago.

But "diversity" is about more than just national, ethnic, and racial diversity: It's about everything people share and don't share. Think about all the ways a group of people who work in the same office are — or, at least, are more likely to be — more diverse than in the past.

- ✔ They can each plug in their headphones and listen, over the Internet, to streaming audio of almost any kind of music. They don't all have to listen to the same radio station.

- ✔ They are more likely to be a mixed group of men and women.

- ✔ Dress codes have been substantially relaxed: Gone are the days when the subway would be filled with men in identical black suits and hats on the way to their jobs.

- ✔ They are more likely to have different employment histories.

- ✔ They are more likely to have lived in different places.

- ✔ They can go down to the bar after work and each choose from a wide array of domestic and imported beverages. You can't just go to the bar and order "a beer" any more.

Those are just a few examples of how the world is growing more diverse. At the same time, as I note earlier, in some ways people are becoming less diverse. People are more likely to have come from different places, but the experiences they had in those different places are more similar than they would have been in the past. People are more likely to have different religious views, but how they actually practice those faiths is more similar than it would have been in the past. You can go to the multiplex and choose from among a dozen movies instead of just one, but they're the same dozen movies that are showing in multiplexes across the country and, increasingly, around the world.

So paradoxically, societies are becoming both more and less diverse. That may be confusing to wrap your head around, but here's the bottom line: Your identity is less and less closely tied to the place you were born or the color of your skin. People everywhere may have, increasingly, the same options to choose among (McDonald's or Burger King?), but they do, in general, have more freedom *to* choose.

The march of technology

You may notice in the first section of this chapter that despite the differences among Marx's, Durkheim's, and Weber's theories of historical change, the theorists do have something in common: They all appreciate the significance of technology in bringing about social change.

When I mentioned that I was working on this chapter, one of my friends asked in only a half-kidding way, "Why don't you just summarize *Guns, Germs, and Steel*?" You may be familiar with that book by geographer Jared Diamond, in which he argues that the history of the world has essentially been shaped by technology and geography. Most sociologists wouldn't agree with Diamond that technological and geographical resources have so definitively shaped human history (Marx would be most likely to agree), but no sociologist can deny that technology and other material resources play a huge role in shaping the social world.

The social world that exists today would not be possible without the technology that has been developed over the past millennia — notably including the communication and transportation technology referenced earlier, but also including medical technology, agricultural technology, manufacturing technology, and, yes, weapons technology. Similarly, in years to come the social world will be affected by technological developments that it's hard to foresee.

Geographers like Diamond correctly point out that a great number of tragic human conflicts have been caused or exacerbated by resource shortages: food, water, fuel. The growth of the world's population is finally beginning to slow — especially in the developed world — but the Earth is still supporting a tremendous number of people, billions of whom are living in poverty. Barring almost unimaginable technological developments, they cannot all live at the standard currently enjoyed by residents of the developed world. You don't need to be a strict Marxist to appreciate that vast disparities in wealth and comfort are bound to be a source of tension, perhaps deadly tension. In the future of global society, much will depend on how successfully famine and disease can be fought using technological development and other means.

Further, the world currently relies to a great extent on irreplaceable fossil fuels like oil and natural gas; this is obviously unsustainable. Eventually the fuels will run out, and many of the technological benefits we currently enjoy — cars, gas heat, electricity — will be out of reach unless we develop other means of power generation.

So on a global scale, the priorities for technological development are clear. But what *else* will happen in terms of technological change? How else will people's lives be affected by advancing technology?

That's, of course, impossible to say. Watch any old sci-fi movie to see how difficult it is to guess how the world will look in the future. What it's safe to say is that while technological development will bring some unwelcome changes and require many adjustments, it will also give people more freedom to live the lives they want to lead — and, in some cases, the freedom to live, period.

The growth of the middle class

If you ask them, most people will tell you that they're members of the "middle class." Can this be possible?

Well, technically, yes — if you consider "class" to be a vertical hierarchy stretching from highest class to lowest class, then everyone in the world can point to both someone "higher class" and someone else "lower class" than he or she is. Also, the "middle class" is where people want to be: It doesn't have the stigma of the "lower class," but nor does it sound as hoity-toity as the "upper class."

Being "middle class" is about more than just being comfortable and unpretentious, though: The middle class is real, and it's been decisive in the economic history of the past couple of centuries. It's been growing over the course of that period, and it's probably a good thing if it continues to grow.

Different sociologists and economists have different definitions of what technically constitutes the "middle class," but the various definitions generally include all these elements:

- A middle-class family is financially stable, but its members still have to work; may, in fact, need to have two incomes.

- A middle-class family can comfortably afford food and shelter, and can further afford a modest number of luxuries like vacations, boats, and home entertainment systems.

- A middle-class job typically requires specialized training or experience, and may involve significant individual autonomy and/or the management of others.

- A middle-class individual likely owns a fair amount of personal property (house, car, furniture) but doesn't have enough assets to draw significant income from investments.

The growth of the middle class is something that Marx did not see coming; he believed capitalist society would continue to polarize between the haves and the have-nots. Marxists today point to the growth of the middle class as one of the reasons there hasn't been a global communist revolution — and it's true, most members of the middle class are pretty happy with capitalism. They may feel like they've been unfairly deprived of something or other at some point, but they probably don't think it would be a good idea to fundamentally change the structure of the economy.(The political views of the lower class and the upper class don't line up exactly as Marx would have predicted, either — but that's another matter.)

From an economic standpoint, the key to the growth of the middle class has been the increasing importance of skilled labor. Advancing technology has increased the overall productivity of society, so that the perks middle-class families enjoy are more readily available; at the same time, it's steadily increased the demand for skilled labor. By developing a useful skill of any sort, a person can lift themselves into the middle class if (and this is a big *if*) an appropriate job is available.

Politicians look to the middle class, with good reason, as a bellwether: In a democracy, if the middle class is unhappy with your policies, you're not likely to stay in office for long. Will the middle class stay happy, and grow, in future years? That's a big, and a very important, question.

For well over a century, members of the middle class in developed countries have enjoyed a steadily rising standard of living. For a long time, middle-class parents have been able to reasonably expect that their children will have bigger houses, better food, and in general a more comfortable lifestyle than the parents did. That's not necessarily the case today, in part *because* of the growth of the middle class around the world. Middle-class jobs require more training and experience than ever, and there is more and more competition for those jobs.

Some countries, like India and China, are booming whereas long-developed countries like those in Europe and North America are reeling from the loss of manufacturing jobs even as they enjoy the many benefits of trade with countries where goods and services can be provided more cheaply. It seems clear that developed countries are going to have to re-imagine themselves to remain economically competitive in the global economy, but it also may be the case that their residents are going to have to accept a significant decline in their standard of living.

The middle class is relatively new, and it may be more fragile than most of its members realize. Technological advances can improve everyone's standard of living — as has been the case for millennia — but technology can only do so much. As aspirants to a middle-class standard of living grow, policymakers around the world are going to have to make some difficult choices. Among them:

✔ Should trade and immigration become more free? Does any given country have more to gain or more to lose by opening its borders to new workers and new trade?

✔ As their economies change, what protections should governments guarantee? Food? Shelter? Transportation? Education? Health care? If these things are provided by the government, where will the money to fund them come from, and how will they be allotted among the needy?

✔ Is it acceptable for inequality to rise, so long as the people on the bottom are adequately well-off; or is rising inequality a bad thing regardless?

When I wrote, at the beginning of this section, that middle-class is something people want to be, I didn't just mean that they want to say they're "middle class;" I meant that they actually want to *be* middle class.

Everyone daydreams of a life of luxury, but very few people expect to achieve it. What people do generally expect is a life where they will be physically comfortable and financially secure, where they have to work for a living but where there's a living to be had for those who will work. They don't expect to have a mansion, but they expect to have a nice home. They don't expect to have diamonds falling out of their pockets, but they expect to be able to splurge on a reasonable luxury item every once in a while. They don't expect to run a big company, but they do expect to work in a job where they're needed and respected, where they learn valuable skills and use those skills to help their employer get ahead; and to be fairly compensated in return.

That's the middle-class lifestyle. Right now, it's a reasonable lifestyle for most people in the developed world, and an increasing number of people in the developing world, to expect. Whether it will continue to be is something no one knows.

A lesson from the past: Work for change, but don't panic

The past few sections may seem a little scary . . . but when it comes to speculation about the future, it can definitely get scarier!

Environmental disaster and economic disaster are possibilities, though (I write with fingers crossed) not probabilities. Other scary possibilities for the future include disastrous warfare, possibly on a global scale. Truly dangerous weapons, weapons that can destroy cities, exist in the world and are perpetually at risk of falling into the hands of people who will use them. In fact, the people whose hands they're in *now* might well use them — they have before. That's a genuine, frightening possibility.

The old-fashioned weapons are still around as well, and unfortunately they are used every day; millions of people around the world live in war-torn places where they justifiably fear for their safety. A machete is scarier than a nuclear warhead if it's held by someone who's threatening you or someone you love. Preventing violent conflict of all kinds is something that anyone concerned about society's future has to work for.

Fortunately, a third world war may not occur; nor may environmental catastrophe or a global economic depression. I certainly hope they don't, and I don't suppose you're rooting for them either. There is, however, one thing that's guaranteed about the future: In your lifetime, you *will* see social change of some sort. The world is not going to stay the same.

If you're old enough to be reading this book, you already have seen social change — and maybe you didn't much care for it.

- ✔ Maybe your country elected a leader you don't like, or passed a law you disagree with.

- ✔ Maybe there's something new that everyone seems to be doing all of a sudden — dressing a certain way, or talking a certain way, or using some new device.

- ✔ Maybe you've seen your favorite local business close, or your favorite drink go out of production, or your favorite TV show go off the air.

- ✔ Maybe you've seen violence flare up in a previously peaceful neighborhood, city, or country.

You're perfectly justified in being concerned about any of those things. Sometimes things do change for the worse, and any kind of change can be stressful and worrisome. If you're a senior citizen, you've seen some dramatic, downright shocking changes in your life — and chances are, you'll see even more to come. If you're still relatively young, just wait and see what happens. It will surely surprise you. (It will surprise me, too.)

It's true that some aspects of social change are hard to control, but it's also true you *do* have the power to influence social change. Whatever world you want to see in the future, you can help make it more likely that it will come about. Whatever power you have to make your voice heard, use it! History books are full of stories about people who fought, sometimes against formidable odds, to bring about the change they wanted to see, and succeeded.

Another thing worth paying attention to in history books, though, is that they are similarly full of people who thought the world was going to hell in a handbasket. It's no exaggeration to say that since the beginning of recorded history, there have been people who thought that the change they were seeing — after all, *everyone's* seen change, no matter when and where they've lived — was absolutely it, the final straw, the end of all that is good and right in the world. You know people like that; in fact, you might *be* a person like that. If so, you have a lot of company.

As it happens, the world hasn't ended. Babies are still being born, teenagers are still disobeying their parents, people are still falling in love (and out of love, and in love again), people are working hard at jobs they're proud of, and fighting and praying and laughing and crying and, eventually, dying. I don't know who you are or where you're living, but even if you're somehow picking this book up in the year 3001, I'll bet you're living in a form of social organization where most people, most of the time, care for one another and work to make the world a better place for everyone. You're probably living in a place where most people are happy most of the time, but even if you're living in a place where some terrible things are happening, you probably have hope for the future, hope that things will get better. And sociologists would say that you have many, many reasons to believe that.

Sociology in the Future

Enough about the possibility of world peace or global catastrophe . . . let's get down to brass tacks. What's the future of *sociology*? In this section, I look in the direction(s) sociology itself might be heading in decades to come.

Will sociology continue to exist?

It may surprise you to find that heading in a book full of useful sociological information: Why *wouldn't* sociology continue to exist? Clearly, it's been useful in the past. Why wouldn't it be useful in the future? I think it will be, and I think sociology will be around for a long, long time. The interesting question is whether people will continue to call it "sociology."

There's no question that the sociological worldview has become more and more common since sociology was founded in the 19th century. The idea that it would be interesting, productive, or even *appropriate* to study human interaction scientifically was something that was not at all taken for granted in the time of Comte or even Durkheim. (See Chapter 3 for more on these thinkers.) Both of those sociologists spent a lot of their time defending the social sciences generally — and sociology specifically — against people who believed the humanities and the natural sciences could together tell the world everything it needed to know about society.

Today, it's safe to say, the basic premise of sociology *is* taken for granted. Can you imagine a university that didn't offer course in economics, psychology, political science, anthropology, geography, education, regional studies, women's studies, or business administration? All of those disciplines, today, are social sciences, built on the same premise as sociology: that society can, and should, be studied scientifically. Further, disciplines ranging from history to law to even theology are using more and more of the tools of the social sciences. As long as human interaction is studied scientifically and systematically, sociology will be around in some form.

But with all those *other* disciplines studying society scientifically, what's the point in having a separate discipline called "sociology"? After all, there's no one thing that sociologists study that isn't studied by people who don't call themselves sociologists. There are political scientists — what's the use of "political sociologists"? There are economists — what's the use of "economic sociology"? There are social scientists working in schools of education — what's the use of "sociologists of education"?

There's a real possibility that "sociology" could go the way of "philosophy." Centuries ago, most scholars were called "philosophers." The ancient Greek and Roman "philosophers" studied everything from society to art to medicine to astronomy. The wide-ranging legacy of the term "philosophy" lives on in the fact that the highest degree in any basic academic is a Ph.D. — its holders are "doctors of philosophy" whether they study plants, people, or Plato. But who, today, actually calls themselves a "philosopher"? Only a relatively few people studying the history of philosophy and highly abstract, theoretical questions.

Way down the line, that could happen to sociology — it could become the very basic science of human interaction in groups and networks, with all the details about ethnicities and governments and places and times left to scholars in other disciplines. For now, though, sociology is standing strong on the basis of its claim to be the only social science that studies *all* aspects of social life.

For me, the most exciting thing about sociology is seeing the connections between how people interact at one time and how they interact at another, how one place is unexpectedly similar to another. To see those connections, you have to be open to studying wildly diverse situations, places, and times; you have to be open to looking, scientifically and systematically, at politics *and* education *and* the economy *and* the family *and* the church *and* everything else about human life. That's what sociologists, and only sociologists, do. It's not easy, but it's tremendously, sometimes unexpectedly, rewarding.

The paradox: More data, less information

Sociologists look at the entire social world — and thanks to advances in technology, there's more and more of the social world to be seen. That sounds like a good thing, but it can also be a challenge.

In his 2000 inaugural address as president of the American Sociological Association, Joe Feagin pointed out that sociologists are used to working with only a small sample of what could possibly be known about the world.

How, he asked provocatively, would things be different if we suddenly knew *everything*? It might actually make sociologists more necessary than they are today.

Of course, sociologists still don't know *everything*, but as more and more of the world moves online, they know vastly more than they could have imagined knowing before. Consider these facts:

- ✔ Not only are social networking sites like Facebook and Twitter becoming more popular, they're increasingly linking with one another and with other sites. As I write, you can use your Facebook account to log on to many other sites — which means that information about what you do on those sites, to some extent, exists on the Facebook servers. Facebook administrators don't know everything about the online social world, but they know a *lot* . . . and what they don't know, their colleagues at Google or Microsoft may well know.

- ✔ Banks have histories of credit card transactions, and various companies track the progress of products from the factory to the warehouse to the retailer and possibly even to the individual home of the consumer.

- ✔ When you buy your car, and when you subsequently take it in for service, its vehicle ID number is recorded. This gives organizations who care to do the legwork access to detailed records of a car's history.

- ✔ Cell phones enabled with GPS can be tracked around the world, and there's serious discussion of implanting trackable microchips under children's skin. (If you think that sounds scary, think about how you'd feel if your child was missing and there was a technology that could tell you precisely where they were.)

What this adds up to is an almost inconceivable amount of information about human activity being — or potentially being — gathered. That has sparked concerns about privacy, but the fun and convenience of being networked seem to be irresistible for most people not to embrace. In the not-too-distant future, there could be in existence a minute-by-minute record of the average person's life. Imprecise tools like surveys would be a thing of the past; already, network surveys ("please list all the people you know") are being replaced by the far-superior data available from social networking sites.

So once the world has all this data, will the mystery of human life be solved? Not likely — without the help of sociologists to draw useful *information* from that mountain of data, those gajillions of bits of data will be about as useful as a phone book that isn't alphabetized. In the new world of infinite data, sociology — a tool for making sense of social life in all its boundless diversity — will be more important than ever.

Part VI
The Part of Tens

The 5th Wave   By Rich Tennant

In this part . . .

Sociology, what can I do with thee? Let me count the ways . . . to be precise, 30 of them. The first ten are books you can read if you're looking for another sociology fix, the second ten are ways you can use sociological insights in your everyday life, and the final ten are myths about society busted by sociology.

Chapter 17

Ten Sociology Books That Don't Feel Like Homework

In This Chapter

▶ Finding books that are fun and informative

▶ Reaching a better understanding of social conditions

*I*f you want to learn more about sociology — and subjects studied by sociologists — you can always pick up a textbook, or one of Talcott Parsons's impenetrable tomes. You'll probably have a better experience, however, and possibly even learn more if you start with one of the many sociological books that are fun and interesting to read.

Your local librarian or bookseller may be able to recommend some, but here are my personal suggestions: ten books that represent a wide range of sociological topics. In each of these books you'll find interesting, eye-opening observations; many of them also tell compelling true stories. Qualitative research is particularly well-represented here because qualitative studies can be easier to relate to — but each of these books takes into account, and has informed, quantitative studies as well. (See Chapter 4 for a description of the distinction between qualitative and quantitative research.)

Some of these titles are relatively obscure, and some are bestselling classics of sociology; they're all well-researched and well-written, and each is a door into the vast, fascinating discipline of sociology.

Randall Collins: Sociological Insight

Randall Collins is a preeminent sociologist in his own right, but he's also helped to communicate sociological theory — thorny as it sometimes is — to a wide audience of students, researchers, and general readers with his publications *Four Sociological Traditions* and *Sociological Insight*.

Sociological Insight is the book that got me hooked on sociology. Here, Collins's goal is to share what he refers to as "non-obvious" insights from sociology, to show why sociology is a unique and powerful way of thinking about the social world. The very readable chapters range over topics such as crime, relationships, and power; in each case, Collins shows why thinking about the topic sociologically lets you understand it in a way you might not otherwise.

What the book *Freakonomics* did for economics a few years ago, *Sociological Insight* did for sociology in 1982. How is being in a romantic relationship like owning property? What is the true nature of power in society? Why is crime inevitable, and maybe even good? You come away from *Sociological Insight* feeling like you're in on a secret — that because of sociology, you now understand the world in a way that most other people don't. It can be a little disorienting, but it's also a lot of fun.

William Foote Whyte: Street Corner Society

This 1943 book is one of the most important books in American sociology. It's one of the best demonstrations of the power of ethnography — a form of qualitative research involving deep immersion in a community. Whyte conducted the research for this book while he was a fellow at Harvard; he spent four years living in Boston's "Little Italy" and got to know the community intimately. *Street Corner Society* is a detailed, fascinating portrait of that community. (See Chapter 14 for more on William Foote Whyte and his place in urban sociology.)

Besides demonstrating the value of patient ethnography, *Street Corner Society* documents the deep complexities of the kind of communities commonly regarded as marginal. Before sociology, people looked to great philosophers or the ancient Romans for models of how society "should" work. Sociologists said, let's take a look at how society *does* work — and that meant, and still means, looking at societies that might not be considered exemplary. By writing about the tremendous richness and depth of society in a neighborhood some might have called a "ghetto" (and that Whyte himself called a "slum"), Whyte proved that society is just as fascinating when viewed from the bottom up as it is when viewed from the top down.

It's also a touching human story, particularly the portion about the "corner boys" whose leader struggles to find his own place in life even as he helps resolve conflicts and knit friendships among gang members. The corner boys do a lot of bowling, and it turns out that the boys held in higher esteem at the moment also tend to score the highest at bowling. Bowling leagues today probably observe the same phenomenon.

William H. Whyte: The Organization Man

This thick but readable 1955 book is more of an extended essay than a traditional sociological study, and in part for that reason, it's more dated than other sociological bestsellers of its time. Still, it's a fascinating portrait of postwar America, where suburbs were sprouting and national corporations were extending their reach with a big and well-trained workforce.

Like other sociologists of his time (including David Riesman, author of *The Lonely Crowd*), William H. Whyte was concerned about the homogeneity of American society in the 1950s. He believed that "the organization man," a man concerned with conformity more than enterprising individuality, was becoming the new model for the American worker.

In the central section of the book, Whyte documents social life in a newly developing suburb; he sees suburbs as the monotonous hubs of the lives of the new "organization men." Almost against his own will, though, Whyte documents the vibrant, bustling social life among the young families who enthusiastically populate the suburban homes of which he's so suspicious. (For more on William H. Whyte and his views on suburban life, see Chapter 14.)

Erving Goffman: The Presentation of Self in Everyday Life

For over half a century, this 1959 book has all but *defined* microsociology. Like a good novel, it reads as though it were written in one sitting, with ideas and inspirations spilling out of Goffman as fast as his fingers could type.

Goffman's central idea is that we're actors on a stage, performing the "characters" we want others to see. That idea is at least as old as *Hamlet*, but what Goffman brings is an acute sociological eye and a drive to push his premise as far as it will go. If we're actors on a stage, when and how do we switch characters? What happens when the "stage" (the setting) or the "costumes" change? If we're *always* acting, then is the "character" at work one who's "played" by the character we are at home? And who plays *that* character? The possibilities might make your head spin, and they'll no doubt be inspiring sociological research for the next 50 years as well.

Elijah Anderson: Streetwise

Elijah Anderson's contemporary classic, published in 1992, is really two studies in one. Anderson writes about two Philadelphia neighborhoods: the gentrifying "Village" and the tough, impoverished "Northton." (See Chapter 14 for more on this study.) Both neighborhoods are facing serious challenges, and Anderson takes the reader deep inside each neighborhood, offering greater understanding but not promising any easy solutions . . . because there are none. Many of the best sociology books are about communities, but Northton and the Village may be more recognizable to you than a Depression-era slum (*Street Corner Society*) or a 1950s suburb (*The Organization Man*).

The Northton section is especially compelling, and has been especially controversial. Anderson's claim that the disappearance of "old head" role models has contributed greatly to the destructive behavior of younger generations has been criticized by some as an argument blaming the young victims of poverty and racism for their own circumstances. Decide for yourself after reading the book — you won't regret it, and you won't forget it.

Arlie Hochschild: The Second Shift

You'll definitely recognize yourself, or your parents, or other people you know in Hochschild's stories of couples managing their household labor. *The Second Shift* is worth reading — especially for couples — if only for acknowledgement that it's not only you who face challenges dividing responsibilities fairly. (See Chapter 15 for more on Hochschild's observations about gender and household labor.)

The Second Shift is also notable in the sociology of sex and gender as one of the first major works to signal that the "sexual revolution" was far from over — not at the book's initial 1989 publication, and not today. Just because men agree that women deserve equal treatment doesn't mean that they actually treat women equally, or that they're willing to take on responsibilities traditionally allotted to women. That situation is happily beginning to change, but as long as there's tension between what people say and what they do, *The Second Shift* will remain relevant.

Viviana Zelizer: Pricing the Priceless Child

A real eye-opener. Forget everything you ever thought you knew about what's "best" for children: Zelizer shows just how very different childhood was prior to the 20th century, and how quickly it changed in just a few decades as rates of childbirth (and also of child death) dropped quickly and children were yanked out of the workforce and off the streets. One of many fascinating stories that Zelizer tells regards the transition in children's life insurance, the value of which was once computed by figuring the amount of income parents were losing with the death of a child. Once children were no longer economically valuable, they became emotionally "priceless." (For more on this idea, see Chapter 15.)

Pricing the Priceless Child is also an excellent example of historical sociology, a method where historical records serve as the evidence to answer a sociological question. Zelizer relies on an array of sources: some of them shocking, some of them amusing, all of them interesting.

Michael Schwalbe: Unlocking the Iron Cage

Although *The Second Shift* shows that even "sensitive men" can be awfully insensitive, *Unlocking the Iron Cage* shows that even "manly" men can be surprisingly sensitive. Schwalbe's fascinating study takes the reader inside the "men's movement," a movement in which men gathered to explore issues of gender and power. Media reports of sweat lodges and drum-beating made the participants sound like insecure sexists, but Schwalbe found that most participants were actually committed feminists who wanted to be as proud of their own gender as their wives, mothers, and daughters were of theirs.

Schwalbe's methodology was participant observation — he actually sat in those circles and hunched in those sweat lodges along with his subjects — and he's honest about the friendships he formed with the men he met. How can sociologists avoid being biased by their personal feelings about their subjects? Suggest *Unlocking the Iron Cage* to your book club; you'll want to debate about it with someone when you've finished reading it.

Richard Peterson: Creating Country Music

In addition to being a top sociologist of culture, Richard Peterson is an ardent music fan — and it shows in this fun book about the history of country music. Country music is often spoken of as "real" music, a music that somehow taps into the heart of America; in this book, Peterson shows that what "real" (or "authentic") means has changed over time, from the music's early hillbilly days to the present, when "real" country musicians wear cowboy hats.

Creating Country Music is a fascinating look behind the scenes of country music, showing that what's "authentic" is actually, in a sense, quite artificial. After reading this book, you'll spend a lot less time worrying about whether a French restaurant, or a dance troupe, or anything is "authentic." What counts as "authentic," Peterson shows, is whatever people happen to decide is "authentic" at any given time.

Katherine Newman: No Shame in My Game

Katherine Newman is a preeminent qualitative sociologist — not that she's a slouch in the quantitative department. In this book, she tells the stories of the working poor: people who work sometimes grueling jobs but still have a hard time getting ahead. Sitting behind the counter at McDonald's and talking with the people who work there may not seem like the most complicated thing to you — unless you've done it, or unless you've read Newman's book. As Whyte did in *Street Corner Society*, Newman reveals a complex world of pride, prejudice, struggle, and success among a group of people who are often ignored or dismissed by those who benefit from their labor.

Each of these books will teach you different things about people from different walks of life, but I'll tip you off as to one of the main lessons to be learned from each of these books: *don't assume that you understand someone until you've walked in their shoes.* By getting up close and personal (or, in some cases, down and dirty) with their subjects, sociologists repeatedly discover that choices (for example, working at McDonald's — or *not* working at McDonald's) that seem hard to understand actually make a lot of sense to the people who are making them.

Chapter 18

Ten Ways to Use Sociological Insight in Everyday Life

In This Chapter

▶ Using sociology to gain a new perspective on your own life

▶ Understanding how sociology affects your daily life

*W*hat's the point of studying sociology? For passing sociology tests, sure. For creating social policy, yes. But for *your* life, when you're not in a sociology class or writing laws? You bet!

Sociology is useful because it can change the way you think about the world. When you understand how sociologists think about the social world and what they've discovered, you may find that sociology gives you a new way to understand the people and situations around you.

In this chapter, I list ten ways that you can use sociological insight to influence your life. In some ways, sociology can help you accomplish tasks or meet goals. In other ways, it can help you know what to worry about and what not to worry about. And, of course, it can simply help you make sense of confusing situations. The more you know about sociology, the more you know about yourself and the world around you.

Sometimes, understanding these situations through a sociological lens is like a light bulb turning on: You suddenly see everything in a new light. In other cases, you may be inspired to read further about a particular topic — or perhaps even to conduct your own sociological research on that topic! There's a huge body of sociological literature in libraries and online, but with a subject as complex as society, there's always room for more.

Think Critically About Claims That "Research Proves" One Thing or Another

You can hardly turn on the TV or read the news without stumbling across a claim that "research proves" one product works better than another, or that drinking certain beverages or eating certain foods is good for you. Most of the time, these claims offer some kernel of truth, but it's usually misleading to claim that existing research really "proves" something beyond any doubt — *especially* when making claims about society.

To be clear, sociologists definitely appreciate the value of research. A good sociologist will insist on empirical verification of any fact about the social world, and after they have that verification, they will critically examine it to see what its strengths and limitations are.

It's precisely *because* sociologists so greatly value high-quality research that they want to see it done as well as possible. A research study can be hugely expensive and time-consuming, and if there's a methodological error or if its results are interpreted inaccurately, all that effort becomes a waste.

Having seen and conducted many research studies, sociologists know just how difficult it is to conduct a convincing study. It's well worth paying attention to the statistical significance of a study's results, but you also have to ask how those results were achieved. When someone tells you that "research proves" something, don't be afraid to ask what that research is and how it was conducted.

Beware of Unprovable Assertions About Society

If research studies are faulty, they can be improved with better research . . . but there are also many statements people make about society that are totally unprovable. A statement is *unprovable* if there is no information that can be gathered to support or refute it. The kind of unprovable statements you typically hear about society are those that are so vague that it's almost impossible to imagine how you would go about verifying whether or not they're correct. For example:

✔ **"Life used to be simpler."** Simpler how? Technology was less advanced and there were fewer career options, but does that mean that people's lives were actually less complicated? If you were to conduct a study measuring how simple life is, what information would you gather?

✔ **"Boys will be boys."** What does it mean to "be a boy"? Boys have Y chromosomes, yes, but is that really what this statement means? Or does it mean that there's a particular type of behavior associated with being a boy that boys always do and have always done? What behavior is that? Can you prove it?

✔ **"The government should stay out of it."** Why? What should the government do, and what should the government not do? The proper role of government is an incredibly complex question, and different people have different views on the question. Data can help determine what works and what doesn't, but there's no clear answer to the question of what any given social institution (government, education, the family) "should" or "shouldn't" do.

When you hear statements like these, think about what kind of information would help to answer the question. Is there an objective way to answer the question with evidence? If not, then it's something that simply must be taken (or not) as a matter of faith.

Sometimes "a matter of faith" is actually a theological question regarding God or the supernatural world, but "having faith" can also mean simply trusting someone or holding on to a hope. In this sense, everyone has faith in something: You may have faith in your friends, or have faith that things will work out in your romantic relationship. Having faith is important, but it's also important to understand the difference between a matter of faith and a matter of fact.

Understand Barriers to Effective Communication

You may have heard it said that everyone's human, and that deep down inside people are the same. It certainly is true that there's common ground to be found even among people from very different walks of life, but it's also true that there are very different languages and customs on Earth, and you can't take for granted that a word or gesture that means something to you will mean the same thing to the next person.

This doesn't just apply to the kind of intercultural differences you'd find between, say, someone from downtown London and someone from the Australian outback. Every household has its own little culture, and it can be frustrating trying to communicate with someone who lives just down the street.

How can you transcend these barriers? Sociology doesn't have any easy answers, but at least it can help you be aware of the barriers. The more you learn about societies and traditions other than your own, the more respect you have for those differences, and the more you appreciate that as difficult as it is to achieve understanding among people from very different social situations, it's critically important.

Chapters 5 and 6 have a lot more information about culture and interpersonal communication.

Know the Difference Between the Identity You Choose and the Identities Others Choose For You

Sociologists draw a clear distinction between *race*, which is something other people look at you and decide to associate with you, and *ethnicity*, which is something that you choose for yourself. The same principle applies to all aspects of identity: People will look at you, or will learn things about you, and will make assumptions — some reasonable, some unreasonable — about who you are. (See Chapter 6 to read about Erving Goffman and his theory that you're an "actor" on a social "stage.")

Sociologists emphasize that "who you are" is shaped by your society and by your place in it, so it's not that you can or should try to ignore your social context. The way you dress, what you say, where you live, who you associate with — those things *do* affect the way other people think about you, and in turn do affect the way you think about yourself. Further, the meanings of those things change from place to place and from time to time. Wearing sneakers to a baseball game and wearing sneakers to a wedding are very different things, and as much as you might prefer not to be judged by what you wear, clothes — along with other lifestyle choices — are symbols, and people will think differently about you depending on how you look.

But that's not to say that you don't have any choices in society! You can, and do every day, shape your own identity by the messages you send and the actions you take.

Many sociologists believe that there is no "you" in any meaningful sense outside of your social context — that is, that you and everyone around you think about you in terms of your society — so it's not necessarily selling out to take social expectations into account when making choices about your life. That doesn't mean, though, that you always have to meet those expectations! You didn't get to choose the society you were born into, but you do get to choose how you navigate through it.

Understanding Art: If It Seems Confusing, That's Exactly the Point

People have strong feelings about painting, music, theater — about all the arts. Everybody knows what they like and, in general, what they don't, but they don't always think very hard about *why*. Sociology probably won't be very helpful in explaining precisely why one song makes you cry and another makes you cringe, but sociologists of culture have spent a lot of time studying how different kinds of art have been used in different ways at different times. Beauty may be in the eye of the beholder, but art is a social institution — and like all social institutions, it makes a lot more sense when you consider it in its social context.

Have you ever looked at a painting or a sculpture that the "experts" say is amazing, but that you can't understand in the slightest and don't even like? Maybe there are works of art, or songs, that even offend you — and probably, you're not alone in being offended by those things. What you may not realize is that the artist probably *knows* it will offend or confuse you and people like you, and that may be part of why the artist is doing it. If you look at a painting and feel angry or confused, it may not be because you don't understand it or you're not smart enough or well-educated enough: making you angry or confused while making other people swoon with delight may be precisely what the artist was trying to accomplish. That doesn't mean you're wrong to feel the way you do.

Art always belongs to its place and its time. Some works of art may be resonant to people for hundreds or even thousands of years, whereas others may seem dated within a few months. If a critic likes something — well, they come from a particular social context, and if that's not a social context you share, it only makes sense that you won't be interested in the same things for the same reasons. It doesn't mean you're "wrong" when you say you don't like a piece of art or a certain song.

Art doesn't have to match your couch — it's more important that it matches your own sense of what is beautiful and interesting.

Be Smart About Relationship-Building

"It's all about who you know" sounds like one of those unprovable assertions, but sociologists are appreciating its wisdom more and more every year. If this book were written 20 or 30 years earlier, it might not have had an entire chapter on social networks; but today, sociologists understand that networks are at the heart of almost every social process. If you live in the United States, then yes, in a sense the United States is "your society." But on a concrete, day-to-day basis, it's the actual people who you know and interact with who are truly "your society." I barely know the woman who lives across the hall from me, but I call or e-mail my friend Whitney across the country in Virginia multiple times a week. My social tie to Whitney makes her much more influential in my life than most people in my home city of Minneapolis. (See Chapter 7 for more on social networks.)

What does this mean for you? It means that it's a good idea to be deliberate about making and maintaining social connections. Think about what social networks you want to be a part of, and work your way in to them through both professional and personal connections. The more people you know, the better your information is and the more powerful you are in those people's social context.

This doesn't mean you ought to spend all your time trying to make friends with people you wouldn't otherwise associate with — but it does mean that if you want to achieve a certain goal in society, it pays to make connections with people who are connected to that job you want or that place you want to be. Be sincere about relationship-building, but also be assertive about making and keeping valuable social ties. It's highly likely to pay off.

Network sociologists agree that it's good to exert some effort to meet people and maintain social connections that you've made, but it's not necessarily beneficial to seem like an over-aggressive "networker." No one likes to feel like they're being used by someone else who only wants information or influence from them. Your most useful social ties are those with people you genuinely have something in common with.

Changing Society: Be Optimistic, But Keep Your Expectations Reasonable

So you have some issues with the world? Yeah, who doesn't? Want to change the world? Go for it! You can do it; at least, you can change *something*.

Still, appreciate that your society is the way it is for a lot of complex reasons. From the things you hate most about your society to the things you love dearly, it's been a long road that's led to your time and place. When dramatic social change happens quickly, it's typically because of very unusual (and possibly quite painful) circumstances. Historical sociologists have spent decades and decades trying to understand the fascinating and mysterious course of social history.

How does A lead to B lead to C? It's not always obvious, but sociologists do believe that somehow it all makes sense . . . and if it *does* make sense, that means you can figure out how to change it. (See the next section for more on social movements.)

A common phrase suggests that you "think globally, act locally." That may sound a little hokey, but it makes good sociological sense — you can have the greatest impact on the people and places closest to you. Making changes in your everyday life can have a big impact over time, on you and on the people around you.

Learn How to Mobilize a Social Movement

Sociologists studying social movements have story after story about individuals and small groups who successfully brought about enormously consequential changes in laws, policies, and customs. The Civil Rights Movement, the movement to end child labor, the pro-recycling movement — all of those had uphill battles to start with, but eventually they turned into spectacular successes.

Of course, they also have story after story about social movements that *didn't* work so well. In the middle of the 20th century, there was a big movement to get the United States to convert to the metric system (kilometers instead of miles, Celsius instead of Fahrenheit) — that one didn't turn out so well, despite the fact that millions of schoolkids were made to memorize the metric system and learn how to convert "standard" units to metric units. Once they finished the fourth grade, the kids all tended to decide that was enough of that.

In social movements as in poker, it's good to remember Kenny Rogers's advice: "You gotta know when to hold 'em, know when to fold 'em; know when to walk away, know when to run."

If you're interested in making social change happen, read Chapter 13 of this book (if you haven't already) and then consider reading more about the sociology of social movements. You'll learn something about what strategies might work and what strategies won't. It pays to try to convince people that you're right, but appealing only to their heads probably won't work: You also have to appeal to their hearts and their bodies. Consider all the different ways you can connect with them and interest them in your cause. With persistence and a little luck, you just might change the world . . . but be patient. It's not apt to happen overnight.

Run Your Company Effectively

In Chapter 12, I explain sociologist Richard Scott's argument that organizations behave as "rational systems," as "natural systems," *and* as "open systems." If Scott is correct — and most organizational sociologists believe that, at least in general terms, he is — your company is a machine, yes, but a machine made up of human beings and a machine that does its work by interacting with other machines. To run your company effectively, you need to understand:

- **Your corporate organization.** Is your company designed to do its job as efficiently as possible? Does information travel accurately and quickly from one part of the company to another? Is there any obvious waste? Does everyone know what their job is?

- **Your corporate culture.** How do people feel about working at your company? Do they like their coworkers? Do they feel like their jobs are healthy, satisfying parts of their lives generally — or are they just punching the clock?

- **Your corporate environment.** What's going on among the companies you deal with as suppliers, customers, and competitors? What are the laws and policies that affect your business, and how are they changing?

Understanding just one — or even two — of these aspects of corporate life won't do it: You have to appreciate all these dimensions of corporate life. In many ways, sociological insight can help you understand how your company works, and (even if you don't own the place) how to be most effective in your job.

Understand How We Can All Be Different, Yet All Be the Same

This is one of the many paradoxes of sociology. On the one hand, sociologists study human societies in all their wild diversity, so sociologists appreciate how very different societies can be. Sociologists love to question assumptions that are taken for granted in their societies: Some of your very deepest values, beliefs, and customs are probably unique to your particular society. Even if it seems like it's "common sense" or "human nature" for norms and values (see Chapter 2) to be the way they are in your society, that's typically not the case.

And still, sociologists know that there *are* commonalities among all people, in all places, at all times. That's why sociologists interested in corporate life in New York City in the 21st century might read books or articles about social networks in Paris in the 18th century or about the spread of a fad across southeast Asia in the 19th century. In the generals — if not the particulars — people are people, and sociology demonstrates the similarities as well as the differences among people in different societies.

Sociology can surprise you by demonstrating just how very different people are in some ways, but it can also — and just as interestingly — surprise you by revealing unexpected connections between people living in very different places at very different times.

Chapter 19

Ten Myths About Society Busted by Sociology

In This Chapter

▶ Discovering the truth behind common myths about society

▶ Using sociology to question erroneous assumptions

*Y*ou may have seen the TV program *Mythbusters*, where scientists and engineers test myths about the world to see if there's any possibility these claims could actually be true. Can you actually survive a fall from a great height into a full dumpster? Can you make a bullet curve by flicking your wrist while you shoot a gun? It's very interesting — and social scientists can do that, too!

Just as many people are convinced, despite all evidence, that tapping on the top of a soda can will make it less likely to fizz over when it's opened, many people are absolutely convinced of the truth of some things about society that are actually not entirely true. In this chapter, I run down a list of ten myths about society that sociologists have shown to be at least partially untrue; in some cases, however, they're complete whoppers.

These myths range across the entire discipline of sociology — so if you've been reading this book from the beginning, you'll recognize some of them as myths right away. There is *some* truth to some of them, but none of them are as completely, unambiguously true as many people are convinced they are. Two centuries of sociological research have shown that long-held assumptions about the social world can actually crumble quite quickly when held up to the light of scientific research.

And these are just a few examples. I hope this book inspires you to question whether all the things you believe about society are actually true, or whether they're just faulty assumptions that you haven't bothered to test or research. They may well be true . . . but sociology can help you to think about how they can be put to the test.

Here are a few that don't pass.

With Hard Work and Determination, Anyone Can Get What They Deserve

This may be the myth that most aggravates sociologists. Especially in established capitalist societies like the United States and Europe, there's a widespread belief that by and large, people get what they "deserve" — that is, that in general, wealth, income, and personal freedom correspond to how hard a person has tried to get ahead in life. It would be nice if it were true because that would mean if you needed a little more money, all you'd have to do would be to try a little bit harder; and if you tried as hard as you possibly could, you'd be fabulously wealthy.

It is true that, in most cases, some effort and dedication and sacrifice are *necessary* to achieve material comfort. There's no question that most people of comfortable (or more than comfortable) means have worked very, very hard to get where they are. Saying that "anyone can get ahead" is a myth is not to diminish the achievements of people who do work hard every day for the money they earn, however much it is.

What makes this a myth is that *there is not a level playing field*. For any number of reasons, some people face challenges that others don't. There is racism, and there are health problems, and there are friends and family members who need to be cared for, and there's just plain bad luck. It happens. Further, what can be hard to appreciate — because few people have been on both ends of the wealth spectrum — is that the disadvantages of poverty are multiplicative, and the advantages of wealth are multiplicative. The more poor you are, the harder it is to climb out of poverty no matter how hard you work; and the more wealthy you are, the harder it is to fall out of that situation no matter how lazy you are.

It is important to make smart, prudent decisions no matter what your financial situation; and to get ahead, you do typically need to work hard. Nonetheless, the idea that people with more money must be somehow working harder or be more deserving than people with less money is a complete and utter myth.

Our Actions Reflect Our Values

I would like to believe that I know who I am and what I value, that there is something consistent and steadfast at my core and that all my actions flow naturally from that. Unfortunately, that's not entirely true.

Not just sociologists, but everyone who closely and systematically examines human behavior — psychologists, economists, political scientists — have found that this is at least partially a myth. It would be very convenient for the social scientists if it weren't a myth because that would mean you could poll someone on their attitudes and beliefs and then safely assume that you know what they're going to do. In fact, again and again and again social scientists have seen that someone can, apparently in all honesty, tell you one thing, and then turn around and do something completely different. Further, people forget what they've done in the past, changing their past actions to be consistent with their present values — which are likely to change in the future. This certainly makes life interesting for novelists and poets, but it's a complete nightmare for social science.

Why don't people act on what they seem to believe? Well, sometimes they do; in fact, *usually* they do. But there are many influences on people's actions, and their core beliefs are only one of those influences. There's peer pressure, there's convenience, there's habit . . . and let's face it, you're a *complicated* human being. You didn't come with a user's manual; you're writing it every day. The bottom line is that you can't look at someone's actions and assume you know "who they are"; and vice-versa, knowing all about someone's beliefs and values tells you only so much about what actions they're going to take in the future.

We're Being Brainwashed by the Media

The ubiquity of the mass media in contemporary society can be frightening. With tens or even hundreds of millions of viewers or listeners, it can seem like TV hosts and radio personalities and pop stars have a huge amount of influence. Those people often get pretty extreme, and it can seem like they're leading the charge in fashion, politics, attitudes, and behaviors. In fact, many people believe that those charismatic figures are *so* influential that everyone is essentially being brainwashed by them, that they can make people do just about anything they want.

That is a myth. Certainly, mass-media celebrities have great influence in certain respects: They can jumpstart trends and influence social attitudes. But there is little sociological evidence to suggest that TV programs, radio shows, or Web sites can influence people in significant numbers to behave entirely uncharacteristically.

Sociologist Stanley Lieberson has found that first names for babies often become popular due to the rising fame of celebrities with those names. And *The Cosby Show* is widely credited with helping to erode widespread stereotypes about African-American families.

Particularly in the present day, when people have an unprecedented number of options, they typically choose to watch, listen to, or read media that are consistent with their preexisting beliefs; if anything, media reinforce the beliefs and habits people had in the first place. Most importantly, though, people — even young children — are active and inquisitive consumers of the media. Do *you* believe everything you hear someone say on TV? Of course not . . . and neither do your neighbors.

Rather than getting caught up in debates over whether some media outlet or another has a political bias, remember that there is no such thing as a purely "objective" source. That's not to say there's no such thing as "the truth" — it's just that there are different ways of telling the truth. With media from around the world available at a click of your computer mouse, you'll do yourself a favor by looking at multiple different news sources, not just relying on any one source.

Understanding Society is Just a Matter of "Common Sense"

Among all these myths, the falsehood of this one should seem most obvious to those of you who have read any or all of this book. It's worth repeating, though — not only because if it were true, every sociologist would be out of a job, but also because it's potentially the most dangerous of all these myths.

There was once a time when it was "common sense" that certain races should be subjugated to others. It was also once "common sense" that women were not suited to vote, and in some societies it's still widely regarded as "common sense" that women are unsuited to choose their own husbands or even their own sexual partners. Should people with mental disabilities be locked away in institutions, or maybe even killed? That, too, was once "common sense."

Those beliefs probably — hopefully! — all seem ludicrous to you now, but it's not enough to dismiss long-refuted beliefs. Sociology challenges you to question the beliefs you take to be common sense *today*. That's a lot harder, but to really understand how society works, and how it might be made better for everyone, you have to be willing to question even your most dearly held beliefs. That's not to say you have to discard them, but you have to keep an open mind. If you don't, not only will you be closed to interesting new ideas, you risk falling victim to destructive myths. They're still out there — for examples, see every other section in this chapter!

For lots of good reasons, it's easy to get caught up in the assumptions and biases of your own society — but it's a certainty that some of those are regarded as nonsense in other societies, and some of the beliefs that people around you take for granted today will seem ridiculous 500 years from now. You don't have to be a relativist — that is, someone who thinks there's no such thing as truth — to appreciate the importance of questioning even assumptions that seem perfectly obvious and normal in your particular society.

Race Doesn't Matter Any More

Just a few decades ago, African-Americans couldn't sit in certain places on public buses or in restaurants. In 2008, an African-American was elected President of the United States. Does that mean race doesn't matter any more? Has Martin Luther King, Jr.'s dream come true: that people may be judged by the content of their character and not by the color of their skin?

It doesn't diminish the amazing achievements of civil rights activists, and the almost unbelievable progress that's been made in social tolerance, but to say that the idea that race "doesn't matter any more" is a myth. Many more options are today available to people around the world regardless of their race, but race remains very much a factor in how people are seen, how they are judged, and how they are treated.

What does this mean for social policy? It's not obvious, except that "race blind" policies, whatever their virtues in particular situations, are not necessarily consistent with the way people see the world. What it means for sociology is that race remains, and will remain for the foreseeable future, something that must continue to be studied.

In Time, Immigrant Families Will Assimilate and Adopt a New Culture

If the falseness of this myth doesn't seem obvious to you, that's okay; for a long time, it didn't seem obvious to sociologists either! For much of the 20th century, sociological studies of immigration were dominated by the theory that one way or another, over time immigrant families would melt into the "melting pot," that they would leave their culture behind and join the culture of their new society.

Today, though, sociologists understand that there are many problems with this theory. The biggest problem is its assumption that there's some kind of path from "less assimilated" to "more assimilated," a path along which all immigrant families can all be located. It's true that immigrant families somehow adapt to their new circumstances, but that adaptation isn't necessarily linear; they may completely change their behavior in some respects while remaining exactly the same in others. Further, it's problematic to assume that there is a single "receiving" culture into which families can assimilate — any culture is really many different cultures, and it's a mistake to think that becoming "American" or "English" or "Japanese" means one thing in particular, one lifestyle or set of values or even one language to which newcomers need to assimilate.

Further, though, the entire concept of "assimilation" suggests a kind of absorption that erases the experiences and values families bring with them. In truth, what happens is that those families' experiences and values are *added* to the culture of their new home. Presuming otherwise can justify a scientifically inaccurate and personally hurtful disregard for those families' contributions. Cultural integration doesn't have to be a win-lose process of "assimilation"; it can be a win-win process of addition and enrichment.

Bureaucracy is Dehumanizing

This myth is touched on in Chapter 12. Like you (I'm guessing), some of the most brilliant sociologists in history have had concerns about the effect of bureaucracy on society. Max Weber called it an "iron cage" that locks people in its cold grip.

But those same sociologists also appreciated its virtues. Most obviously, there's the fact that bureaucracy allows people to do more, more efficiently; Marx, Durkheim, and Weber all understood this and alluded to it in one way or another. By raising productivity, the widespread adoption of bureaucracy has meant a higher standard of living for people around the world. If business was still done through informal understandings and personal contact, it would take much more time and be much more expensive to get *anything* done, and accordingly, prices of goods and services would skyrocket.

It's also true, though, that sometimes a little dehumanizing can be a good thing. It may seem infuriating when you can't get a human being on the phone, or can't convince anyone to bend a policy when you accidentally miss a credit card payment — but that "dehumanizing" property of corporate bureaucracy also makes it much harder for those companies to discriminate or mistreat people for arbitrary reasons. Bureaucracy can sometimes feel cold and impersonal, but it also gives you a tremendous amount of freedom to be who you want and do what you want, to be treated simply as a number rather than as a person about whom others have expectations and to whom they will extend only certain privileges. In that way, bureaucracy can actually allow you to be *more* human.

People Who Make Bad Choices Are Just Getting the Wrong Messages

There's a persistent belief that people who make "bad choices" — whether they're choices you simply disagree with, or choices that seem to actively contradict their values or goals — are "getting the wrong messages," that they're somehow under the influence of people or publications that are persistently misleading them about what the "right choices" are. And some-times they are.

Most people, however, in most societies, are getting a *lot* of messages from a *lot* of sources. Those sources may include:

- ✔ Friends
- ✔ Family members
- ✔ Teachers
- ✔ Coworkers
- ✔ Spiritual leaders
- ✔ Physicians or counselors
- ✔ The media

Among those messages, the ones they pay attention to may vary from situa-tion to situation, and from day to day.

Sociologist David Harding's study, mentioned in Chapter 7, shows that people who get conflicting messages are often more confused and may have less pre-dictable behavior than people who are hearing consistent messages; but every-one has a number of different sources of information to inform their decisions.

If you make poor decisions, it probably does mean that you're getting "the wrong messages" . . . but you're probably getting "the right messages" as well. Which messages you choose to act on is up to you.

Society Prevents Us From Being Our "True Selves"

Some psychologists believe that the process of growing up is, at least in con-temporary society, almost universally traumatic — that as people learn to adapt to social expectations, they are forced to betray their "true selves."

It certainly feels like that sometimes, but most sociologists believe that it doesn't even make sense to think about a "true self" that stands outside of society. Who you are and what you do is fundamentally social, from the moment you are born. It's your society that gives meaning to your life, that gives you a language, history, friends, and family. For your entire life, even your most intimate, personal thoughts are deeply wrapped in your social life. Your "true self" *cannot be separated* from your society: Even if you leave your society, your experiences there will continue to give shape and meaning to your experience for the rest of your life.

This may be the very best reason to study sociology because unless you understand your society, you cannot really understand yourself. And if you don't understand yourself, how can you understand anything else?

There Is Such a Thing as a Perfect Society

Auguste Comte, the man who coined the term "sociology," thought that one day we'd get it all figured out, that with enough effort and study we'd achieve the perfect society and that would be that. Needless to say, sociologists would be the ones in charge. (See Chapter 3 for more on Comte.)

Comte's intellectual descendents, those being sociologists today, don't believe that any more. Never in the history of the world has there been a society without inequality, conflict, crime, and unhappiness. Whatever you might consider to be a "perfect" society, we haven't figured it out yet and we almost certainly never will.

Why? Because we're not perfect people. People are selfish, foolish, and inconsistent, and they make mistakes. Building a perfect society out of human beings is like trying to build a cathedral out of Gummi Bears. It's just not going to happen.

But that doesn't mean you should give up hope! With the help of sociology and the other social sciences, we've come a long way since Comte's time, and you and I have every reason to think that social conditions will get better yet. People aren't perfect, but nor is there reason to think they're fundamentally wicked or destructive. By working together, and by asking tough questions and demanding the best answers we can get, we can make the world a better place to live. It will never be *perfect*, but you know what? I'm okay with that.

Index

• *M* •

• N •

● **S** ●

Notes

Notes

Notes

Notes

Business/Accounting & Bookkeeping

Bookkeeping For Dummies
978-0-7645-9848-7

eBay Business
All-in-One For Dummies,
2nd Edition
978-0-470-38536-4

Job Interviews
For Dummies,
3rd Edition
978-0-470-17748-8

Resumes For Dummies,
5th Edition
978-0-470-08037-5

Stock Investing
For Dummies,
3rd Edition
978-0-470-40114-9

Successful Time
Management
For Dummies
978-0-470-29034-7

Computer Hardware

BlackBerry For Dummies,
3rd Edition
978-0-470-45762-7

Computers For Seniors
For Dummies
978-0-470-24055-7

iPhone For Dummies,
2nd Edition
978-0-470-42342-4

Laptops For Dummies,
3rd Edition
978-0-470-27759-1

Macs For Dummies,
10th Edition
978-0-470-27817-8

Cooking & Entertaining

Cooking Basics
For Dummies,
3rd Edition
978-0-7645-7206-7

Wine For Dummies,
4th Edition
978-0-470-04579-4

Diet & Nutrition

Dieting For Dummies,
2nd Edition
978-0-7645-4149-0

Nutrition For Dummies,
4th Edition
978-0-471-79868-2

Weight Training
For Dummies,
3rd Edition
978-0-471-76845-6

Digital Photography

Digital Photography
For Dummies,
6th Edition
978-0-470-25074-7

Photoshop Elements 7
For Dummies
978-0-470-39700-8

Gardening

Gardening Basics
For Dummies
978-0-470-03749-2

Organic Gardening
For Dummies,
2nd Edition
978-0-470-43067-5

Green/Sustainable

Green Building
& Remodeling
For Dummies
978-0-470-17559-0

Green Cleaning
For Dummies
978-0-470-39106-8

Green IT For Dummies
978-0-470-38688-0

Health

Diabetes For Dummies,
3rd Edition
978-0-470-27086-8

Food Allergies
For Dummies
978-0-470-09584-3

Living Gluten-Free
For Dummies
978-0-471-77383-2

Hobbies/General

Chess For Dummies,
2nd Edition
978-0-7645-8404-6

Drawing For Dummies
978-0-7645-5476-6

Knitting For Dummies,
2nd Edition
978-0-470-28747-7

Organizing For Dummies
978-0-7645-5300-4

SuDoku For Dummies
978-0-470-01892-7

Home Improvement

Energy Efficient Homes
For Dummies
978-0-470-37602-7

Home Theater
For Dummies,
3rd Edition
978-0-470-41189-6

Living the Country Lifestyle
All-in-One For Dummies
978-0-470-43061-3

Solar Power Your Home
For Dummies
978-0-470-17569-9

Internet
Blogging For Dummies,
2nd Edition
978-0-470-23017-6

eBay For Dummies,
6th Edition
978-0-470-49741-8

Facebook For Dummies
978-0-470-26273-3

Google Blogger
For Dummies
978-0-470-40742-4

Web Marketing
For Dummies,
2nd Edition
978-0-470-37181-7

WordPress For Dummies,
2nd Edition
978-0-470-40296-2

Language & Foreign Language
French For Dummies
978-0-7645-5193-2

Italian Phrases
For Dummies
978-0-7645-7203-6

Spanish For Dummies
978-0-7645-5194-9

Spanish For Dummies,
Audio Set
978-0-470-09585-0

Macintosh
Mac OS X Snow Leopard
For Dummies
978-0-470-43543-4

Math & Science
Algebra I For Dummies,
2nd Edition
978-0-470-55964-2

Biology For Dummies
978-0-7645-5326-4

Calculus For Dummies
978-0-7645-2498-1

Chemistry For Dummies
978-0-7645-5430-8

Microsoft Office
Excel 2007 For Dummies
978-0-470-03737-9

Office 2007 All-in-One
Desk Reference
For Dummies
978-0-471-78279-7

Music
Guitar For Dummies,
2nd Edition
978-0-7645-9904-0

iPod & iTunes
For Dummies,
6th Edition
978-0-470-39062-7

Piano Exercises
For Dummies
978-0-470-38765-8

Parenting & Education
Parenting For Dummies,
2nd Edition
978-0-7645-5418-6

Type 1 Diabetes
For Dummies
978-0-470-17811-9

Pets
Cats For Dummies,
2nd Edition
978-0-7645-5275-5

Dog Training For Dummies,
2nd Edition
978-0-7645-8418-3

Puppies For Dummies,
2nd Edition
978-0-470-03717-1

Religion & Inspiration
The Bible For Dummies
978-0-7645-5296-0

Catholicism For Dummies
978-0-7645-5391-2

Women in the Bible
For Dummies
978-0-7645-8475-6

Self-Help & Relationship
Anger Management
For Dummies
978-0-470-03715-7

Overcoming Anxiety
For Dummies
978-0-7645-5447-6

Sports
Baseball For Dummies,
3rd Edition
978-0-7645-7537-2

Basketball For Dummies,
2nd Edition
978-0-7645-5248-9

Golf For Dummies,
3rd Edition
978-0-471-76871-5

Web Development
Web Design All-in-One
For Dummies
978-0-470-41796-6

Windows Vista
Windows Vista
For Dummies
978-0-471-75421-3

Available wherever books are sold. For more information or to order direct: U.S. customers visit www.dummies.com or call 1-877-762-2974.
U.K. customers visit www.wileyeurope.com or call (0) 1243 843291. Canadian customers visit www.wiley.ca or call 1-800-567-4797.

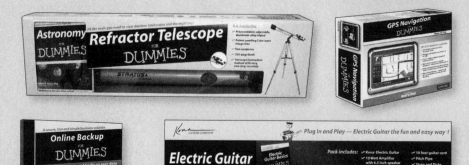